Series Ten

Reprinted for

American Philosophical Society

by

University Microfilms International
Ann Arbor, Michigan, U.S.A.
London, England
1978

Library of Congress Cataloging in Publication Data

Coe, Joffre Lanning.
    The formative cultures of the Carolina
Piedmont.

    (Books on demand : Series 10)
    Reprint of the ed. published by the American
Philosophical Society, Philadelphia, as v. 54, pt. 5 of its
Transactions, new ser.
    1. Indians of North America—North Carolina—
Antiquities. 2. North Carolina—Antiquities. I. Title.
II. Series: American Philosophical Society, Philadelphia.
Transaction ; new ser., v. 54, pt. 5.

E78.N74C63   1978   975.6'5   78-8460
ISBN 0-8357-0315-0

TRANSACTIONS

OF THE

AMERICAN PHILOSOPHICAL SOCIETY

HELD AT PHILADELPHIA

FOR PROMOTING USEFUL KNOWLEDGE

NEW SERIES—VOLUME 54, PART 5
1964

THE FORMATIVE CULTURES OF THE CAROLINA PIEDMONT

JOFFRE LANNING COE

Director, Research Laboratories of Anthropology, University of North Carolina

THE AMERICAN PHILOSOPHICAL SOCIETY
INDEPENDENCE SQUARE
PHILADELPHIA

AUGUST, 1964

Library of Congress Catalog
Card Number 64–21423

ACKNOWLEDGMENTS

When a project has extended over as many years as this one, it is inevitable that many people will have contributed to its fruition. A word of encouragement, a moment of assistance, and a helpful suggestion all become ingredients in the final results but are frequently forgotten or overlooked in the writing of the study. It is for this reason that I should like to acknowledge my appreciation to the many people who have been helpful in making our work in the field easier and our work in the laboratory more successful.

I am especially indebted to Mr. H. M. Doerschuk formerly of Badin, North Carolina, who from 1927 to 1952 located most of the known sites in the Uwharrie area. His contribution of specimens to the University of North Carolina and his intimate knowledge of these sites have been invaluable to this study.

Mr. J. S. Holmes, Manager of the Carolina Aluminum Company, has been very cooperative in arranging permits for the University of North Carolina to conduct excavations on the Company's properties. The interest and enthusiasm of the late Mr. J. G. Holtzclaw, President of the Virginia Power and Electric Company, was a major factor in the successful completion of the Roanoke Rapids Basin survey. The support given this program by Mr. Thomas W. Morse, formerly Superintendent of State Parks, has also been of great importance. The use of the facilities of the state parks has made a great deal of work possible that could not have been accomplished otherwise.

I am also indebted to Mr. Stanley South who, as my very capable assistant, became indoctrinated in archaeology in the Roanoke Rapids Basin and who participated in much of the field work for the next three years. I am appreciative of Mr. Lewis Binford's enthusiasm and for his assistance in the Roanoke Rapids work as well as for the preparation of the maps for the Roanoke project.

Finally, I should like to express my gratitude to my wife, Sally Denton Coe, for the many hours of typing as well as her helpful comments and criticisms on the organization and presentation of the report, and to Dr. James B. Griffin, not only for the radiocarbon dates published in this study but more especially for his friendship and sound advice throughout these formative years.

J. L. C.

THE FORMATIVE CULTURES OF THE CAROLINA PIEDMONT

Joffre Lanning Coe

CONTENTS

INTRODUCTION

In a sense, this study is the culmination of a quarter of a century of effort on the part of the author to gain some knowledge of the aboriginal occupation of North Carolina. When he entered into this venture in 1934, the prehistory of the Piedmont lay entirely in the ground, and the archaeology of the southeastern United States was in its infancy. Since that time, remarkable progress has been made in archaeological research, and the basic patterns of cultural development for the ceramic communities are now well known throughout most of the Eastern Woodlands. Today only the Archaic and earlier cultures remain virtually unknown for this area.[1] In North Carolina, the first efforts were directed toward identifying the archaeological remains of the historic tribes of the Piedmont, but for the last decade our efforts have been more concerned with the identification of earlier cultures and the verification of their antiquity.

The first systematic excavation in the Piedmont was undertaken in 1936 at the site of the historic Indian town of Keyauwee in Randolph County.[2] This resulted in the identification of the cultural complex of the early eighteenth-century Keyauwee Indians and its ancestral form. The former was named Caraway for Caraway Creek upon which it was situated, and the latter was named Uwharrie for the surrounding Uwharrie Mountains. The next year, excavations were begun on the protohistoric temple mound site on Little River in Montgomery County.[3] Excavations have continued at this site and a restoration program is in progress there at the present time. The Lamar-like complex found at this site was given the name Pee Dee after the major river system on which it was located, and it should not be confused with the name Pedee which has sometimes been applied to a tribe of Indians that once lived along the lower courses of this river.

In 1938 other historic Siouan villages in the Piedmont were located and investigated with the assistance of a grant from the Indiana Historical Society. The seventeenth-century towns of the Occanneechi and Saponi on the Roanoke River and the Sara on the Dan River were partially excavated. Subsequently, the early eighteenth-century towns of the Occanneechi on the Eno River and the Saponi on the Yadkin River were also investigated.

From 1939 to the beginning of World War II an intensive program of site surveys and excavations was carried out in the Piedmont region of North Carolina with the aid of N.Y.A. and W.P.A. funds, and, by the time all archaeological acitivities were suspended in June of 1942, the nature of the cultural complexes of the historic and protohistoric tribes were well known for the Piedmont. At the same time, a considerable body of data was accumulated on earlier complexes that could not, at that time, be properly identified.

When work was resumed in North Carolina in 1948, emphasis was placed upon identifying and defining certain of those earlier complexes. During the following year a thorough study was made of collections from over a hundred sites in the Uwharrie area in an attempt to see whether the presence, absence, or repeated association of specific traits on those sites could identify a recurring cultural complex. It was assumed that, if a significant number of traits were found to occur together on a series of sites, then they were probably the physical remains of the activities of a particular group of people at a particular period of time. The first results of this effort appeared to be rewarding and the Guilford and Badin foci were first defined on the basis of this assumed association of traits.[4] It was disappointing, therefore, when this small bubble of success was punctured by the irrefutable evidence that those recurring complexes of traits were in reality the remains of recurring occupations on those sites by the same sequence of people.

In the Piedmont the nature of the topography is such that the great majority of sites are situated on knolls, ridges, or terraces and have been subjected to continuous erosion. This condition has resulted in the remains of all prior occupations being kept on or near the surface. It would be unrealistic to assume that any of these sites were occupied only once during the 10,000 years with which we are concerned. This is what may be determined *after* the cultural complexes have been defined and proven. It cannot be assumed beforehand. It is for this reason that seriation studies, such as Holland's analysis of projectile points in Virginia, are primarily clerical exercises and contribute mainly to compounding confusion.[5] Seriation has meaning only when it can illustrate the relative use, or popularity, of two or more styles of a given product at one time in a single community. It is unlikely that any two of Holland's types were ever used at the same time. His percentages and graphs, therefore, reflect either the predilection of the collector or the relative size and length of the multiple occupations, or both. The resulting order of data, then, had no validity in itself but was based upon intuition or prior knowledge. This was a lesson that had to be learned in the Piedmont.

This uncritical lumping of traits together into assumed complexes has not been limited to surface collections. All too often the fact that two artifacts have been found in physical proximity to each other has been taken as *prima facie* evidence that they were functionally related, even though this proximity may have been entirely fortuitous. In this fashion, middens that have accumulated to a depth of several feet over a span of hundreds of years appear to be "culturally homo-

---

[1] Byers, 1959a.
[2] Coe, 1937.
[3] Coe, 1940.

[4] Coe, 1952 : 304–307.
[5] Holland, 1955.

6

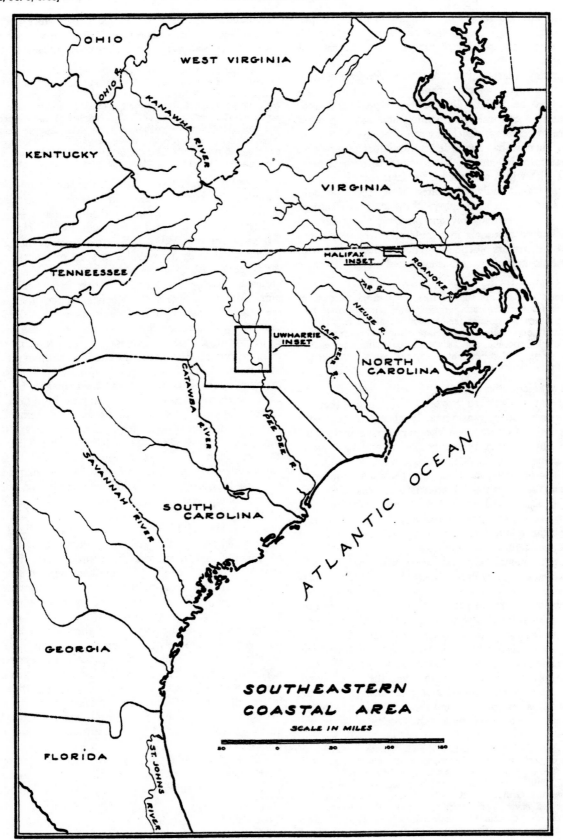

FIG. 1

geneous," and the variety of hunting and fishing implements assigned to some of those primitive people rivals the selection of sporting equipment at Abercrombie and Fitch.

For many years pottery has been recognized as a cornerstone upon which archaeological cultural complexes may be built. The pottery type has formed the basis for cultural identification and has become a measure of temporal development. The use of pottery for this purpose has succeeded so well that other items in the cultural inventories have tended to become mere ribbons with which to dress up the formal report. This situation was vividly illustrated in a recent monumental study on the archaeology of the lower Mississippi Valley. The fact that only one paragraph was devoted to nonceramic materials in a publication of 472 pages was, to the authors, justified. Their concern was with the ceramic materials, and they stated that:

In this report the word "collection" may be read "potsherds." . . . This sounds like the familiar excuse of the ceramist for neglecting other categories of material, but at present we do not feel apologetic about it. It will undoubtedly be possible to correlate stone and pottery types as the work proceeds, and as we get back into the earlier periods stone, and other materials, are certain to become increasingly important.[6]

This prediction was not long in being realized. Subsequent reports on the Poverty Point and Jaketown sites, where pottery was virtually absent in the early period, relied heavily upon the nonceramic materials.[7]

It is obvious that the technique of pottery making was learned relatively late in the Southeast,[8] and that the studies of earlier cultures must be based upon other categories of artifacts—as unsatisfactory as they may be. Of all the items manufactured by those preceramic people, only the projectile point was produced in sufficient quantity and with sufficient diversity of style to be useful as an index trait.

Projectile points, however, lacked many of the qualities that endeared pottery to the archaeologist. Pottery was made in a profusion of shapes and decorations while the variations in projectile point styles were limited by the nature of the material from which they were made and the function that they were intended to serve. Pottery was seldom transported great distances and broke easily, leaving many fragments to mark the time and the place. Projectile points, on the other hand, were frequently transported and when broken only the basal end is useful for identification. Furthermore, projectile points were made and scattered over the

Piedmont landscape a full 10,000 years before the first pottery was made. Therefore, it is little wonder that Jones in his *Antiquity of the Southern Indian* felt that:

It is hardly proper, however, to pursue this attempt at classification any further. Were we to note all the varieties which suggest themselves, we would be led into a multiplicity of illustrations which would do little more than represent the individual skill and fancies of the respective workmen, the various casualties to which these implements have been subjected during the process of manufacture and subsequent use, and the modifications of form consequent thereupon.[9]

Sixty-two years later, David Bushnell published a study on the location of certain historic Indian villages in the Piedmont of Virginia and illustrated a series of artifacts that he believed were made by the Manahoac Tribes around 1608.[10] It is now known that those specimens actually represented a span of several thousand years. Although Bushnell was only a part-time archaeologist, he was using the best data available to him. Many full-time archaeologists, on the other hand, are still creating mythical complexes today. The author's own illustration for the Badin period has proven to be one of the better examples of this kind of error in interpretation.[11] While he intended to illustrate the nonceramic artifacts associated with the first pottery-making in the Uwharrie area, he managed to show about everything else. For example: in figure 163, *Archaeology of the Eastern United States*, items A, G, P, and Q have now been identified as Hardaway: items B, D, E, M, and N are associated with the Kirk horizon; and items H, T, and X belong to the Stanly Complex. All of these items can now be demonstrated to have an antiquity of over 6,000 years while the pottery of the Badin component is probably less than 1,500 years old.

By the end of 1948, therefore, it was realized that the distribution of the early nonceramic artifacts was so general that there was little probability that any specific complex could be identified with reasonable certainty in this area on the basis of collections from the surfaces or by excavations of shallow midden deposits. The preliminary test pits dug at the Lowder's Ferry and Doerschuk sites during the summer of 1948, however, indicated that the answer to some of those problems lay close at hand. In 1949 the systematic excavation of a section of the Doerschuk Site was completed and the analysis of the data collected at that time is presented in Part One. Later, during the same year, excavations were continued at the Lowder's Ferry Site, and the results obtained there confirmed the Doerschuk Site sequence.

The work at these sites demonstrated two important facts: first, that stratified sites of depth and antiquity do exist in the alluvial flood plains of the Piedmont;

---

[6] Phillips, Ford, and Griffin, 1951: 45. Another example of the use of pottery as a prime indicator of cultural identity is Evan's "Ceramic Study of Virginia Archeology," 1955.

[7] Ford, Phillips, and Haag, 1955; Ford and Webb, 1956.

[8] Crane and Griffin, 1958b: 1122. Charcoal sample, M-236, was reported having a radiocarbon date of 1812 ± 200 B.C. and associated with a plain fiber-tempered pottery at the Dulany Site, Chatham County, Georgia.

[9] Jones, 1873: 267.

[10] Bushnell, 1935.

[11] Coe, 1952: fig. 163.

and second, that when an occupation zone can be found that represents a relatively short period of time the usual hodgepodge of projectile point types are not found —only variations of one specific theme. In the light of this evidence, there can no longer be any doubt as to the diagnostic value of projectile points, but to be useful the types must be defined with precision. Except for the work of Krieger and others in Texas, the Southeast has been unusually lackadaisical in developing working types in this category.[12] With the present emphasis on preceramic cultures, however, the miscellanea of projectile points are becoming increasingly important as an index of culture change or continuity. Finally, it must be realized that projectile points can never be as sensitive an indicator of change as pottery for, while the latter may reflect variations of style within a decade or generation, the former may continue in use with little obvious change for centuries.

The success in finding stratigraphy in depth at the Doerschuk and Lowder's Ferry sites was due largely to good luck. Although test pits were dug for that purpose, there was no known procedure for locating sites of this type. In the beginning, the intent was to test as many sites as possible until some evidence of stratigraphy was found. Those two sites were tested first because of the variety of specimen types that had been found on the surface and collected from the eroding banks. The depth of the upper midden was visible at the Doerschuk Site, but the presence of the underlying levels came as a surprise.

After the excavations were completed at the Doerschuk and Lowder's Ferry sites, their topographic position in the flood plain was given a thorough review in consultation with geologists from the University of North Carolina for the purpose of determining some criteria that would increase the archaeologist's probability of finding other sites that contained stratified levels of human occupation. The result was a working hypothesis that has produced surprisingly good results.

In developing this hypothesis, however, it was necessary to find at least a partial explanation for two problems. First, since a number of different culture groups did inhabit the same location at the Doerschuk Site over a period of several thousand years,· there must be some physiographic factors that would tend to concentrate those aboriginal people into that locality. Second, under certain conditions there must be depositional factors involved in the building of flood-plain deposits that would tend to preserve the evidence of their former existence.

In regard to the first problem in the Uwharrie area this concentration of primitive populations was due to at least three factors. The Yadkin Basin (fig. 2) is an area of approximately 4,490 square miles, but it is ultimately drained through a gorge at the Narrows, like sand in an hourglass. People, of course, are not

12 Newell and Krieger, 1949; Suhm and Krieger, 1954.·

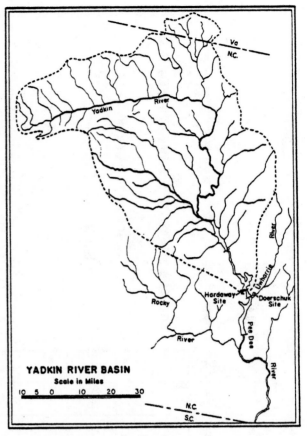

FIG. 2

fish and they are not confined to the river course. Nevertheless, it appears that their movements were frequently with the river and when this was true they ·inevitably passed ·in the vicinity of the Narrows. The second factor was the presence of the falls and rapids in the river (fig. 3). Shallow water such as this was a major attraction to primitive people who lived in part upon the fish and mollusks gleaned from the river. The third, and most important, factor was the narrow valley and barriers to shore traffic. Any people moving up or down the river would be funneled into a relatively narrow neck which limited the space available for camps until they moved away from the river into the surrounding hills. The Doerschuk Site was at the very neck of the Pee Dee "funnel." It was the last bit of level ground on the east side of the river below the Narrows and anyone desiring to live in that vicinity would, of necessity, arrive at about the same location.

The second problem concerns the preservation of the occupational remains. The lower part of the Pee Dee River, where the bed is aggrading and the valley is wide, is transversed by a mature meander system. The probability of finding stratified sites in this area is poor. There are no physiographic factors present that would concentrate a scattered population at one place, and the sites that were situated along the river were

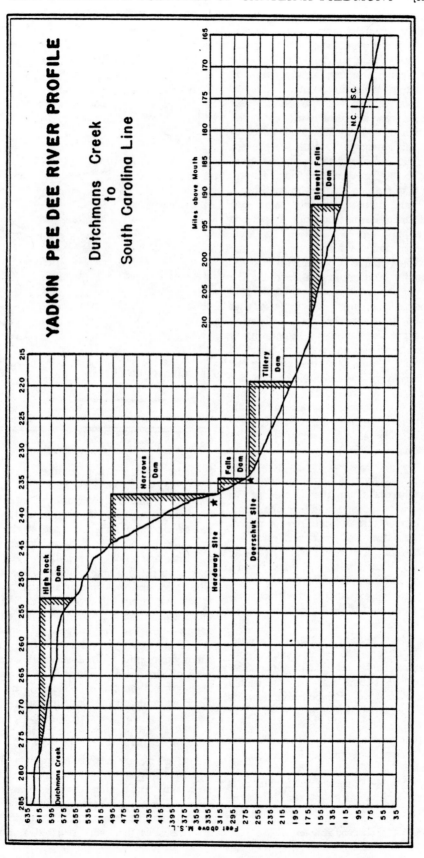

FIG. 3

frequently lost with the erosion of the banks and the shifting and cutting of new channels. Those that managed to escape destruction were buried and their locations were lost in the homogeneity of the flood plain. Only sites that were located along the edge of the valley were likely to survive or to be discovered.[13] These sites, if located above the flood plain upon older terraces, would not be subject to overflow and, therefore, would not develop natural stratification. If they were located in the flood plain, but lost to the main course of the river, they would be subjected only to overbank deposition which is usually inconsequential.[14] In any event, the broad aggraded or stable river valleys are unprofitable places to search for sites that contain the stratified remains of former human occupation of considerable antiquity.

In areas where the rivers fall rapidly, however, such as along the fall line of the Carolina Piedmont, their beds are being cut rather than filled. In this situation the valleys are narrow and rocky and the high velocity of the water prevents the development of characteristic meander patterns. These rivers are usually confined to a relatively broad but shallow bed that is interspersed with outcropping rocks and small islands. As

these streams move from one side of their confining valley to the other, they frequently pass places where fingers of resisting rock extend from the valley wall to the edge of the river. Behind these projecting rocks the river forms large eddies when it is in flood and deposits sand and silt at a faster rate than elsewhere along the narrow flood plains. Since these areas build up faster, their rate of flooding becomes progressively less until eventually a point is reached where they are higher than the normal flood stage. It is a curious fact that many of these deposits which began building early in the Holocene are still preserved and have continued to build, at a progressively slower rate, to the present. It suggests that there has been comparatively little change in the courses of these rivers through the fall line since the end of the last glaciation and that there are many places where the remains of aboriginal man have been buried and preserved.

An opportunity to check this hypothesis in another drainage system occurred in 1955 when salvage work was begun in the Halifax area on the Roanoke River (fig. 4). This is an area of rapids where the river, flowing in a narrow valley, crosses the fall line and spreads out into the Coastal Plain. Topographically, this area is similar to the Uwharrie region. At this point, the Roanoke River drains a large fan-shaped basin of over 8,000 square miles that lies to the west and north of the rapids (figs. 4 and 5). Although this

---

[13] Phillips, Ford, and Griffin, 1951: 296–306.
[14] Wolman and Leopold, 1957: 97–101. The great flood on the Ohio in 1937 was supposed to have deposited an average thickness of only 0.008 foot.

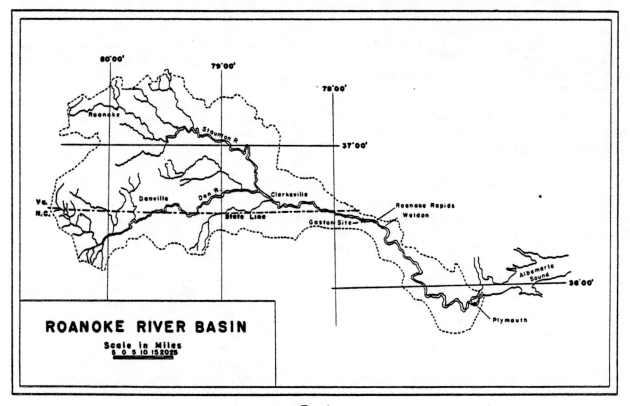

ROANOKE RIVER BASIN

Scale in Miles
5 0 5 10 15 20 25

Fig. 4

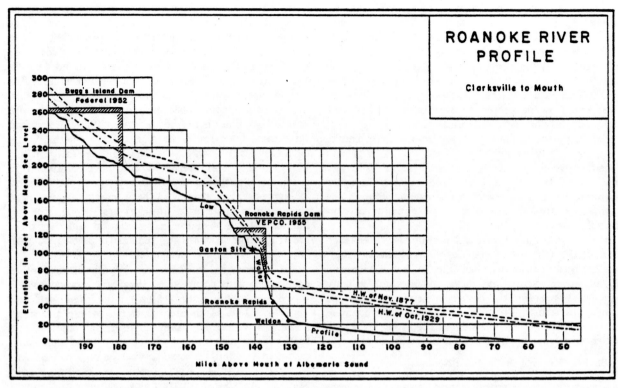

FIG. 5

gorge is considerably wider than the Narrows on the Yadkin, it still constitutes a major restriction in the drainage system. After the preliminary survey of the basin was completed, a site (Hxᵛ7) on the south bank of the river, approximately six miles above the town of Roanoke Rapids, was selected for intensive excavations. In view of the experience on the Yadkin River, it was felt that there was an excellent chance that this site would contain evidences of stratified occupation zones, since it seemed to fit all of the requirements of the suggested hypothesis. The results of this excavation are described in Part Three, and it will suffice to state here that three preceramic zones of occupation were discovered underlying the midden deposit of the later ceramic periods. The deepest zone was found at a depth of six feet, but there were traces of still earlier occupations. If time had permitted a more thorough search, it is quite likely that still earlier and deeper occupation zones would have been located.

This hypothesis has also been checked to a limited extent in other river systems. In 1947 Carl Miller excavated two test pits at the Lake Spring Site which was situated on the Georgia side of the Savannah River about one and a half miles above the Clark Hill Dam. This was in an area of rapids and narrow valleys similar, in many respects, to the Uwharrie and Halifax areas. The primary occupation of the site was that of the Savannah River Archaic and Miller stated that specimens "continued to a depth of five feet . . . [and

that] . . . both pits were driven well into undisturbed subsoil, which proved to be a former sand bar laid down earlier by the Savannah River." [15] In 1951 Joseph Caldwell revisited the site at the suggestion of the author and dug another test pit to a depth of eight feet. At this place on the site, the Savannah River midden was about three feet thick and rested on a bed of sterile sand that varied three to four feet in depth. Below this, however, ". . . . at a surface depth ranging from 5.9 to 6.4 feet was a visible midden strip containing numerous broken pebbles, quartz chips, and a relatively homogeneous group of 34 quartz artifacts." [16] In 1957 the author visited the area below the Clark Hill Dam and located several sites that showed substantial stratigraphic evidence in their eroded bank profiles.

A final illustration may be mentioned for the lower Chattahoochee River. In 1953 Ripley Bullen excavated test pits on site J-5 situated on a natural levee along the west bank of the river about a half mile from the Jim Woodruff Dam. Although this area is not identical to those described above, it is an area where the river still moves rapidly and the valley is constricted. The Flint River joins the Chattahoochee opposite this site, just above the point where the valley has its maximum restriction. The eddies resulting from the confluence apparently produced a long bar or "natural levee" similar in structure to those found on

[15] Miller, 1949: 39–40.
[16] Caldwell, 1954: 37–39.

the Yadkin and Roanoke rivers. At this site, Bullen examined a profile eighteen feet deep and found that it contained four stratified zones of occupation. The earliest was buried approximately fifteen feet below the surface but, unfortunately, did not yield any diagnostic artifacts. The three other zones, however, were identified as belonging to the Orange, Deptford, and Fort Walton periods, and they were clearly separated from each other by thick deposits of sand and clay.[17]

The third site described in this study was not situated in a flood plain but on top of a hill high above the river (fig. 6). It was named Hardaway after its last occupants—the Hardaway Construction Company.[18] Although erosion and other agencies have destroyed most of the original site, there still remains, in a few places, a midden deposit nearly three feet thick. There had been so many different groups of people living on this site in the past, however, that it was not until after the stratified sites in the flood plains had been excavated

that any satisfactory progress could be made in the interpretation of the cultural remains found there. As cultural units were recognized and isolated elsewhere, they could then be extracted from the medley at this site. Finally, with the completion of the 1958 excavations, the first three occupational periods were isolated and defined. Even though this site was not stratified in the same sense as those found in the alluvial plains, there was sufficient separation and superposition to verify the priority of these earliest cultures over all others thus far identified in the Carolina Piedmont.

In summary, therefore, this study is concerned with the identification and antiquity of certain discrete cultural units as they were represented at three sites in the Carolina Piedmont. It is further concerned with the continuity or discontinuity of these units, particularly in the relatively unknown Archaic stage. Finally, it is concerned with the development of a hypothesis that will increase the probability of finding stratified sites in the river flood plains, since that is where the answers lie to the problems of early cultural developments in the eastern United States.

---

[17] Bullen, 1958: 334, 350.
[18] The construction company that built the Narrows Dam had its barracks and shops built on this site.

PART ONE

THE DOERSCHUK SITE

Mgᵛ22

I. THE NATURAL SETTING

A. LOCATION

The Yadkin River rises on the eastern slope of the Blue Ridge Mountains in western North Carolina and flows four hundred and thirty-five miles to enter the Atlantic Ocean through Winyah Bay near Georgetown, South Carolina. Two hundred miles from its source and two hundred and thirty-five miles from the sea, the Yadkin funnels its turbulent and muddy waters into the Narrows near the present town of Badin. For a distance of four miles these waters rush through this rock-walled gorge then spew forth into the broad valley below. One mile farther downstream the Uwharrie River joins the Yadkin from the east and from this point to the ocean the river is called the Pee Dee.

The sources of the headwater streams that form the Yadkin River are at elevations ranging from 3,500 to 4,000 feet above mean sea level. These streams descend rapidly to an elevation of 1,500 feet to form the head of the Yadkin Valley proper at the foot of the Blue Ridge Mountains near the small town of Patterson, North Carolina. Twenty-five miles farther to the northeast, near the town of North Wilkesboro, the river has descended to an elevation of 934 feet above mean sea level. The river continues in a northeasterly direction for a distance of fifty-five miles with a steady fall of 3.4 feet per mile until it reaches the "great bend." Here the course of the river changes abruptly to flow in a southerly direction for the next sixty miles with the rate of fall decreasing to 2.3 feet per mile. Below this point the river is joined from the west by the South Yadkin River and turns to flow in a southeasterly direction for the rest of its journey to the sea. The rate of fall increases as the river flows into the Carolina Slate Belt giving the thirty-eight miles from the junction of the South Yadkin to the mouth of the Narrows an average fall of 6.6 feet per mile. The greatest fall, however, lies in the Narrows itself where the bed of the river drops ninety-one feet in four miles or at a rate of 22.75 feet per mile. The elevation of the river upon the completion of this drop is 280 feet above mean sea level.

Nestled in a small cove on the eastern bank of the river at the foot of the Narrows is the Doerschuk Site. To the north and to the east the steep slopes of the Uwharrie Mountains rise abruptly to tower above it more than five hundred feet. On these slopes a small stream originates and flows swiftly through a narrow and rocky ravine to join the river at the southern edge of the site. Farther to the south, the river, now called

the Pee Dee, meanders out of the confining Uwharrie Mountains into a broad shallow valley in the Coastal Plain. It falls at an average rate of 3.1 feet per mile until it reaches the vicinity of Cheraw, South Carolina, sixty-six miles below the Narrows. At this point the river has passed over the "fall line" and stands at an elevation of sixty-four feet above mean sea level. For its remaining length of 167 miles, it has an average rate of fall of only 0.38 foot per mile.[1]

B. DESCRIPTION

In its natural condition the valley of the Yadkin near the Doerschuk Site was narrow and rugged. It was an area where the eroding river had cut through alternate layers of hard and soft rock, developing falls, rapids, and cascades. Immediately above the mouth of the Narrows the river turned slightly to flow in a southwesterly direction; its rate of fall decreased, and it entered a relatively broad, elliptically shaped basin that lay roughly parallel to the general strike of the underlying geologic structure. In this basin the river spread to a width of 1,000 feet and flowed through and around a number of small islands. At the mouth of the Narrows, however, the Yadkin turned abruptly to the southeast and entered a narrow, steep-sided canyon. Throughout its four-mile length, the bed of the river in this gorge did not average over one hundred and fifty feet in width, and in one place, its maximum width was only sixty feet (figs. 6, 46).

At the foot of the Narrows the width of the valley floor increased allowing the river to fan out and form into a series of shallow rapids, which were interspersed with outcropping rocks and small sand-filled islands. This increase in the width of the river together with a sudden leveling of its bed formed an effective brake to the velocity of the water as it poured out of the gorge. Sand and silt were deposited along the edge of the river forming narrow flood plains. These, in turn, were eroded and redeposited as the force of the water meandered from one side of this narrow valley to the other.

At the present time, for a distance of about a mile below the foot of the Narrows, there are only traces of flood plain deposits on the western side of the river. On the eastern side, at the Doerschuk Site, the flood plain is about eighty yards wide. Its width increases gradually to about 250 yards near the mouth of Dutch John Creek. Below this point, however, the width decreases until the flood plain disappears about one

[1] United States Army Corps of Engineers, 1933: 15.

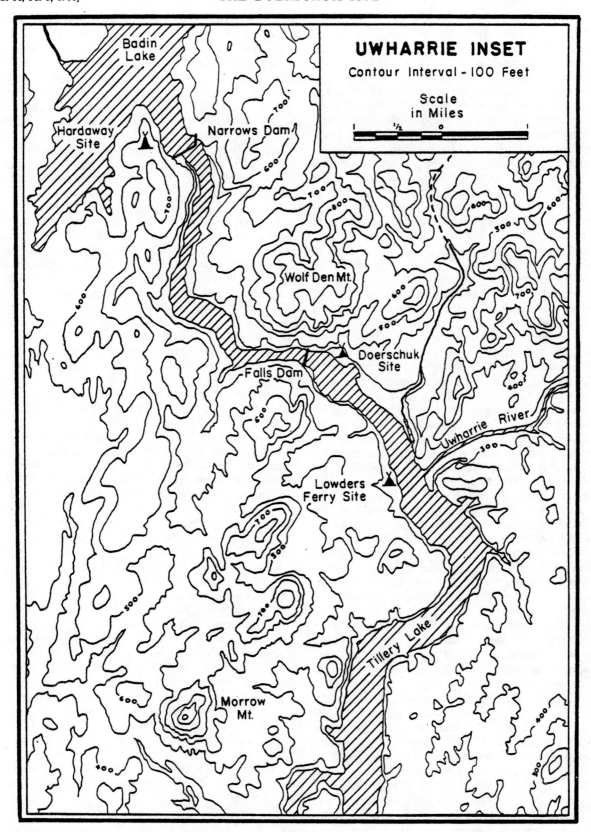

FIG. 6

quarter of a mile above the mouth of the Uwharrie River (fig. 6). From the Uwharrie south to the mouth of Rocky River, a distance of nineteen miles, the total width of the valley floor and the flood plain deposits gradually increase. The river, as it meanders from one side of the valley to the other, flows first along the steep rocky slopes on its western bank then along those on the eastern side. The flood plain deposits also alternate with the river and occur as a series of semilunar strips separated from each other by the meandering of the river. Both banks of the river, from the mouth of Rocky River to the foot of the Narrows, are formed by high rocky hills alternating with flat alluvial plains. As the Narrows are approached from downstream the width of these plains decrease and the height and slope of the hills increase.

The Doerschuk Site is situated on the last strip of alluvial deposit below the Narrows. Since it was impossible, under ordinary conditions, to continue up the river either by boat or along its bank by foot, this barrier at the top of the Pee Dee Valley made it quite likely that any people moving along the river would stop at this point. The area suitable for camping was limited and any occupation of it by people in the past would necessarily be concentrated and superimposed.

The natural structure of the Doerschuk Site is in many respects similar to that of the Gaston Site on the Roanoke River (see page 86). Both were built by overbank deposition in an area protected by an upstream escarpment of resistant rock. Both sites also contain a series of occupational levels separated one from the other by sterile flood deposits of sand and silt. At the Doerschuk Site, however, the occupation began earlier and remained concentrated in a smaller area. The majority of the evidence for these early cultures was found in a narrow strip that begins at the foot of Wolf Den Mountain and runs parallel to the river for about three hundred feet (fig. 6). Altogether, this is an area of less than one acre with its present surface eighteen feet above the normal level of the river. It is separated from the foot of Wolf Den Mountain on the north by a gully five feet deep. To the east the surface also slopes downward slightly, but then rises again at the foot of the mountain slope (fig. 7). To the south the height of the surface continues to drop until it reaches a small stream where the bank is only four feet higher than the river.

The surface of the site was covered with weeds and corn stubble when it was first visited by the author in 1937. There is no information available concerning the date this site was first cleared and plowed. Local tradition suggests that cultivation may have begun as early as 1800. It was in cultivation in 1928, however, when it was first visited by H. M. Doerschuk, and it was plowed last in 1936. When this excavation was begun thirteen years later, the site was covered with a thick natural growth of young pines. In the summer of 1958 these trees were large enough for saw timber, averaging over twelve inches in diameter.

Archaeological evidence indicates that the site was occupied last at the beginning of the eighteenth century by a band of eastern Siouan Indians, probably the Keyauwee. No objects of European or colonial manufacture have been found, however, and no further occupation of this site appears to have taken place. As late as 1824, on the other hand, ". . . bands of ten or more [Indians] were frequently met with on their way to Fayetteville, armed with bows and arrows, and ready for a reward to display their dexterity in hitting, before it came down, a piece of coin tossed up in the air." [2]

The first settlers came into what is now Stanly and Montgomery counties around 1750. Part of these people were Dutch, Scotch-Irish, and German who had moved south from their earlier homes in Pennsylvania and New Jersey. The others were English who had moved east from the Cape Fear settlements. The first public Inn or Ordinary was built by John Colson near the junction of the Pee Dee and Rocky rivers and, for many years, it was the only place identified on maps of this area. It appeared first as "Coulson Ord" on John Collet's map of 1770. By 1800 a number of communities had developed on both sides of the Pee Dee near the mouth of the Uwharrie River. Just below its confluence there was a good ford which made this crossing of the "old stage coach road" a center of commerce for the area. On the west side of the Pee Dee the community was first known as Tindalsvale and then later as Laurensville. On the east side the communities were known as Blakely and Henderson. All four places served as county seats for the young Montgomery County between 1779 and 1841. The County was divided in 1841, however, and that part which lay to the west of the Pee Dee River was called Stanly. [3]

After the Revolutionary War a sixteen-room inn was built by George Kirk in Tindalsvale near the Pee Dee ford, and it was operated by the Kirk family until 1845. The property was later bought by Dave Lowder who built and operated a ferry across the Pee Dee from Tindalsvale to the south shore of the Uwharrie River. [4] This ferry continued to be operated as one of the major crossings until the Swift Island Bridge was constructed eight miles down the river in 1926.

Of all the activities of man in the Yadkin-Pee Dee Valley, the construction of modern hydroelectric dams has altered the configuration of the land and water most. The first attempt to harness the power of the Yadkin was made by George I. Whitney in 1901. He began the construction of a stone masonry dam about four miles up the Yadkin above the mouth of the

---

[2] Kron, 1875: 390.

[3] Corbitt, 1950: 152–155, 195.

[4] The Lowder's Ferry Site, St'7, is located here. See fig. 6.

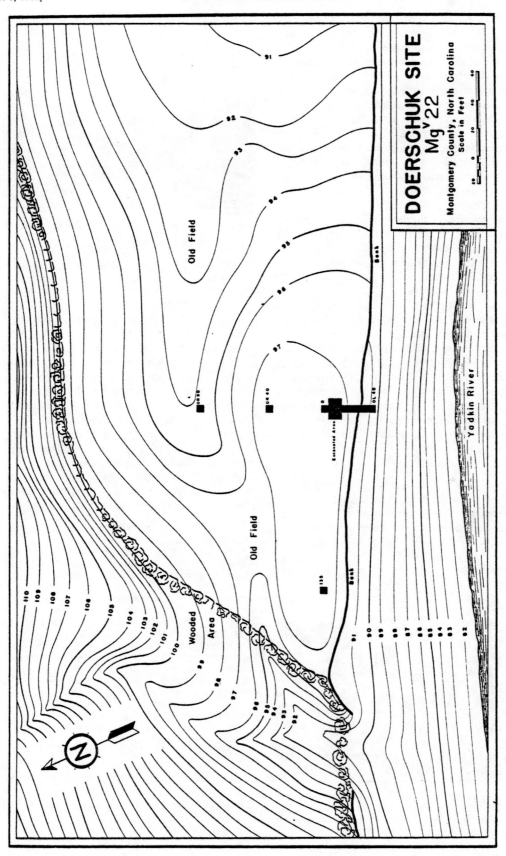

DOERSCHUK SITE
Mg^V 22
Montgomery County, North Carolina
Scale in Feet

FIG. 7

Narrows near the small town of Palmerville. Six years later the Whitney Company failed and the dam, though nearly complete, was never finished.

In 1912 the French Aluminum Reduction Company purchased the Whitney holdings and began the construction of a major dam in the mouth of the Narrows. World War I began two years later and the French engineers and technicians were called home. All work on the project was discontinued. The Aluminum Company of America bought out the French interests a year later. They redesigned the dam and power plants and began work on a grand scale. When the dam was completed in 1917, its power head of 179 feet was the highest in the South.

Upon the completion of the Narrows Dam work was begun on the Falls Dam at the foot of the Narrows. This dam was completed in 1920 with a power head of seventy-nine feet. It was located about one quarter of a mile above the Doerschuk Site, and it, as well as the site, may be seen in figure 9.

Fifteen miles below the Falls Dam the Carolina Electric and Power Company began the construction of still another dam across the Pee Dee in 1926. This project was completed two years later and formed a lake that was seventy feet deep at the dam and that backed water all of the way to the edge of the Doerschuk Site. A large number of aboriginal sites were covered by the backwaters of this lake. The Doerschuk and Lowder's Ferry sites, however, were sufficiently far upstream to be unaffected and were available for excavation.

C. PHYSIOGRAPHY

The Piedmont Plateau is a region of mature topography with well rounded hills, gently sloping valleys, and graded streams. There are, however, local exceptions that are characterized by narrow ridges with steep, rocky slopes and valleys with gorges and courses

FIG. 9. The Falls Dam at the Doerschuk Site. The Falls Dam of the Carolina Aluminum Company was built across the foot of the Narrows. Wolf Den Mountain rises in the background on the right, and the Doerschuk Site is situated on the edge of the river to the right of the dam.

of rapids. The Uwharrie Mountain region is one of those exceptions.

There is a high degree of correlation between the surface configuration and the nature of the underlying rocks. The ridges are, without exception, composed of harder and more resistant rock than the lower country and valleys. The present relief in the area, therefore, appears to be the direct result of the same processes of weathering and erosion that are now going on. The wide bands of sedimentary, slatelike rock have weathered fastest to form the valleys. Intercalated with these occur strips and lenses of volcanic rock which have been more resistant to decay and which now form the backbone of the ridges and hills.

The region has suffered a period of severe dynamic metamorphism or mashing, consequent upon a great compressive force which squeezed the beds into enormous folds: followed by a time of chemical alteration and mineralization, which in turn was succeeded by a long period of erosion and weathering. The rocks have suffered to a variable degree from all these factors. In general, each formation has a massive and a mashed or schistose phase, with every gradation between the two. The passage of heated solutions has affected all formations, as evidenced by the mineralized zones, the abundance of quartz veins, and the high degree of silicification in many belts of rock, and the universal occurrence of infiltrated iron ores. Finally, erosion has planed off all the upper portion of the folded series; but weathering has proceeded in excess of erosion to such an extent that the region is now deeply decayed. so that only here and there do rocks project through a thick mantle of decomposed rock or soil.[5]

When this great series of slates, tuffs, breccias, and flows were compressed and thrown into enormous folds, a complex and mountainous surface was formed. This was attacked even during its formation by the forces of erosion, and in time denudation was carried to such

FIG. 8. The Valley of the Pee Dee River. View of the Valley of the Pee Dee looking southeast from the top of Wolf Den Mountain. The Doerschuk Site is on the left side of the river at the extreme bottom of the photograph.

---

[5] Pogue, 1910: 26–27.

an extent that the region was leveled across hard and soft formation alike to form what is called a peneplain. Following this cycle of complete erosion, there began a slight tilting or rising of the land and a new system of drainage was inaugurated. This system, of which the Yadkin is the remnant, was not controlled by the nature of the underlying rocks which were then near sea level but by the direction of the tilt or slope of the land. This direction was in a northwest-southeast line and cut directly across the alternate layers of hard and soft formations.

The establishment of this line of drainage was followed by a progressive elevation of the land to its present height.[6] Throughout this long period of time there was a constant competition on the part of the drainage to maintain its original direction and on the part of the slowly rising land to divert the drainage from its anomalous course into conformity with the underlying rock structure. The configuration of the present surface suggests that these two opposing forces were nearly equal. The cutting of the Narrows shows that the rise of the land did not greatly exceed that of the down-cutting of the river, and the presence of rapids in the gap shows that the rate of down-cutting did not exceed the rate of rise of the land.

During this contest between the rising Piedmont Plateau and its drainage system, the Yadkin River emerged as the master stream which receives the drainage of the area. At the same time, however, the chemical and mechanical forces of weathering continued their attack upon the region. Streams subordinate to the Yadkin were developed. These found their easiest path to lie in agreement with the structure and carved their valleys along the softer bands of rock in a northeast-southwest direction. Thus, as a result of the elevation of the land and the down-cutting of the streams, the present topography of the Uwharrie Mountains came into being.

The development of the Uwharrie region of the Piedmont Plateau has been a very long process. The original beds of slatelike rock were apparently laid down in a slowly sinking basin until they reached a depth of ten to eighteen thousand feet.[7] No fossils have been found in these slates, and it is generally believed by geologists who have worked in the area that this series of rock was laid down in Pre-Cambrian time.[8] The great intruding magmas of greenstone were followed by the folding and schistosity of the older slate during the lower Paleozoic, and ". . . the Wadesboro Triassic Basin was faulted downward into the older volcanic-sedimentary rocks and the Neward Series was deposited in the trough . . ." during late Triassic times.[9] There appears to have been no further structural change in this area since the Triassic period and the subsequent

alteration of the surface has been primarily the result of weathering and erosion.

If the above observations have been correctly interpreted, then there has been very little change in this land form during the period of human occupation of the Western Hemisphere. It is reasonable to expect, therefore, that some evidence should be found in this area of any people who may have lived there in the past. Even though erosion has been insignificant during the past 10,000 years in a geologic sense, it has been considerable from an archaeological point of view. When these early occupations occurred on elevated places, the evidence lies on or near the surface since the soil has gradually eroded downward. On the other hand, when these people lived on the flood plain, their remains would be buried under the more recent alluvial deposits. The Hardaway Site (see Part Two) which is situated on top of a hill overlooking the mouth of the Narrows is an example of the former situation. The Doerschuk Site situated on the flood plain at the foot of the Narrows is an example of the latter.

The base of the present depositional sequence at the Doerschuk Site is the former river bed. It is an area of eroded bed rock strewn with gravel and large boulders upon which the first phase of deposition began as channel deposits or point bar formations as the force of the river's current gradually moved toward the west. These deposits of sand and gravel continued to build until they reached the height of about six feet above the normal level of the river where they were covered only by the higher annual floods.

The second phase of building consisted of overbank deposition which was laid down as thin horizontal laminae to a depth of four feet. This thick bed of varve-like deposits is not a general characteristic of flood plains, but, instead, is the result of a local configuration of the river channel to its flood plain and valley walls.[10] At the time this material was being deposited, the river flowed along the western side of the valley. The site was separated from it by natural levees or bars of sufficient height to impound flood waters until much of the materials held in suspension settled to the bottom. Following each flood a thin layer of sand was deposited after which it was covered by the finer particles of clay which settled out of the water last. These deposits were nearly uniform in thickness but followed the irregular contours of the older sand level upon which they were laid. This would not have been the case if the water carrying these sediments had continued to move. The surface of the site at this time, therefore, must have been swampy and covered with standing water following periods of flood.

Although this general sequence of varvelike deposits continued until it reached a depth of four feet and stood ten feet above the normal level of the river, it was interrupted at least twice by major flooding of the whole

[6] White, 1953: 561–580.
[7] Bowman, 1954: 75.
[8] Pogue, 1910: 95.
[9] Bowman, 1954: 76.

[10] Wolman and Leopold, 1957: 97–98.

FIG. 10. The eroded river bank at the north edge of the Doerschuk Site. This bank has a maximum height of forty feet and is composed of angular, flat fragments of highly weathered slate consolidated in a clayey matrix. Numerous chips and a few scrapers have been recovered from this eroding face.

FIG. 11. The eroded river bank west of the main trench at the Doerschuk Site. These stone specimens were derived largely from the upper half of the stratified deposits.

valley. The first change occurred about midway in the deposit and suggests a series of floods of sufficient magnitude to overflow the protective levee system and carry large quantities of coarse sand into the area. The height to which these sand bars were built is not known because the second period of major flooding resulted in extensive erosion to the sand and clay deposits alike. Following this, however, the older levees were apparently reinforced and the still water deposition of sand and clay varves continued, resting unconformably upon the older sequence (fig. 17).

The age of this deposit can only be estimated. No charcoal was collected from this level and no samples of pollen could be found. Evidences of human occupation, however, were unmistakable, and the culture type (Stanly) found incased in the upper foot of this deposit has an estimated antiquity of 7,000 years.[11] Another estimate may be made, however, of the time necessary for the building of this deposit. The more than 200 sets of sand and clay varves in this zone represent separate periods of flooding, and an approximation of the length of time necessary for this number to accumulate may be made on the basis of the observed magnitude and frequency of floods on the Pee Dee River since 1890. Data recorded at Cheraw, South Carolina indicate that floods of sufficient height to cover the lower part of this deposit could be expected once every two years, while floods high enough to cover the upper part of this zone would not occur more than once in twenty-five years.[12] When these data are plotted on a frequency curve, they indicate that approximately 1,536 years would be required for the building of this

deposit.[13] Since it is believed that the cultural material covered by the upper part of these varves was being made around 5000 B.C., then it must be assumed that this second phase of deposition began before 6000 B.C. and that the other fragments of worked stone recovered from the underlying sand and gravel of the first phase are even older.

The third and final phase of deposition began when the force of the river shifted back toward the center of the valley and buried the clay deposits of the second phase under a foot thick mantle of coarse sand (fig. 13, Zone X). This surface then remained stable for a long period of time until the growth of vegetation and the occupational debris of humans (Morrow Mountain) living upon it developed into a dark and thick zone of humus (fig. 14). Subsequent to this, a second major flood deposited nearly two feet of sand upon the site in the form of a long high ridge (Zone VIII). This formed the base and began the delineation of the present surface configuration which, for nearly two thousand years, has remained essentially unchanged. It was occupied in succession by three cultural groups (Morrow Mountain; Guilford, ca. 4000 B.C.; and Savannah River, ca. 2000 B.C.) with each leaving considerable evidence of their daily life in the slowly growing humus and midden zone. This slow accumulation of occupational debris was interrupted twice more by major floods that deposited mantles of sand a foot or more thick over the surface of the site. The first of these occurred before 1000 B.C. (Zone IV) and the last occurred around A.D. 1000 (Zone II). There is no indi-

---

[11] This estimate of the age of the Stanly Complex is based upon its stratigraphic priority to the Guilford Complex and the carbon dates secured for the Gaston Site.

[12] United States Army Corps of Engineers, 1933: 100.

[13] In evaluating this estimate of time two sources of error must be considered. First, no allowance was made for the deposits lost to erosion, and second, the data on flood frequencies were collected at a point sixty-three miles downstream from the Doerschuk Site where the Pee Dee River drains 3,240 additional square miles. This estimate of 1,536 years, therefore, should be considered only in terms of the minimum amount of elapsed time.

cation that the site has been flooded since that time. The highest flood on record occurred in 1908 and reached a height of 17.3 feet above flood stage at Cheraw, South Carolina. According to the U. S. Army Corps of Engineers' estimate, this flood was of such magnitude that it could be expected to occur only once in 670 years; yet it fell at least a foot below the present surface of the site. The Corps of Engineers also estimated that a flood of 1,000 year magnitude would crest at only 17.9 feet, still nearly a half foot below the surface of the site.[14]

It should be emphasized that in trying to evaluate the amount of elapsed time represented by this sequence of alluvial deposits the relative ages of the known cultural complexes were used as the primary guides. There is nothing inherent in such deposits that would allow one to use them as an absolute measure of time. It is important to realize, however, that there are localities such as this on the flood plains where deposits do build up rapidly in their lower levels then gradually slow down until they reach a point where they are no longer covered by floods of normal magnitude. At the same time recent studies have shown that flood plains as a whole do not build up to this maximum height.[15] The rate of deposition equals roughly the rate of erosion and the height of the flood plain above the river bed tends to remain static.

It is obvious, therefore, that there must be other factors that control these isolated build-ups on the river flood plain. In the case of the Doerschuk Site the projecting outcrop of rock formed a large eddy area during the period of major floods. This resulted in the deposition of greater quantities of coarser materials than would have been true in the open flood plain. A second factor to be considered is that the narrow valley and projecting rock outcrops have prevented the formation of mature meanders and this area has been largely protected from lateral or bank erosion. Once such a deposit has reached its mature height, it appears that a major tectonic change in the river system would be required for its destruction.

II. THE EXCAVATIONS

A. THE PROBLEMS AND METHODS OF EXCAVATIONS

In the summer of 1948 Mr. Paul Strieff, a graduate student at the University of Michigan, began working with the author on an archaeological survey of the Morrow Mountain area. The primary purpose of this work was to reexamine the various known sites along this section of the Yadkin-Pee Dee River with the hope that some evidence of cultural stratigraphy or superposition might be found. The first site to be examined was at the old Lowder's Ferry landing on the west bank of the Yadkin opposite the mouth of the Uwharrie

[14] United States Army Corps of Engineers, 1933: 100.
[15] Wolman and Leopold, 1957: 100.

River (fig. 6). A series of fifteen test pits were dug throughout the site, and, for the first time in the Carolina Piedmont, conclusive evidence was found for the association of cultural materials with natural stratigraphic levels (see fig. 117). Here the remains of a Guilford occupation was found buried nearly three feet below the surface. This old land surface had been covered subsequently by eighteen inches of flood deposited sand, after which it was reoccupied by people who have been identified with the Savannah River type culture. This level, in turn, was buried by ten more inches of flood deposits before the site was again occupied. The final occupations were components of the Uwharrie, Pee Dee, and Caraway cultures.[16]

After completing the tests at the Lowder's Ferry Site attention was turned to the Doerschuk Site. situated about two miles upstream and on the opposite side of the river. This site was known to have a thick midden deposit, so it was anticipated that this should show some change in the ceramic styles from top to bottom. The first test was a five-foot-square pit (0L10) located in the approximate center of the site.

[16] The Lowder's Ferry Site, St'7, was extensively excavated in 1949. The above sequence was fully corroborated, but no other cultural components were found.

FIG. 12. The 1948 excavation at the Doerschuk Site. This photograph shows Mr. Paul Strieff standing on top of Zone XI in which was to be found the evidence of the Stanly occupation. The large sterile zone (Zone VIII) may be seen directly behind his head.

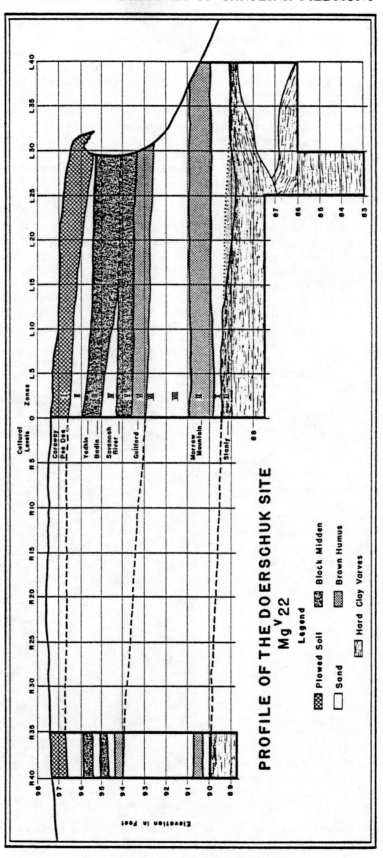

PROFILE OF THE DOERSCHUK SITE
Mg^V 22

Legend

Plowed Soil   Black Midden
Sand   Brown Humus
               Hard Clay Varves

FIG. 13

When this was excavated to the bottom of the midden (Zone VI) it became evident that for the second time in the Carolina Piedmont cultural materials were being found in a stratified context. Evidence of the relatively well-known Caraway and Pee Dee components were found in the plowed zone and pottery of earlier periods were found in the lower levels. Below these pottery complexes evidence was again found for a Savannah River and a Guilford occupation. At this point in the test, the sequence found at Lowder's Ferry had been duplicated and extended by the presence of two additional ceramic periods.

As work in this test pit continued below the midden it became obvious that the underlying soils were not all sterile of cultural debris. A new type of projectile point was found in Zone VII (52″) and again below a very thick sand deposit in Zone IX (84″). These points were later named for the nearby Morrow Mountain. Below this level and at an average depth of eight feet below the present surface there was found still another distinctive cultural complex to which the name Stanly has been given. Work in the test pit continued to a total depth of ten feet (fig. 12). Stone chips were

FIG. 15. The excavation of zones in the main trench at the Doerschuk Site. The worker in the foreground has begun excavation of Zone XI at the Stanly level. The caved-in section on the left occurred after the 1948 excavation and before the excavation of the main trench. The block in the background is Square 0L20 and illustrates the effort made to correlate the excavated levels with the natural zones of deposition.

FIG. 14. The main trench of the 1949 excavation at the Doerschuk Site. The deepest portion of this trench has exposed the top of Zone XI, and the midden deposit of the Morrow Mountain occupation (Zone IX) may be seen in the near profile. The majority of the trench in the background has been excavated to the top of Zone VIII.

found throughout this sand deposit, but no earlier occupation was discovered below Zone XI.

The procedure for excavating this original test pit was simply to remove the soil in six-inch arbitrary levels, since the natural stratigraphy was unknown at at that time. The soil in the upper levels was thrown by shovel into a screen where it was sifted, but as the excavation deepened, it became necessary to remove the loose soil with a bucket and a rope. In order to facilitate this work, a second five-foot square (0L15) was excavated at the western edge of the original pit to a depth of fifty inches. This provided a working platform about halfway down and lessened the danger of a cave in.

Work at the Doerschuk Site was suspended when the excavation of this test pit reached a point ten feet below surface. The depth of the deposits and the sandy nature of the soil made this type of well-digging operation hazardous, and it was too late in the season to extend the excavations over a larger area. An insight into the importance and natural structure of the site

FIG. 16. The main trench at the Doerschuk Site after the 1949 excavation. The exposed profile is between 0L15 and 0L40.

had been gained, however, and plans were made to return the following year for the continuation of the excavations on a more systematic basis.

On June 1, 1949, camp was set up on the edge of the site and work was begun cleaning out the caved in area in the original test pit and cutting sight lines through the dense underbrush.[17] After some effort a reasonably accurate contour map was completed for the site based on an arbitrary bench mark with an assumed elevation of 100 feet (fig. 7).[18] A base line was then established ten feet to the east of the original test pit and parallel to the river bank. A second line was placed at right angles to this so that it crossed the southern edge of the test pit. The intersection of these two lines was designated zero and the grid system thus formed incorporated the previous excavation as square 0L10 (ten feet left of zero). This grid, however, was not oriented north and south, but was laid to conform to the natural axes of the land which ran from the northwest to the southeast.

When the surveying of the base lines was completed an area five feet wide and forty feet long was staked out to extend from zero to a point ten feet beyond the

edge of the eroding bank. This area lay over the original test pit and extended its profile in both directions (fig. 13). It also provided an open end to the trench so that the soil from the lower levels could be removed by wheelbarrows.

In beginning the actual excavation in 1949, the first effort was directed toward separating the cultural materials from the various natural levels of deposition. The plowed soil was all removed as a unit and an attempt was made to identify the underlying deposits as they were excavated. This soon proved to be impractical since it was not always possible to distinguish accurately each of the natural zones in the upper midden during the moment of excavation. The tops of Zones VIII and XI were clearly recognizable at every point of contact, however, so it was decided to excavate the remainder of the trench in three separate stages (fig. 14). The first stage removed all of the upper midden (Zones II through VII) in six-inch arbitrary levels. The second stage removed the sterile sand zones (Zone VIII and X) as units but divided the Morrow Mountain midden (Zone IX) into two arbitrary levels. The third stage removed Zone XI and all succeeding levels in six-inch arbitrary units. Square 0L20, however, was left standing until is was exposed on both sides

FIG. 17. A detail view of Zone XI between stakes 0L30 and 0L40 at the Doerschuk Site. Note the regularity of the sand and clay varvelike deposits and the unconformity in the background.

---

[17] The excavation crew consisted of four college students: Fred Gilliam, Tom Lilly, Buck Swaringe, and James Wood.

[18] The height of the assumed datum point has been estimated to be 297 feet above mean sea level.

then each natural deposit that could be identified was carefully isolated and excavated (fig. 15). When the excavation of the whole trench was completed, the profiles were cleaned, photographed, and drawn to show the true relationship of these superimposed land surfaces. In the analysis of the cultural materials each arbitrary level was considered first then these were translated into terms of their natural zones of deposition as illustrated in figure 13.

In addition to the excavation of the main trench, additional test pits were dug at 0R40, 0R90, and 135 (fig. 7). These confirmed the stratigraphy of the first excavation for the area as a whole, and they also indicated that the greatest concentration of cultural material was in the vincinity of the 0-0L40 trench.

B. THE NATURAL ZONES OF OCCUPATION

The antiquity of man in the Valley of the Pee Deè is very great and only a small part of his activities has been captured by the flood deposits at the Doerschuk Site. Nevertheless, these deposits do represent a span of approximately 8,000 years. Some evidence of man's activities has been found at the bottom of every test made as well as in the matrix of the slump at the base of Wolf Den Mountain (fig. 10). This matrix has a depth of over forty feet and underlies all of the later flood deposits. The origin of this slump, which has been found to contain many stone chips and a few stone scrapers, is not known. Since the material in the matrix is not sorted and shows no sign of water erosion, it cannot be considered to have developed as an alluvial fan. It could have originated, however, during the climax of the last glaciation as a result of the longer periods of colder weather.

In the area of the 0–0L40 trench small quantities of stone chips were found throughout the sand and gravel of the first phase of deposition, but it was not until near the end of the second phase of deposition (page 20) that this land surface was actually occupied by man. Even here no hearth or other such evidences of camp life was found, but the quantity of chips, blades, and projectile points of the Stanly Complex clearly indicated a concentration of human activity in that area (Zone XI).

Following this period of occupation the artifactual remains were covered by a series of thin compact layers of fine clay silt to a depth of two to three inches. This was followed by a period of minor erosion and the cutting of a shallow gulley into Zone XI. This may be seen on the profile in figure 13 between stakes 0L15 and 0L30.

The third phase of deposition began with the flood that deposited a bed of sand over the whole site. In time, this land surface was also lived upon and considerable refuse accumulated to form Zone IX; then, it too, was buried beneath another thick bed of sand.

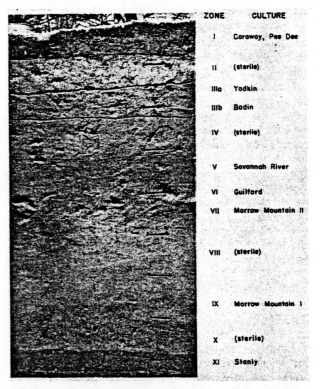

ZONE	CULTURE
I	Caraway, Pee Dee
II	(sterile)
IIIa	Yadkin
IIIb	Badin
IV	(sterile)
V	Savannah River
VI	Guilford
VII	Morrow Mountain II
VIII	(sterile)
IX	Morrow Mountain I
X	(sterile)
XI	Stanly

FIG. 18. East profile of Square 0 at the Doerschuk Site. Natural zones of deposition are indicated by numbers. The names refer to the culture types found buried in these zones.

The "Morrow Mountain" people, however, reappeared after this flooding to occupy the top of the sand bed that had buried their former home, and this disturbance has been designated Zone VII.

The Guilford occupation (Zone VI) appeared next in this sequence of events, and it was followed by a long period of surface stability which allowed the development of a humus zone approximately six inches thick over the whole site. This, again, was covered by a thin deposit of flood sand as shown in square 0R40 and subsequently occupied by people now identified with the Savannah River Culture. This occupation, as indicated by Zone V, was extensive, and for the first time a truly thick midden of human refuse accumulated at this site. Then, as was true many times before, the remains of the Savannah River Complex was covered by a deposit of flood sand.

When this site was occupied again it was by people who knew how to manufacture pottery. A second thick midden deposit (Zone III) developed as a result of their activities over a period of several hundred years. This deposit was not homogeneous, however, as it was found that a distinction could be made in the distribution of both pottery and projectile points. The lower half of the midden, IIIb, contained the largest per cent of the complex called Badin while the upper half, IIIa, contained a later stage, the Yadkin Complex. A final flooding deposited Zone II over the site after which the Yadkin occupation continued. Finally, between A.D. 1500 and A.D. 1700 it was occupied, for the last time, by small components of Pee Dee and Caraway cultures.

Throughout the ceramic era the occupants of the site engaged in various kinds of digging activities and the clean-cut segregation found in the lower levels did not exist above Zone IV. The later stratification was obscured by the intrusion of pits into lower levels and the bringing up of earlier material to the surface. Even though this situation was realized and every effort was made to isolate the intruded materials, the final analysis may still contain some error. The belief that intrusions tend to average out and that distribution measured by the rule is alone sufficient has led to some interesting, if questionable, interpretations in southeastern archaeology.[19]

III. THE ANALYSIS OF ARTIFACTS

A total of 6,841 specimens was collected from the Doerschuk Site. Of this collection, 2,539 were recovered in 1948 (acc. no. 301) and 4,302 were excavated in 1949 (acc. no. 312). Many of these specimens were not finished artifacts, but, rather, raw materials in the process of manufacture. One of the major activities at this site, from the earliest occupation to the last, was the manufacture of chipped stone implements, and, as a result, there was left in each deposit large quantities of chips, cores, and discarded or broken specimens (fig. 11). Obviously, only a representative amount of this discarded material could be retained and catalogued for each excavated unit. Otherwise, the total inventory would have been nearer 600,000.

[19] Phillips, Ford, and Griffin, 1951: 291.

It should also be explained that in the final analysis of the various artifact types only the specimens recovered from relatively undisturbed positions in the occupation zones were used. All of the artifacts found on the surface, in caved-in areas, from aboriginal pits, or other disturbances were excluded. The only exception being the material from the excavated plowed soil or Zone I, for although obviously disturbed it contained the evidence for the last occupations.

A. POTTERY

The total pottery collection from the Doerschuk Site consisted of 2,314 sherds. Of this total, 781 were found on the surface or in some other disturbed context and the remaining 1,533 were from excavated levels that showed no physical evidence of intrusion. The distribution of these sherds according to the levels in which they were found is illustrated in table 1 and figure 19. These data should make it crystal clear that the sequence of ceramic development at the Doerschuk Site was from Badin to Caraway.

The details of this development, however, are not so clear. As stated above, the content of any particular level should not be considered as a cultural unit, i.e., the product of one people at one time. The softness and unevenness of present and past surfaces, together with the pitting and the everyday activities of the occupants, would certainly mingle any contemporary debris with that of the earlier inhabitants. The presence of 242 sherds in Zone II which began its existence as a barren flood deposit should, by itself, indicate the extent of the intrusions that were not detected during the excavation. Loose sand is a joy to sift, but it also creates many problems for archaeological interpretation.

The data illustrated in table 1 and figure 19 would

TABLE 1

PERCENTAGE DISTRIBUTION OF POTTERY SERIES BY ZONES AT THE DOERSCHUK SITE*

Natural Zone	Excavated Level	Total	Caraway Series	Dan River Series	Pee Dee Series	Yadkin Series	Badin Series	Dentate** and Linear Check	Steatite
I	1	100.0 (805)	18.9 (174)	1.0 (8)	28.0 (218)	49.8 (387)	2.3 (18)		
II	2	100.0 (242)	4.1 (10)	0.4 (1)	7.4 (18)	69.8 (169)	15.0 (36)	3.3 (8)	
IIIa	3	100.0 (347)			1.4 (5)	15.8 (54)	68.0 (234)	14.2 (49)	0.6 (5)
IIIb	4	100.0 (129)				6.9 (9)	86.2 (112)	4.6 (6)	2.3 (2)
	5	100.0 (10)					50.0 (5)	20.0 (2)	30.0 (3)
IV	6	--------	--------	--------	----- Sterile -----		--------	--------	------

* Individual count given in parentheses.   Total sherds: 1,533.
** One dentate sherd found in Zone IIIa.

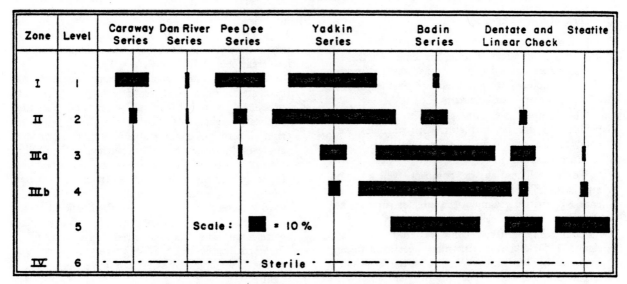

Zone	Level	Caraway Series	Dan River Series	Pee Dee Series	Yadkin Series	Badin Series	Dentate and Linear Check	Steatite
I	1	▬	▪	▬▬	▬▬▬	▪		
II	2	▪		▪	▬▬▬	▪	▪	
IIIa	3			▪	▪ ▬▬▬		▬	▪
IIIb	4				▪ ▬▬▬		▪	▪
	5			Scale: ▪ = 10 %	▬▬		▬▬	▬▬
IV	6	· — · — · —	· — · —	· —	Sterile · + — · — ·	— · —	· — · — ·	— ·

FIG. 19. Distribution of pottery series by zones at the Doerschuk Site.

suggest at first glance that the Badin and Yadkin Series are free variations of a single ceramic tradition—that the use of the Badin type declined as the popularity of the Yadkin variety increased. This, however, was not the case at the Doerschuk Site. While it is true that the Badin and Yadkin Series are part of one ceramic tradition, they represent two separate periods of development and not a continuum between them. Unlike the Vincent-Clements transition at the Gaston Site (fig. 94) the Badin and Yadkin types can be placed, for the most part, in mutually exclusive categories. The presence of a few Badin sherds (54) in the upper levels was undoubtedly the result of the same intrusive actions that dropped the Yadkin sherds (63) into the lower levels. Although there are some suggestions of change, the transition in style must have occurred at some place other than the Doerschuk Site, and it is quite possible that there was a gap of several centuries between the major part of these two occupations.

1. Badin Series

This pottery (figs. 21, 22) consisted of two principal types: Badin Cord-Marked and Badin Fabric-Marked. The paste was hard and compact with a fine sandy texture. The color tended to be dark brown with some areas burned to a light tan. The vessel form was that of a simple straight sided jar with a conical base. The rims were irregular but smoothed and rounded. No decoration was used.

These types are similar in appearance and manufacture to the Vincent Series found in the Roanoke Rapids Basin. They also appear in the same stratigraphic context, and it is presumed that they were made at about the same time. It is significant to note that this earliest pottery, while crude in appearance, was nevertheless, very well made and much more durable than

much of the pottery that was to follow. The techniques of pottery-making, therefore, must have been well developed before they were introduced to the Indians of the Carolina Piedmont.

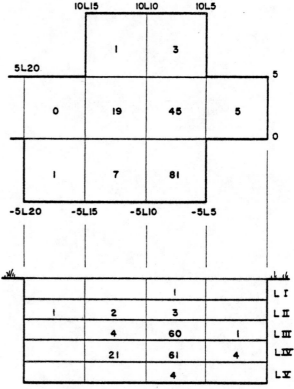

FIG. 20. Horizontal and vertical distribution of the potsherds found at the Doerschuk Site and used in the reconstruction of the Dan River Net-Impressed vessel illustrated in Figure 27. This distribution clearly shows that these sherds lay within the configuration of a large, shallow pit although its outline was not visible at the time of excavation.

Badin Cord-Marked (fig. 21):

Method of manufacture: Annular segments built upon a starting coil or disc. Paddle malleated on the exterior surface; scraped and smoothed on the interior surface. Fractures were frequent along the junction of the coils or annular segments.

Paste: (1) Temper: Very fine sand with an occasional pebble 2–3 mm. in diameter. All particles were rounded and appear to be river sand.

(2) Hardness: 2.5 to 3.5.

(3) Texture: The clay was compact, well kneaded, and hard. The surface was sandy to touch but not coarse or gritty. Many of the interior surfaces had a slick or clayey feel.

(4) Color: The exterior color varied from a light tan to a dark brown with most specimens falling into the lighter range. A few specimens had a slight orange tint. The interior surfaces were usually the same color as the exterior, but in a few cases they were darker. The core was uniformly the same color as the surfaces. Where the interior surface was darker, there was a gradual change from dark to light in the core cross section.

FIG. 21. The pottery type Badin Cord-Marked from the Doerschuk Site. *A.* The fragments of this specimen were found in Zone III*b* in Squares 0, 0L5, and –5L5. *B.* Square 0R40, Zone III*a*; Sq. –5L5, Zone III*b*; Sq. 0R40, Zone III*b*. *C.* Square 0L5, Zone III*b*; Sq. –5L10, Zone III*a*; Sq. 0R40, Zone III*b*.

Firing: Fired upright in an open fire. The firing was well controlled and the core, as well as all the surfaces, appears to have been thoroughly oxidized.

Surface treatment:

(1) Exterior: The whole exterior surface was malleated with a cord-wrapped paddle. The impressions of the cords are clear and the final application was made roughly at right angles to the rim. There was considerable overpaddling and the angle of the cord tended to become more oblique toward the base. The diameter of the cords used for wrapping the paddles varied from 1.5 to 3 mm. These cords were considerably larger than those used on the Vincent Cord-Marked, and they are one of the distinguishing traits. A few specimens were found with traces of a red clay coating filling the cord impressions. Since there was no red clay at the Doerschuk Site it must have been applied deliberately.

(2) Interior: All interior surfaces were carefully smoothed. There is clear evidence that a scraping tool was used to dress the surface prior to finishing it with the hand. This latter process tended to float the finer clay particles and gave the interior surface its characteristic clayey feel. There was no evidence of cord impressions on the interior surface.

Decoration: None.

Form: (1) Lip: Slightly thinned and rounded. Smoothed with the fingers, but irregular and undulating.

(2) Rim: More or less straight and vertical.

(3) Body: Globular bowl tending toward a conical base.

(4) Base: Semi-conical.

Vessel size: Only one vessel could be reconstructed sufficiently well to allow an estimate of its overall shape and size. It was a bowl 28 cm. in diameter and 20 cm. in depth. The wall thickness varied from 0.8 to 0.9 cm. but thickened at the base to an estimated 2 cm. The range of wall thickness for all specimens was 0.5 to 1.0 cm., with the average being about 0.8 cm.

Badin Fabric-Marked (fig. 22):

Method of manufacture: Same as Badin Cord-Marked. The segments appeared to have been better bonded, however, since fractures along the coil were not as frequent.

Paste: Same as Badin Cord-Marked. The color, however, tended toward the darker shades with a larger percentage having dark gray to black interior surfaces. The cores were also much darker and in many cases they were completely black from surface to surface.

Firing: While some of these vessels appeared to have been fired in the same fashion as the Badin Cord-

Marked type, many were not. The majority of the specimens suggest that the vessels were fired in an inverted position or were otherwise covered preventing the extent of oxidation previously noted for the cord-marked type.

Surface treatment:

(1) Exterior: The entire exterior surface was malleated with a wicker-type fabric. This matlike material was sufficiently stiff to serve as a paddle when folded or rolled. The heavy warp rods varied from 5 to 10 mm. in thickness with an average diameter of about 7 mm. The weft was usually a twisted cord with a diameter of about 1 or 1.5 mm. In a few specimens the weft appeared to have been made from a soft nontwisted material which was about 4 mm. in diameter (leather?). It is possible that all of these latter specimens were from the same vessel and that this represents a variation in weaving technique quite incidental to its use on the pot.

(2) Interior: Similar to Badin Cord-Marked. Some specimens show definite signs of scraping with a tool and all interiors were hand smoothed, even where the contours were irregular.

Decoration: None.

Form: (1) Lip: Thinned and rounded, and in some cases rolled slightly outward. All were finger smoothed.

(2) Rim: Straight and vertical. In the case of jars with more abruptly restricted necks the rims were recurved to a vertical position.

(3) Body: Bowl forms were rounded and shallow. The jars were deeper with slightly restricted necks.

(4) Base: Bowls were rounded, jars were conical.

Vessel size: Same as Badin Cord-Marked.

Badin Net-Impressed (fig. 22 C):

In the original analysis, 246 net-impressed sherds were examined. Nine of these were recognized as Dan River Net-Impressed (A.D. 1650) and one as Uwharrie Net-Impressed (A.D. 1500). Later, 161 other net-impressed sherds were found to be parts of one Dan River pot (fig. 20), and they were excluded from the level analysis. This left a total of 75 net-impressed sherds still unidentified. Their paste and interior finish closely resembled that of the Badin Series and for that reason they were included in that tabulation. Their distribution was as follows: Zone II, 3; Zone IIIa, 62; and Zone IIIb, 10. This has less significance, however, when it is recalled that 90 sherds of the previously mentioned Dan River pot were found in Zone IIIb. It has been the author's observation that net-impressing, as a ceramic technique, appeared relatively late in the Piedmont, and it is not believed that this is an exception. According to the criteria set up for the identification of the Badin Series, however, these sherds should be included. A larger sample, however,

FIG. 22. The pottery types Badin Fabric-Marked and Badin Net-Impressed from the Doerschuk Site. *A*. Badin Fabric-Marked rim sherds. Sq. 5L10, Zone IIIa; Sq. –5L5, Zone IIIa; Sq. 0L5, Zone IIIb. *B*. Badin Fabric-Marked base and body sherds. Sq. 5L5, Zone IIIb; Sq. –5L5, Zone IIIb. *C*. Badin Net-Impressed body and rim sherds. Sq. –5L5, Zone IIIa; Sq. 0L15, Zone I.

together with a better understanding of their association will probably show that they are a local variation of the Dan River Series, similar to the reconstructed pot previously mentioned (fig. 27).[20]

Badin Plain:

A second group of sherds that were placed reluctantly in the Badin Series consisted of 57 specimens with smoothed exteriors. They, like the net-impressed sherds, resembled the Badin pottery in the composition of the paste and the treatment of the interior surface, and they were also small body sherds that lacked diagnostic features of rim and body shape. The distribution of the "Badin" Plain sherds was as follows: Zone I, 1; Zone II, 3; Zone IIIa, 30, and Zone IIIb, 23. If these sherds should prove to be part of the Badin Complex, then it is the first instance of the occurrence of this type of surface finish in such an early context in the Carolina Piedmont.

[20] Coe and Lewis, 1952: 1.

2. *Yadkin Series*

This group of pottery is without a doubt a continuation of the same basic techniques and styles that were practiced earlier by the people who produced the Badin pottery. A total of 619 sherds, or nearly half of the total sample used for analysis at the Doerschuk Site, have been classified as belonging to this group. Their stratigraphic position relative to the earlier Badin pottery is shown in table 1 and figure 19. When the percentages of distribution are figured vertically by type, instead of horizontally by levels, they show that 89.8 per cent of this group was found in Zones I and II while 86.7 per cent of the Badin Series was found in Zone III. This certainly indicates that Zone III was primarily the result of a Badin occupation, and that, while the Yadkin occupation may have begun at the top of Zone III, it certainly continued for the major part of its existence on or near the present surface after the deposition of Zone II.

Fig. 23. The pottery type Yadkin Cord-Marked from the Doerschuk Site. *A*. Yadkin Cord-Marked rim sherds. Sq. –5L15, Zone II; Sq. 0L10, Zone II; Sq. 0L15, Zone III*b*; Sq. 5L5, Zone I. *B*. Yadkin Cord-Marked rim sherds. Sq. 0L15, Zone I; Sq. –5L15, Zone II; Sq. 5L10, Zone I; Sq. 0L5, Zone I. *C*. Yadkin Cord-Marked body sherds. Sq. 0L15, Zone III*a*; Sq. –5L15, Zone I; Sq. 0R40, Zone I. *D*. Yadkin Cord-Marked body sherds, paste type "B." Sq. 0L20, Zone I; Sq. –5L15, Zone III*a*; Sq. 0L15, Zone II.

This Yadkin pottery was also made with cord-marked and fabric-marked surface finishes, with each occurring in about equal proportion. The shape and dimensions remained essentially the same as those of the earlier Badin types, but there was a major change in the preparation of the clay. Crushed quartz was used for temper, and it was added in such quantities that it frequently would constitute 30 to 40 per cent of the body of the paste (fig. 26 *B*). On cord-marked sherds, the size of the cord was smaller and the surface of most of these sherds was burnished or smoothed over after the application of the cord-wrapped paddle. The weave of the fabric was also finer on most of the fabric-marked sherds and in appearance they were very similar to the Roanoke and Clements types on the Roanoke River (fig. 99). A few sherds, however, were still impressed with a coarse woven fabric similar to that commonly used on the Badin sherds and this may suggest the nature of the transition. Only two of the 285 Yadkin Cord-Marked sherds, however, resemble the Badin type of cord-marked surface.

It was during this period that a few traits common to the southern coastal area made their first appearance. Sixty-four sherds with the characteristic Yadkin shape and texture were finished on the exterior with a linear check stamp (fig. 26). Forty-six of the Yadkin Fabric-Marked sherds also had the addition of a quantity of clay temper mixed with the crushed quartz (fig. 25 *C*). Finally, one other sherd made from this clay-quartz tempered paste was decorated with a dentate stamp (fig. 25 *C*).

Yadkin Cord-Marked (fig. 23) :

Method of manufacture: Annular segments, well bonded. Fractures were irregular and seldom occurred along the junction of the segments. The exterior surface was malleated with a cord-wrapped paddle and the interior surfaces were scraped and smoothed.

Paste: (1) Temper: Large angular fragments of quartz that appeared to have been broken especially for tempering material. The particles varied from 1 to 8 mm. in diameter with the majority being about 3 mm. in their dimension.

(2) Hardness: 2 to 3.

(3) Texture: The clay was well kneaded and compact, but the high percentage of quartz temper resulted in a coarse and friable paste.

(4) Color: The exterior color varied from brown to light tan with a few tints of orange and yellow. As a whole these sherds ranged darker than the earlier Badin Cord-Marked. A high percentage of the pottery was dark gray or black on the interior surface and the cores were black through one-half to two-thirds of the wall thickness.

FIG. 24. The pottery type Yadkin Fabric-Marked from the Doerschuk Site. *A*. Yadkin Fabric-Marked rim sherds. Sq. –5L10, Zone I; Sq. –5L10, Zone II. *B*. Yadkin Fabric-Marked rim sherds. Sq. 0L10, Zone II; Sq. 135, Zone I; Sq. 0L10, Zone II. *C*. Yadkin Fabric-Marked body sherds. Sq. 0L25, Zone I; Sq. 135, Zone I; Sq. 0L15, Zone II.

Firing: Many vessels appeared to have been inverted when fired and variation of exterior color indicates that the firing was probably not as thorough as that indicated for the Badin pottery.

Surface treatment:

(1) Exterior: The whole exterior surface was covered with cord impressions that varied from 0.5 to 2 mm. in diameter. These impressions were aligned, more or less, at right angles to the rim. There was no crisscrossing but the surface was thoroughly beat, leaving deep and clear impressions. This paddling was followed by the smoothing down of the irregularities with a bone or stone burnishing tool. The cord impressions, however, were never completely removed.

(2) Interior: The majority of the sherds were from pots that had been carefully smoothed on the inside. This appeared to have been accomplished by scraping and tooling so that the large particles of quartz temper were pushed into the clay rather than pulled or dragged. This was then followed by smoothing with the hand. There was no attempt to produce a finished burnished surface and in some specimens the clay was smoothed over the quartz leaving the surface quite irregular.

Decoration: None.

Form: (1) Lip: Rounded and finger smoothed with a slight tendency to bevel outward.
(2) Rim: Straight and vertical.
(3) Body: Hemispherical bowls and semi-conoidal jars.
(4) Base: Probably round for the shallow bowls and conoidal for the deeper jars. No good specimens were recovered.

Vessel size: Although 241 sherds of this type were found, none were large enough to give a reasonable estimate of the vessel size. The range of wall thickness, however, was from 4 to 8 mm. The average was about 6 mm.

Yadkin Fabric-Marked (figs. 24, 25, and 54):

Method of manufacture: Same as Yadkin Cord-Marked except that a wicker fabric was used to malleate the exterior surface instead of a cord-wrapped paddle.

FIG. 25. Variations of the Yadkin Fabric-Marked pottery type from the Doerschuk Site. *A*. Yadkin Fabric-Marked rim and body sherds (coarse fabric variety). Cave in; Sq. 0L5, Zone IIIb; Sq. 0L5, Zone IIIa. *B*. Yadkin Fabric-Marked body sherds (coarse fabric variety). Sq. –5L15, Zone II; Sq. 5L10, Zone IIIa; Sq. 0, Zone IIIb. *C*. Yadkin Fabric-Marked rim sherds and Yadkin Dentate Stamped body sherds (clay-tempered variety). Sq. 0, Zone IIIa; Sq. –5L5, Zone IIIa; Sq. –5L10, Zone II (and) Sq. –5L5, Zone I.

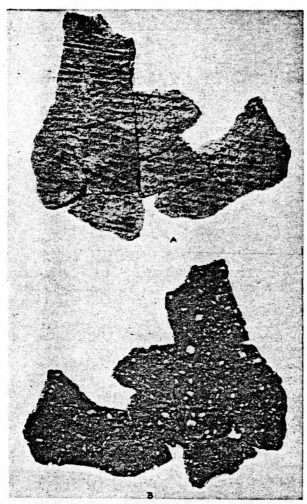

FIG. 26. The pottery type Yadkin Linear Check Stamped from the Doerschuk Site. *A*. Yadkin Linear Check Stamped body sherd. Exterior surface. These fragments were found in Sq. –5L10, Zone IIIa; Sq. 0L15, Zone IIIa; and Sq. 0L15, Zone IIIb. *B*. Interior surface.

Paste: (1) Temper: Same as Yadkin Cord-Marked. About ten per cent of the total number of Yadkin Fabric-Marked type sherds, however, contained particles of clay temper.
    (2) Hardness: 2 to 2.5.
    (3) Texture: Same as Yadkin Cord-Marked.
    (4) Color: Same as Yadkin Cord-Marked.
Firing: Same as Yadkin Cord-Marked.
Surface Treatment:
    (1) Exterior: The exterior was completely covered with wicker fabric impressions. The size of the stiff warps was considerably smaller than those used on the Badin Fabric-Marked and averaged only 4 mm. in diameter. These impressions were made at random over the surface without any attempt to orient them in any specific direction. Frequently, they would be applied parallel to the rim for 5 or 6 cm., then vertically or obliquely over

the rest of the pot. Fifty-seven sherds, or about 12 per cent of the total Yadkin Fabric-Marked type, were impressed with a coarse fabric similar to that used earlier on the Badin Fabric-Marked. Since these may represent a transition in style and technique between the Badin and Yadkin series, they were not included in the tabulation given in table 1.
    (2) Interior: Similar to Yadkin Cord-Marked. One sherd, however, was scraped with a serrated tool leaving deep striations similar to those so characteristic of the later Uwharrie pottery. A few other specimens were impressed with fabric along the inside of the rim; as would be expected, the stiff warp impressions were vertical to the rim.
Decoration: None.
Form: (1) Lip: Usually round and smooth, but occasionally flattened with the fabric paddle. Those specimens whose lips were flattened were also the ones that were marked on the inside of the rim with the fabric.
    (2) Rim: Usually straight and vertical, but occasionally recurved to vertical on pots with restricted necks.
    (3) Body: The most frequent form used was a shallow hemispherical bowl. Deeper jars with slightly restricted necks were also made.
    (4) Base: Round and semi-conical.
Vessel size: One reconstructed bowl size measured 33 cm. in diameter, 24 cm. in depth, and 1.0 cm. in average wall thickness. The wall thickness for all sherds of this type varied from 0.5 cm. to 1.2 cm., but averaged about 0.8 cm. The fabric-marked pottery as a whole was thicker than the cord-marked variety.

Yadkin Linear Check Stamped (fig. 26):

Sixty-four sherds or about 4 per cent of the tabulated pottery from the Doerschuk Site were finished on the exterior with a linear check stamp. In all other respects these sherds were similar in appearance and manufacture to the other Yadkin type pottery and must have been made locally. Since the use of a linear check stamp was unique in this area of the Yadkin-Pee Dee Valley, the distribution of these few specimens were shown in a separate column in table 1. The fact that 49 or 75 per cent of these specimens were found in Zone IIIa may be misleading. Most of those were found to belong to only two large sherds.

3. Uwharrie Series

One sherd of the Uwharrie Net-Impressed type was found in Zone I of square 5L10. This almost total absence of Uwharrie pottery was surprising since the type site for this material was barely two miles away at the mouth of the Uwharrie River. Pottery of this type was also absent on the surface. This suggests that the

lack of evidence for a Uwharrie occupation was true
for the whole site and not the result of the chance location of the excavated area.

4. *Pee Dee Series*

The third most numerous pottery ware found at the
Doerschuk Site was the product of the Pee Dee Culture (A.D. 1550–1650) of the upper Pee Dee River
basin. This type was described briefly in *The Archaeology of Eastern United States* and a more detailed
statement has been prepared for publication elsewhere.[21]
The most characteristic feature of this ware was its
paste. Large quantities of fine quartz sand were mixed
thoroughly with the clay and gave it a granular or
sugary appearance. It was well fired, however, and
the result was a hard and durable pottery.

The Pee Dee pottery was made in a variety of shapes
and finishes. The most frequent finish used on small
pots and bowls was smoothing and burnishing while
complicated stamped designs were paddled on the larger
jars. A number of different stamp designs were used,
but the two most common were the filfot cross and
opposing arcs and angles. At the Doerschuk Site a
total of 241 Pee Dee sherds were found. Of this
group, 155 were Pee Dee Plain and 79 were Pee Dee
Complicated Stamped. Three other sherds were
brushed on the exterior, and the final four were finished

---

[21] Coe, 1952: 309, fig. 165; Coe, n. d.

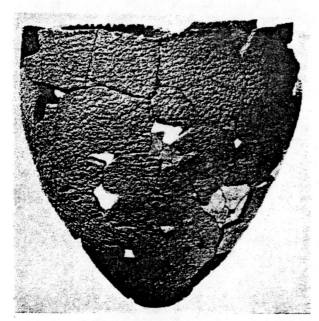

FIG. 27. A restored vessel of the Dan River Net-Impressed
pottery type (height: 32 cm.). This pottery vessel was
reconstructed from 161 sherds which were recovered from
twenty separate units of the excavation. See figure 20 for
the horizontal and vertical distribution of these sherds. The
largest number of sherds (56) was found in Sq. –5L5,
Zone IIIa.

FIG. 28. Pottery types of the Pee Dee Series at the Doerschuk
Site. *A.* Pee Dee Complicated Stamped rim and body
sherds. Sq. 0L10, Zone I; Sq. –5L15, Zone I; Sq. –5L10,
Zone I. *B.* Pee Dee Plain rim sherds. Sq. 0R40, Zone I;
Sq. 0L5, Zone I; Sq. 0, Zone I; Sq. –5L15, Zone I. *C.*
Pee Dee Plain and Pee Dee Cord-Marked (center) rim
sherds. Sq. 5L10, Zone I; Sq. 0L15, Zone I; Sq. 0L5,
Zone I.

with a check stamp. This pottery is very similar to that
found on the Wateree River near Camden, South Carolina and along the Georgia coast near Savannah.[22]

5. *Dan River Series*

This pottery was represented at the Doerschuk Site
by 170 net-impressed sherds. One hundred and sixty-
one of these, however, belonged to one pot (figs. 20,
27). A detailed description of the Dan River Net-
Impressed type can be found in the *Prehistoric Pottery
of the Eastern United States* series for 1952.[23] This
pottery developed out of the earlier Uwharrie type and
was roughly coeval with the Pee Dee occupation of the
area.

6. *Caraway Series*

The final pottery used at the Doerschuk Site was
made around A.D. 1700. This was the culmination of
the Badin-Yadkin-Uwharrie-Dan River tradition, which
incorporated in its form and surface finish certain elements of Pee Dee influence.[24] The paste was compact,
hard, and tempered with very fine particles of sand.

---

[22] Caldwell and McCann, 1941.
[23] Coe and Lewis, 1952.
[24] Coe, n. d.; Coe and Lewis, 1952.

FIG. 29. Pottery types of the Caraway Series at the Doerschuk Site. *A.* Caraway Plain rim sherds. Sq. 0L20, Zone I; Sq. 0L10, Zone I; (center) Sq. 0, Zone I; Sq. –5L5, Zone I; Surface. *B.* Caraway Brushed rim and body sherds. Sq. 5L10, Zone I; Sq. 0L5, Zone I; Sq. 0L10, Zone I (and) Sq. 5L5, Zone I. *C.* Caraway Complicated Stamped (left) and Caraway Simple Stamped rim sherds. Sq. 0L5, Zone I; Sq. 135, Zone I; Sq. 0L5, Zone I.

This pottery had a pronounced ring, even when broken, and clearly was the best of all aboriginal pottery made in this area. The Caraway vessel forms and finishes were not as sophisticated as the Pee Dee but their hardness and durability was greater.

One hundred and eight of the 184 sherds of this group were Caraway Plain, a type finished by smoothing and burnishing. As a whole, however, this type was not burnished as thoroughly as the late prehistoric and historic Catawba ware. The remaining 76 sherds were of the following types; Caraway Complicated Stamped, 27; Caraway Simple Stamped, 18; Caraway Brushed, 27; Caraway Corncob-Impressed, 2; and Caraway Net-Impressed, 2.

B. PROJECTILE POINTS

There was a total of 971 chipped-stone projectile points collected from the Doerschuk Site. Of this number 348 were used for the final analysis and the remaining 623 were eliminated because they were found on the surface or in other disturbed areas. This analysis, however, proved to be one of the most rewarding aspects of the work at the Doerschuk Site, and it resulted in an unusually clear insight into the relative age and association of these projectile point types. The high degree of correlation between the point types and the natural soil zones is illustrated in table 2 and figure 30. In general, it appeared that almost every zone was occupied by a distinctly different cultural group after what must have been long periods of disuse. For example, all of the Stanly type points were found in Zone XI and they did not reappear above the flood deposition of Zone X. The Morrow Mountain points were an exception. Although the majority of them were found in Zone IX, they were also found in Zone VII which followed a period of major flood deposition. The Morrow Mountain I points did not occur any higher in the deposit and only four Morrow Mountain II points were found in Zones V and VI. Zone VI contained the remains of the Guilford component and Zone V those of the Savannah River component. The fact that some Guilford points were found in both Zone V and Zone VII reflects the inability always to translate correctly arbitrary excavated levels into natural zones of occupa-

TABLE 2
PERCENTAGE DISTRIBUTION OF PROJECTILE POINT TYPES BY ZONES AT THE DOERSCHUK SITE

Zone	Count*	Caraway	Pee Dee	Yadkin	Badin	Savannah River	Guilford	Morrow Mt. II	Morrow Mt. I	Stanly
I	79	70.9	16.4	1.3	5.1	2.5	1.3	2.5		
II	22	36.4		36.4	27.2					
IIIa	45	8.9		48.9	42.2					
IIIb	21			19.0	81.0					
IV						– – – Sterile – – – –				
V	81					82.7	12.4	4.9		
VI	24						83.3	16.7		
VII	21						14.3	9.5	76.2	
VIII						– – – – Sterile – – –				
IX	24							16.7	83.3	
X						– – – Sterile – – – –				
XI	31									100.0

* Total projectile points: 348.

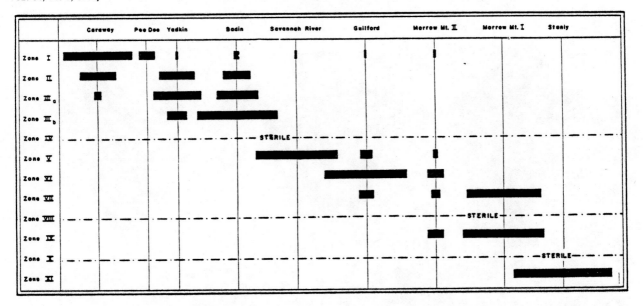

Fig. 30. Distribution of projectile point types by zones at the Doerschuk Site.

tions. In the areas where the excavation was controlled by natural zones, all Guilford points were found in Zone VI. In either case, all of the Savannah River points were found in Zone V except two, and they were found in the plowed soil. Zone IV was composed of sterile flood sand and all of the triangular point types were made subsequent to this deposition. Approximately 80 per cent of the large triangular types were found in Zone III, and about 85 per cent of the small triangular types were found in Zone I. With these data it was no longer necessary to group the various projectile point forms into a single illustration and label it "typical."

1. *Stanly Stemmed* (fig. 31)

Summary Description: A broad triangular blade with a small squared stem and a shallow notched base. A typical "Christmas tree" shape.

Form: (1) Blade: Triangular and broad. The ratio of width to length varied from 1:1 to 1:1.5. The sides were concave and frequently had an angular projection at the shoulder. Most specimens were serrated slightly along the sides of the blade, a few were serrated deeply, and some specimens were beveled as a result of resharpening. The blades were all well formed and symmetrical.

(2) Base: Concave and thinned. No evidence of grinding.

(3) Stem: Small with parallel sides. The ratio of stem width to blade width varied from 1:2 to 1:5. The stem height was usually equal to its width.

(4) Shoulder: Wide and straight, usually at right angle to the stem but sometimes sloped toward the point.

Size: (1) Length: Range, 40–80 mm.; average. 55 mm.
(2) Width: Range, 25–45 mm.; average, 35 mm.

Material: Igneous rocks: rhyolite and andesite, usually porphyritic. Quartz and argillite were not used.

Technique of manufacture: Apparently a combination of pressure and percussion techniques were used. Large flakes were struck off in the initial shaping, but the final edge, together with the serration, was made by pressure flaking. The quarry blades, types I and II, were associated with this point, and presumably these were to have been worked into points at a later date.

Comment: This point type was the earliest found at the Doerschuk Site. It was associated with a semi-lunar type atlatl weight and with quarry blades, types I and II. It had a wide distribution throughout the Piedmont Plateau, but it does not appear to have been recognized as a type. The larger points of this type tend to blend with the smaller points of the Savannah River type, and it may well be that they are related. At the Hardaway Site (Part Two) the Stanly points were found on the surface and in pits intrusive into the original midden deposit. There the broader and less serrated Kirk type points from the earlier midden tended to resemble the narrower and more serrated Stanly forms. At the Doerschuk Site four Kirk type points (fig. 32 B) were found in the Stanly level, Zone XI. This association and similarity of form also suggested that the Kirk type may have been the ancestral form. If these assumptions can be proved in fact, then the Kirk-Stanly-Savannah tradition would have had an existence of over 5,000 years.

FIG. 31.   The Stanly projectile point type at the Doerschuk Site.   *A*. Sq. 0L5, Zone XI.   *B*. Sq. 0L25, Zone XI.   *C*. Surface.   *D*. Sq. 0L20, Zone XI.   *E*. Sq. 0, Zone XI.   *F*. Sq. 0L20, Zone XI.   *G*. Sq. 0L30, Zone XI.   *H*. Sq. 0L20, Zone XI.   (Natural size.)

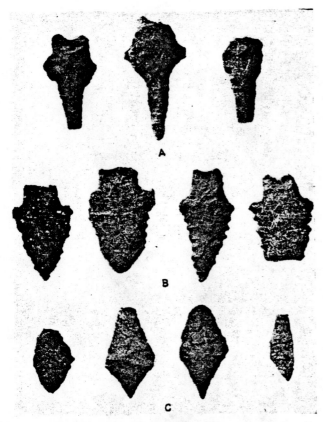

FIG. 32. Stanly drills and earlier projectile point types at the
Doerschuk Site. *A.* Stanly drills. Sq. 0L10, Zone I; Sq.
0L25, Zone XI; Sq. 0L5, Zone XI. *B.* Kirk Serrated
projectile point type. Sq. 0L25, Zone XI; Sq. 0L35, Zone
XI; Sq. 0L15, Zone XI; Sq. 0L30, Zone XI. *C.* "Lake
Mohave" projectile point type. Sq. 0L25, Zone VIII; Sq.
0L15, Cave in; Surface; Sq. 0, Zone VIII. (½ natural
size.)

2. *Morrow Mountain I Stemmed* (fig. 33)

Summary description: A small triangular blade with a
short pointed stem.

Form: (1) Blade: Usually broad and triangular. Sides
were usually rounded slightly, but on a small per
cent of the specimens the sides were straight or
slightly concave. Serration along the sides of the
blade was faint and irregular. The greatest width
of all points was at the shoulder. The ratio of
width to length varied from 1:1 to 1:2, but averaged 1:1.5.

(2) Base: Pointed.

(3) Stem: Short and tapered, frequently in the form
of an equilateral triangle. The length of the stem
was from 1/5 to 1/10 of the length of the specimen.

(4) Shoulder: Wide and sloping. The shoulder usually curved into the stem without a noticeable break
or angle.

Size: (1) Length: Range, 30–70 mm.; average, 45 mm.

(2) Width: Range, 22–45 mm.; average, 30 mm.

Material: Usually igneous rock, rhyolite, and andesite,
though a small per cent of the specimens were made
from argillite and novaculite. Porphyritic stone with
large phenocryst of quartz or felspar was rarely used,
and quartz was not used at all.

Technique of manufacture: The larger points appeared
to be the result of direct percussion and, in general,
were crudely made (fig. 33 *C*). The smaller points
were all finished by pressure flaking and were very
symmetrical in form (fig. 33 *A*). There was slight
grinding along the edge of the shoulder and stem
on some specimens, but it was never pronounced.

Comment: At the Doerschuk Site, this type occurred
stratigraphically higher than the Stanly and lower
than the Guilford. It is a form that has a wide distribution over most of North America, but, with a
few exceptions, its age and association is unknown.
In the West, the points from Gypsum and Manzano
caves are similar in style and must have been in use
at about the same period. In the East this same type
has also been found in another stratified context,
three feet below a shell midden of the Savannah
River Focus at the Lake Springs Site in Georgia.[25]

3. *Morrow Mountain II Stemmed* (fig. 34)

Summary description: A long narrow blade with a long
tapered stem.

Form: (1) Blade: Long and narrow with straight or
slightly rounded sides. Some specimens tend to
flare or curve outward at the shoulder giving the
impression of a crude cross. The relatively short
blades on some specimens appeared to be the result
of having been reworked or resharpened (fig. 34
A). The ratio of width to length varied from 1:1.3
to 1:5 but averaged 1:3.

(2) Base: Pointed.

(3) Stem: Long and tapered. Although the shoulder
and stem tend to curve together, there is a more
definite break or angle than was true for the Morrow Mountain I type. In some specimens this was
quite pronounced. The length of the stem was
from 1/3 to 1/2 the length of the specimen.

(4) Shoulder: Wide, straight, and at right angle to
the stem.

Size: (1) Length: Range, 30 mm.–80 mm.; average,
60 mm.

(2) Width: Range, 18 mm.–30 mm.; average, 20
mm.

Material: Same as for Morrow Mountain I.

Technique of manufacture: Same as for Morrow
Mountain I, however, on the specimens from the
Doerschuk Site there was no evidence of grinding or
smoothing on the shoulders or stem.

Comment: There seems to be little doubt that this form
is a variation of the Morrow Mountain type, although
its distribution at the Doerschuk Site was somewhat

[25] Caldwell, 1954: 37–39.

FIG. 33.   The Morrow Mountain I projectile point type at the Doerschuk Site.   *A.* Sq. 0L25, Zone IX; Sq. 0L10, Zone VII; Sq. 0L25, Zone IX; Sq. 0L15, Zone IX.   *B.* Sq. 0L5, Zone IX; Sq. 0L20, Zone IX; Sq. 0L10, Zone IX; Surface.   *C.* Sq. 0L10, Zone VII; Sq. 0L10, Zone IX; Sq. 0L10, Zone IX.   (Natural size.)

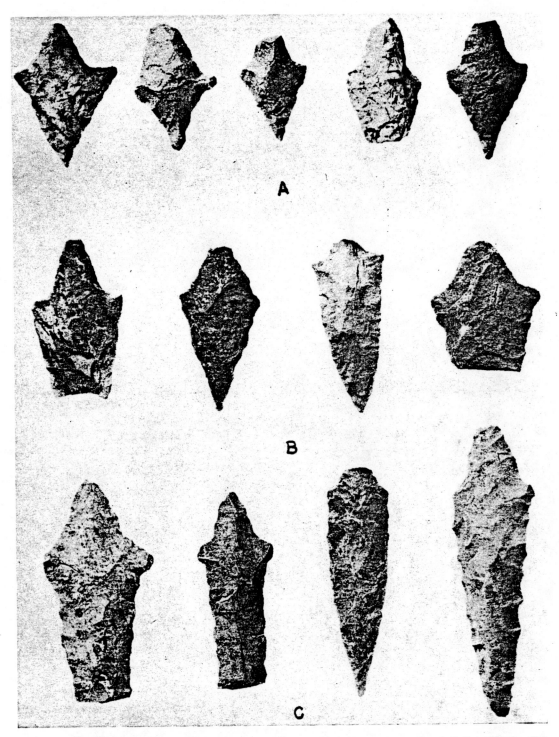

FIG. 34.　The Morrow Mountain II projectile point type at the Doerschuk Site.　A. Sq. 0L25, Zone VI; Sq. 5L5,
Zone VI; Sq. 0L30, Zone IX; Sq. 5L5, Zone VI; Sq. 0L25, dist. soil.　B. Sq. 5L10, Zone VI; Sq. 0L15, cave-in;
Sq. 0L15, Zone V; Sq. 0L10, Zone VII.　C. Sq. –5L10, Zone VI; Sq. –5L10, Zone I; Sq. 0L20, Zone VII; Sq.
–5L10, Zone VI.　(Natural size.)

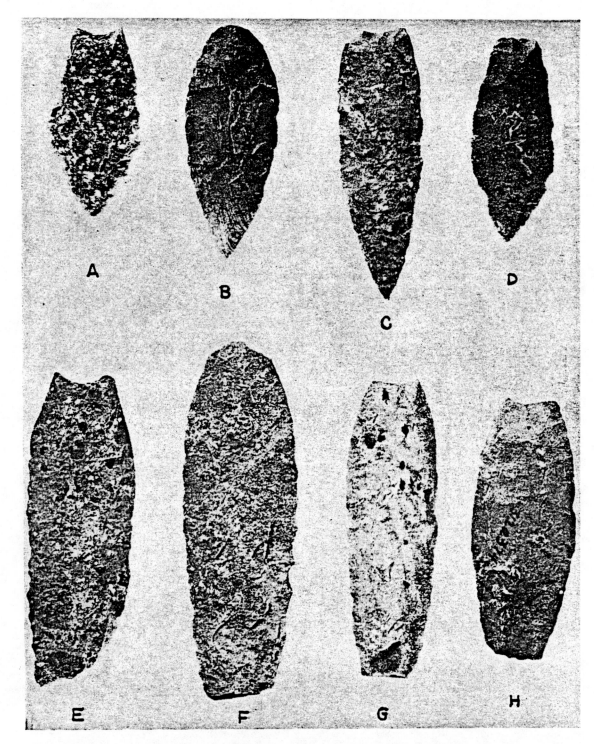

FIG. 35.   The Guilford projectile point type at the Doerschuk Site.   *A.* Sq. 0L10, cave-in.   *B.* Surface.   *C.* Sq. 0, Zone VI ;
   D.   Sq. 0L25, Zone VI.   *E.* Sq. 5L10, Zone VI.   *F.* Sq. –5L15, Zone VI.   *G.* Sq. 0L5, Zone VI.   *H.* Sq. –5L5,
Zone VI.   (Natural size.)

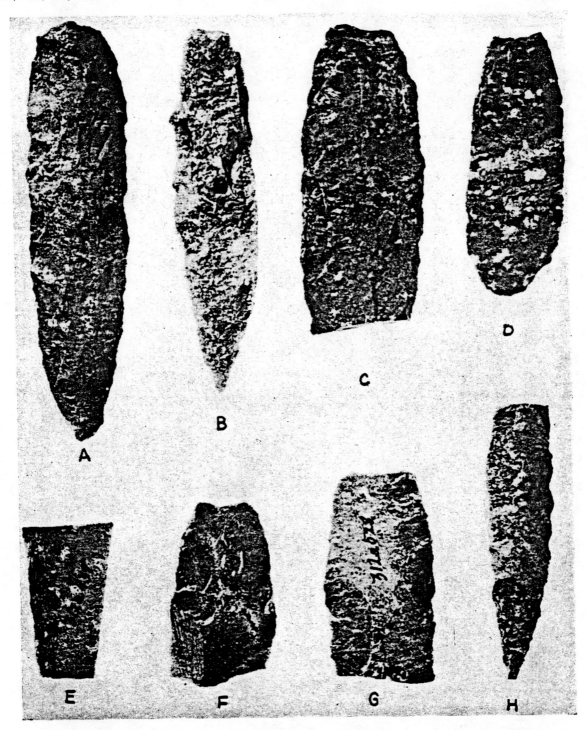

FIG. 36. Guilford blades and unfinished projectile points from the Doerschuk Site. *A*. Quarry blade, Type VII; Sq. −5L5, Zone VI. *B*. Quarry blade, Type VII; Sq. 5L5, Zone VI. *C*. Quarry blade, Type VII; Sq. −5L10, Zone VI. *D*. Quarry blade, Type VII, finished into a scraper at the point end. Sq. 0, Zone VI. *E*. Unfinished blade. Sq. 5L10, Zone VI. *F*. Unfinished blade. Sq. 0L10, cave-in. *G*. Unfinished blade. Sq. 0L10, cave-in. *H*. Quarry blade, Type VII; Sq. −5L15, Zone VI. (Natural size.)

FIG. 37. The Savannah River projectile point type at the Doerschuk Site.   A. Sq. 0L25, dist. soil.   B. Sq. 0L15, Zone V.   C. Sq. 0L25, dist. soil.   D. Sq. 0R40, Zone V.   E. Surface.   F. Sq. –5L15, Zone V.   (Natural size.)

42

confusing. Only sixteen specimens of this type were available for the analysis shown in table 2 and their actual distribution was as follows: Zone I, 2; Zone V, 4; Zone VI, 4; Zone VII, 2; and Zone VIII, 4. Their presence in the later zones may have been the result of intrusive disturbances or it may indicate that this form was transitional and survived to a later date. Evidence from other sites in the area supports the latter interpretation. This form also has a wide distribution throughout North America, but there seems to have been a greater concentration of this type in the Mid-Atlantic coastal area. In general, previous publications have not distinguished between the Morrow Mountain I and II forms or other similar types. In Virginia, however, Holland's type K appears to be of the long tapered stem variety.[26] In New Jersey, Cross has illustrated many specimens of this type but did not define them specifically.[27]

4. *Guilford Lanceolate* (figs. 35 and 36)

Summary Description: A long, slender, but thick blade with straight, rounded, or concave base.

Form: (1) Blade: Long, narrow, with slightly rounded and smoothly contoured sides. A small per cent of the specimens of this type, however, have a shoulder or break in the contour of the sides (fig. 35 A, D, E). The blades are usually thick but symmetrical and carefully chipped. The ratio of thickness to width varied from 1:2 to 1:3, and the ratio of width to length varied from 1:2 to 1:4.5 but averaged 1:3.

(2) Base: Concave, rounded or straight. The majority of the specimens had rather precisely shaped concave bases, about ten per cent had rounded bases, and straight bases were rare.

Size: (1) Length: Range, 50 mm.–120 mm.; average, 90 mm.

(2) Width: Range, 20 mm.–35 mm.; average, 30 mm.

Material: At the Doerschuk Site most specimens were made from porphyritic rhyolite and andesite. At other sites, quartz, quartzite, and varieties of argillite or novaculite (Carolina Slates) were the materials most commonly used.

Technique of manufacture: Although it is generally difficult to tell much about the actual technique of manufacture from a finished projectile point, a great deal can be told from the discarded or partly finished specimens. A number of these were recovered from the Guilford zone at the Doerschuk Site, and they suggest that the following steps were used in the production of this point type. The first step involved striking a long thin flake from a prepared flat platform. The parent rock at this site was secured from both the cliffs back of the site and the bed of the river. In the latter case, boulders were split in half

to form the necessary surface from which to detach these initial flakes. The second step consisted of roughly shaping the point by direct percussion. This was done along one edge at a time for the full length of the specimen. Figure 36 E shows the mid-section of an unfinished point with the reverse side and the left side shaped but the original flake scar may still be seen on the right side. Figure 36 F illustrates a specimen shaped on the reverse and right side but only partly finished on the left. The base, however, was shaped before starting down the final edge. The specimen illustrated in figure 36 H was shaped on both sides, but not the base which still showed the old striking platform. The three specimens shown in figure 36 A, B, and C were completely roughed out and have been called quarry blades, type VII. At this point, they were apparently stored for future work ("cache blades") when the craftsman was unable to finish them on the spot. The third step toward producing a completed point consisted of retouching the edges by pressure flaking. This resulted in a general reduction in width, but not in thickness and gave to these specimens their characteristic almond-shape cross section. The primary flakes were broad and shallow and, as illustrated above, were worked to a median line. The secondary chipping, while finer, was also shallow and seldom extended more than halfway to the center. There was no appreciable thinning of the base. The fourth and final step was the grinding of the basal edges of the points. At least a third of the known specimens of this type have pronounced grinding at the base and along the sides for about one-third of the length of the blade.

Comment: Points of this general shape are known to occur in an early context throughout much of North America. Comparisons have been made with the Eden, Angostura, and other western forms without a great deal of satisfaction. Although the estimated difference in age is not very great, there are many differences in the chipping techniques that cannot be attributed solely to the poorer quality of the raw materials. The Nebo Hill points in Missouri, however, appear to have more characteristics in common.[28] The El Jobo points found in northwestern Venezuela appear to be still closer, typologically, than other specimens known outside of the Piedmont area.[29] In the east these points have been found in great numbers in the south Appalachian area, but they have hardly been mentioned in the literature. The first brief description of this type was not published until 1952.[30] In Holland's analysis of the Virginia specimens, however, he describes a lanceolate form (type F) which certainly belongs in the Guilford Complex.[31]

[26] Holland, 1955: 170.
[27] Cross, 1941.

[28] Shippee, 1948: 29–32.
[29] Cruxent and Rouse, 1956: 172–179.
[30] Coe, 1952: 304.
[31] Holland, 1955: 168–169.

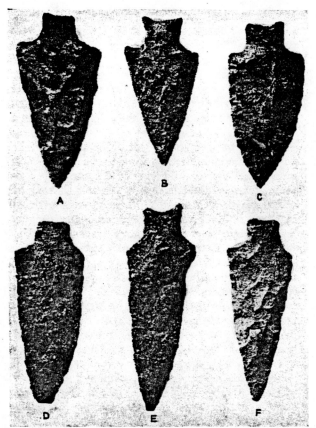

FIG. 38. The Savannah River projectile point type at the Doerschuk Site. *A.* Sq. 0L15, Zone V. *B.* Sq. 0L5, Zone V.
C. Sq. 0L10, Zone V. Slender variety. *D.* Sq. 0L15,
cave-in. *E.* Sq. 5L5, Zone V. *F.* Surface. (½ natural
size.)

Radiocarbon dates at the Gaston Site (table 15) suggest a minimum date of 4000 B.C.

5. *Savannah River Stemmed* (figs. 37–40)

Summary description: A large, heavy, triangular blade
with a broad stem.

Form: (1) Blade: Large broad blade, triangular in
shape with rounded sides. Frequently the sides
ran parallel for ⅓ to ½ of the length of the blade
before curving to the point. In a few instances the
sides were straight and formed a more precise triangle (fig. 38 *A, B*). Although the blades were
large and heavy, they were relatively thin. The
average ratio of thickness to width was 1:10. The
relative width to length varied from the long blades
illustrated in figure 40 to the extremely short blades
illustrated in figure 37. Their ratio varied from
1:1.2 to 1:4. The average was about 1:2.

(2) Base: Occasionally straight but usually concave.

(3) Stem: The sides of the stem were always straight
and the stem itself was nearly always square. A
few large blades, however, had very short rectangular stems (fig. 39 *D* and *E*).

(4) Shoulder: Straight and at right angle to the
stem. The angle made by the shoulder to the stem
and blade was always acute in the finished and un-
broken specimen. Figure 40 *A* and *C*, illustrates
two blades that have had their stem and shoulder
roughed out but not finished. These may well be
knife forms rather than projectile points.

Size: (1) Length: Range, 70 mm.–170 mm.; average,
100 mm.

(2) Width: Range, 35 mm.–70 mm.; average, 50
mm.

Material: At the Doerschuk Site all specimens were
made from local igneous rock, usually porphyritic
rhyolite or andesite. At the Hardaway Site a few
specimens were made from argillite, and at the Gaston Site most of the specimens of this type were made
from quartzite.

Technique of manufacture: These points were made
almost entirely by percussion flaking. Retouching
and pressure flaking was relatively insignificant and
served only to smooth out irregularities along the
sides and to straighten the stem and shoulder. Quarry

FIG. 39. The Savannah River projectile point and knife types
from the Doerschuk Site. *A.* Bottom half *only* is deeply
weathered. Sq. 0L15, cave-in. *B.* Sq. 0L10, Zone V. *C.*
Sq. –5L5, Zone V. Broad, weak-stemmed variety (hafted
knives?) *D.* Sq. 5L5, Zone V. *E.* Sq. 0L10, Zone V. (½
natural size.)

blades, type II and III (fig. 44 *A* and *B*), appeared to have been prepared prior to the finishing of the point.

Comment: This projectile point type has been recognized in many areas of the eastern United States. Its first detailed description was published in 1931 by William H. Claflin, Jr. as a result of his work on Stallings Island in the Savannah River.[32] Subsequent work in that area by Fairbanks, Caldwell, and Miller have made this one of the best identified points in the southeast.[33] In Tennessee this same style point has been called Appalachian Stemmed, Benton Stemmed, and Kays Stemmed, depending, apparently, upon the part of the State in which it was found.[34] At the Marcey Creek Site in the Potomac Valley similar points were found,[35] and in New Jersey they were the majority type found at the Koens-Crispin Site.[36] Throughout the eastern area this type has appeared, with little modification, as the dominant projectile point type of the late Archaic period.

6. *Badin Crude Triangular* (fig. 41)

Summary description: A large, crudely made triangular point.

Form: (1) Blade: Triangular in shape, sides usually straight but occasionally rounded.

(2) Base: Usually concave and thinned, but occasionally straight.

Size: (1) Length: Range, 40 mm.–80 mm.; average, 55 mm.

(2) Width: Range, 25 mm.–40 mm.; average, 35 mm.

Material: Porphyritic rhyolite and andesite.

Technique of manufacture: All specimens of this type were made by direct percussion, and they were not retouched or otherwise finished by secondary chipping. The flake scars were all large, broad, and shallow.

Comment: See Yadkin Large Triangular.

7. *Yadkin Large Triangular* (fig. 42)

Summary description: A large, symmetrical, and well-made triangular point.

Form: (1) Blade: Triangular and broad. Most of these points were nearly equilateral, but a few were narrow. The ratio of width to length varied from 1:1 to 1:2.5. The average was about 1:1.5.

(2) Base: Usually concave. In many instances the bases were extremely concave, but a few of the narrower points had bases that were nearly straight.

Fig. 40. The Savannah River knife type at the Doerschuk Site. *A.* Sq. –5L15, Zone V. *B.* This specimen had an estimated length of 18 cm. Sq. 0L25, Zone V. *C.* Sq. –5L15, Zone V. (½ natural size.)

Size: (1) Length: Range, 30 mm.–60 mm.; average, 45 mm.

(2) Width: Range, 20 mm.–40 mm.; average, 30 mm.

Materials: Only fine-grain and non-prophyritic rock was used. Rhyolite and andesite were used most frequently, but argillite and novaculite were also used.

Technique of manufacture: All specimens of this type appeared to have been made by pressure flaking. The flake scars were small, narrow, and well controlled. The edges were even and symmetrical.

Comment: The Badin and Yadkin projectile points were both found in the same zones (table 2). In Zone III*b*, however, there were a substantially larger number of Badin points, while the Yadkin points were in the majority in Zone III*a*. Although it is possible that the points that have been called Badin might have been only a crude and unfinished form of the Yadkin point, this does not seem to have been the case. The distribution of these two types in Zones III*a* and III*b* indicated that the Badin type was earlier and these two types differed greatly in the material used and in the technique of their manufacture. For the most part, the Badin points were made from a coarse grain porphyritic rock while the Yadkin points were invariably made from a dense, fine-grained rock. The Badin points were also made by percussion techniques which left large and broad flake scars. The Yadkin points, however, were all made by pressure flaking which left only small and thin flake scars. None of the Yadkin points showed any evidence of

[32] Claflin, 1931: 33–39.

[33] Caldwell, 1954: 38; Fairbanks, 1942 223–254; Miller, 1949; 38–50.

[34] Kneberg, 1956: 25–26; 1957: 66.

[35] Manson, 1948: 223–227.

[36] Cross, 1941: 81–90.

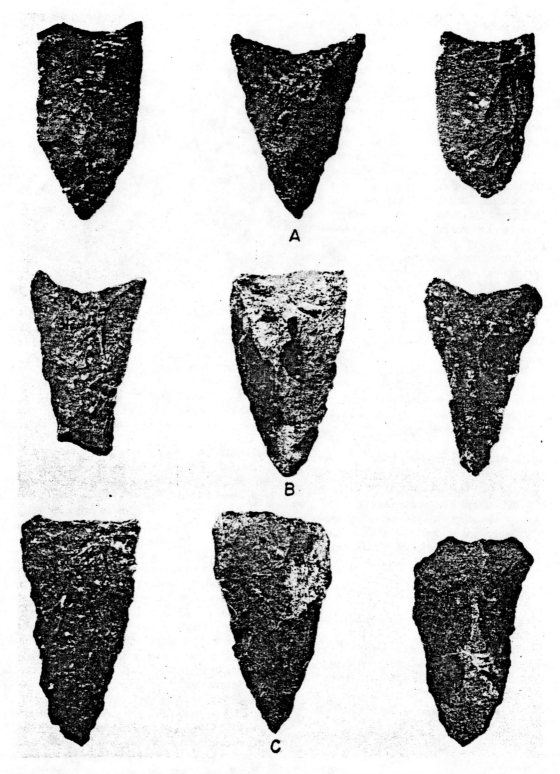

FIG. 41.   The Badin projectile point type at the Doerschuk Site.   *A*. Surface; Sq. 0L15, Zone III*b*; Sq. 0L10, Zone III*a*.   *B*. Sq. 0, Zone III*b*; Sq. 0L10, Zone III*b*; Sq. 0L10, Zone III*a*.   *C*. Sq. 0L5, Zone III*a*; Sq. −5L10, Zone III*b*; Sq. 0L20, Zone II.   (Natural size.)

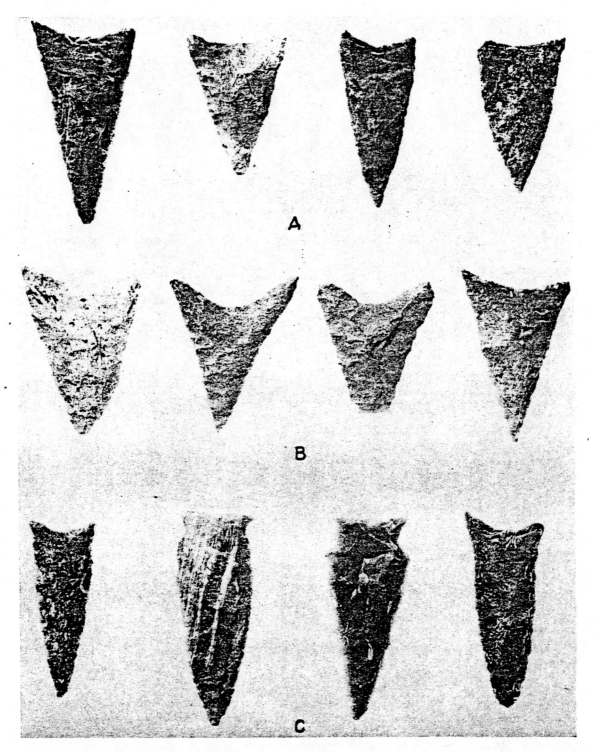

FIG. 42. The Yadkin projectile point type at the Doerschuk Site.   *A*. Sq. –5L15, Zone IIIa; Sq. 0R40, Zone IIIa; Sq. 0L10, Zone IIIa; cave-in.   *B*. Sq. 0L10, cave-in; Sq. 0L20, Zone II; Sq. 0L20, Zone II; Sq. 5L10, Zone IIIa. *C*. A-typical eared variety. Sq. 5L10, Zone II; Sq. 5L10, Zone II; Sq. 5L10, Zone II; Sq. 0L25, Zone II.   (Natural size.)

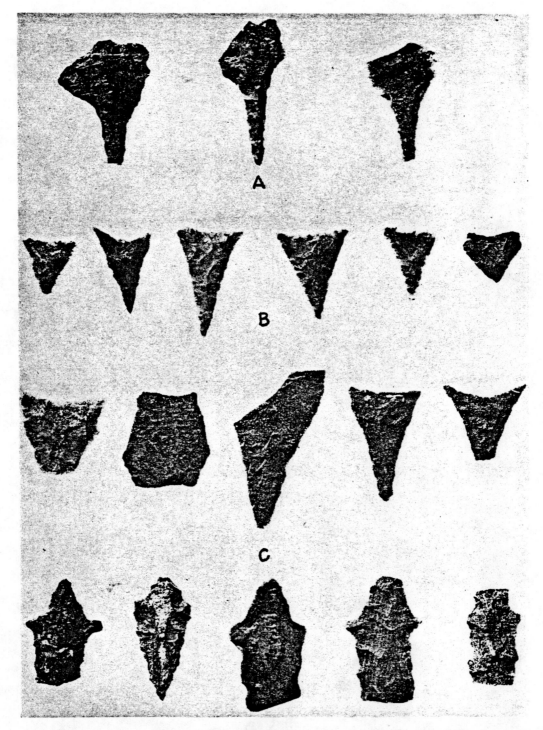

FIG. 43. Drills and projectile points of the historic period at the Doerschuk Site. *A.* Chipped stone drills. Sq. 0L25, Zone I; Sq. -5L5, Zone I; Sq. 0L25, Zone I. *B.* Caraway Triangular. Sq. -5L15, Zone I; Sq. -5L15, Zone I; Sq. 0L15, Zone II; Sq. -5L5, Zone I; Sq. 5L5, Zone I; Sq. 0L25, Zone I. *C.* Pee Dee Pentagonal and Pee Dee Triangular. Sq. -5L15, Zone I; Sq. 0L5, Zone I; Sq. -5L5, Zone I; Sq. -5L5, Zone I; Sq. 0L20, Zone I. *D.* Randolph Stemmed. Sq. 0L10, Zone II; Sq. 0R90, Zone I; Sq. 0L20, Zone I; Sq. 0L25, dist. soil; Sq. 135, Zone II. (Natural size.)

having been roughed out (Badin style) before being finished in their present form.

Points of this type have a wide distribution along the Appalachian slope from Georgia northward into New England. They also occur in the Appalachian Mountains and in eastern Tennessee, but are surprisingly rare in the Mississippi River Basin.[37] No points of this type were mentioned or illustrated in either the Wheeler Basin or Pickwick Basin reports.[38] They were also absent from the various reports that have been published on the lower and central Mississippi Valley. In the Piedmont area, at least, there is a high degree of correlation between the first known appearance of these broad triangular projectile points and the first known appearance of cord and fabric-marked pottery.

The Yadkin point is very similar to the Camp Creek point in Tennessee, and they both should have been in use at about the same time.[39] The "pointed ear" variety illustrated in figure 42 C is the same basic point, but had shallow side notches toward the base that gave it its characteristic appearance. These points also have their counterpart at the Camp Creek Site and have been called Nolichucky.[40] In Virginia, Holland has also described similar types. His type C, Triangular, corresponds to the previously described Badin point.[41]

8. *Pee Dee Pentagonal* (fig. 43 C)

Summary description: A small asymmetrical and carelessly made point.

Form: (1) Blade: Pentagonal in form, usually asymmetrical. Some specimens, however, were very carefully and symmetrically made. The points were broad and thin with a ratio of width to length that varied from 1:1.2 to 1:1.5.

(2) Base: Varied from straight to concave.

Size: (1) Length: Range, 25 mm.–46 mm.; average, 30 mm.

(2) Width: Range, 20 mm.–30 mm.; average, 25 mm.

Materials: Varieties of the Carolina Slates, argillite and novaculite were used almost exclusively.

Technique of manufacture: All points of this type were made by fine pressure flaking on a thin primary flake. Frequently, the original flake scar was not removed entirely from either one or both faces. There was, as a rule, only a minimum amount of work done to bring these flakes into an acceptable shape and this resulted in the frequent lopsided appearance. Only about ten per cent of these points were carefully and symmetrically finished.

Comment: This point is associated with the protohistoric Pee Dee occupation of the area.[42] Only thirteen specimens of this type were found in the excavated squares at the Doerschuk Site and used in the analysis, and all of them were found in Zone I. Although this is a very small number, the type is well known. Over 10,000 specimens of this type have been recovered from the Town Creek excavations alone. It is most probably that the pentagonal points recovered by Miller and Holland in the Virginia area were inspired by this Pee Dee tradition rather than the Folsom tradition that was first suggested.[43]

Occurring with these pentagonal forms was another type called Pee Dee Triangular. This type blended with the Uwharrie and later Caraway types and was not always identifiable when found out of the Pee Dee context. The typical point, however, was distinctive. It was broad and had concave sides which were frequently serrated. The Uwharrie-Caraway types on the other hand were longer, narrower, and straight sided.

9. *Caraway Triangular* (fig. 43 B)

Points of this type were associated with the historic occupation of the area by the Keyauwee and Saponi Indians at the beginning of the eighteenth century. The Caraway point was first described on the basis of 665 specimens collected during the excavation of the Keyauwee Town on Caraway Creek in Randolph County in 1936.[44] The average point was a straight-sided isosceles triangle that measured about 20 mm. wide and 30 mm. long. The bases were either straight or slightly concave, but the extreme concavity and deep serrations that were characteristic of the Pee Dee Triangular form did not occur on these points.

There was a distinct difference between the Uwharrie-Dan River-Caraway (Sara and Keyauwee) tradition in the southern Piedmont and the Roanoke-Clarksville-Hillsboro (Occanneechi and Saponi) tradition of the northern Piedmont. In the former instance, the terminal projectile points were small but narrow triangles that measured between 20 and 30 mm. in length. In the latter instance, the terminal projectile points were equilateral triangles that seldom measured over 15 mm. in length. The two specimens in figure 43, at the left and right end of row B, are of this type.

10. *Randolph Stemmed* (fig. 43 D)

The aboriginal cultures of the Piedmont disintegrated rapidly after A.D. 1700, and within a decade, as the gun

[37] Lewis and Kneberg, 1957.

[38] Webb, 1939; Webb and DeJarnette, 1942.

[39] Kneberg, 1956: 23; Lewis and Kneberg, 1957: 17–24. The C-14 date given by Lewis and Kneberg for Level C of the Camp Creek Site was 2050 ± 250 years or approximately 100 B.C. This seems too early a date for our comparable component.

[40] Lewis and Kneberg, 1957: fig. 14, b.

[41] Holland, 1955: 167.

[42] Coe, 1952: fig. 165, k, l.

[43] Holland, 1955: 176; Miller, 1949.

[44] Coe, 1937.

replaced the bow and arrow, the craft of stone working declined. Between 1725 and 1800, however, there were still a large number of Indians in the Piedmont living in small destitute bands. As a result of their inability to continue to supply themselves with adequate guns and ammunition, they found it necessary to return to the bow and arrow for hunting and exhibition (see page 16). While some of these people probably continued to manufacture traditional triangular points, at least one group achieved a different result, and this point type has been called Randolph Stemmed. These points looked like crude miniature versions of the old Morrow Mountain II type. They had a roughly tapered stem, and they were narrow and thick. The chipping was exceedingly rough and crude, and most of the flakes were irregular and poorly controlled. In many instances this produced a saw-toothed edge. The most interesting characteristic about these points, however, is that they almost always show that they had been made from old flakes or broken points of an earlier period.

C. OTHER MISCELLANEOUS ARTIFACTS

Quarry Blades

A total of 465 large blades was recovered from the Doerschuk Site. Of this total 310 were found on the surface or in areas of recent disturbance. The remaining 145, however, were found in the excavated zones and their distribution is shown in table 3. The term "quarry blade" seemed appropriate in this instance, since most of the effort of the aboriginal occupants of this site was directed toward the gathering of rock and the manufacturing of blades and finished points. These quarry blades are similar to other blades that have been found in large caches in many nearby sites. One cache, found on the Uwharrie River ten miles east of the Doerschuk Site contained 1,026 type III blades. Another cache found about fifteen miles above the

Fig. 44. Quarry blade types from the Doerschuk Site. *A.* Savannah River variety (Type III). Sq. 5L10, Zone V; Sq. 0. Zone V; Sq. –5L15, Zone V. *B.* Unspecialized variety (Type II). Sq. 0L35, Zone IX; Sq. –5L5, Zone V; Sq. 0, Zone VI. *C.* Stanly variety (Type I). Sq. 0L30, Zone XI; Sq. 0L35, Zone XI; Sq. 0L30, Zone XI. (⅓ natural size.)

Doerschuk Site on the Yadkin River contained 814 type II blades. There is little doubt that these aboriginal stone chippers reduced their raw material to as light and compact form as possible without taking the time to finish their points completely. These blades could then be transported and finished at leisure at places other than the source of the material.

These blades have been grouped into seven types based upon their general shape (fig. 44). All blades were made by direct percussion, and even though this was just a preliminary step in their manufacturing procedure, some of these forms can be identified with the final product. Other forms appeared to be so general that they occurred in all levels. As it would be logical to expect, the material used for the quarry blades conformed to the materials previously described for the finished points.

At the Doerschuk Site twenty-one of the twenty-eight type I blades were found in Zone XI in association with Stanly points. The remaining seven specimens were found in the Morrow Mountain zones. This type

TABLE 3

PERCENTAGE DISTRIBUTION OF QUARRY BLADE TYPES BY ZONES AT THE DOERSCHUK SITE

Zone	Count*	Type I	Type II	Type III	Type IV	Type V	Type VII
I	7		85.7	14.3			
II							
IIIa	6		33.3	66.7			
IIIb	7		14.3	85.7			
IV	----	----	----	Sterile	----	----	----
V	31		35.5	32.2	9.7		22.6
VI	12		25.0	8.3			66.7
VII	9	33.3	66.7				
VIII	----	----	----	Sterile	----	----	----
IX	15	26.7	73.3				
X	----	----	----	Sterile	----	----	----
XI	58	36.2	62.1			1.7	

* Total rough blades: 145.

tended to be rather egg-shaped and was somewhat better made than most of the others (fig. 44 C). It has been found in caches all over the Piedmont, but, heretofore, it has not been identified with any cultural group.

Quarry blade, type II, was by far the most numerous type found at the Doerschuk Site (fig. 44 B). In shape, it was longer, the sides were nearly parallel at the midsection, the base was rounded, and, in general, it was more crudely done than type I. This type was found in all zones, but thirty-six of the total of seventy-six specimens were found in the Stanly level, Zone XI.

Quarry blade, type III, on the other hand, was quite different. These were rather precisely shaped in the form of a large elongated triangle with a straight base (fig. 44 A). Eleven of twenty-two specimens of this type were found in the Savannah River level, Zone V, and it would require little imagination to see how these type III blades could become finished Savannah River points by the simple procedure of chipping out the corners to form the stem.

Quarry blade, type IV, was a rough triangular blade similar to type III, but broader and thicker. Only three specimens of this type were found, but they were also found in the Savannah River level, Zone V.

Quarry blade, type V, was represented by only one specimen at the Doerschuk Site. It was a thick, rough, double-pointed blade, and it was found in the Stanly level, Zone XI.

Quarry blade, type VII, is a long, slender blade with a squared-off base. This type has previously been described in association with the Guilford Lanceolate point (see page 43) and all fifteen of these specimens were found in the levels that contained Guilford points. Eight of the fifteen were found in the Guilford level, Zone VI. The remaining seven were found in Zone V. As previously stated, however, the arbitrary excavated levels did not coincide exactly with the natural zones and the presence of Guilford points and blades in the Savannah River zone is an illusion created by the excavation when the arbitrary cut included a part of both zones.

Chipped Stone Hoes

Twenty-six chipped stone blades with soil polish on the bit end have been identified as hoes. These were heavy triangular blades with a slightly rounded edge or bit. These specimens averaged about 14 cm. long and 6 cm. wide. The average thickness was about 3 cm. Twenty-three of these specimens were found on the surface and the remaining three were found in Zone I of the excavated area. These hoes were used by either the Pee Dee or Caraway or by both, since their hoe types appear to be essentially the same. It is important to note that hoes did not occur earlier in the deposit than Zone I, and there is no other evidence for agriculture at this site. In reviewing all of the known sites in the Piedmont, it seems quite certain that agriculture

was not practiced until very late, probably after A.D. 1000.

Chipped Stone Axes

Although chipped and notched axes have usually been found in association with Guilford points (fig. 110) very little evidence was found for them at the Doerschuk Site. Three fairly complete specimens were found on the surface, but only seven small fragments were found in the excavation. Of this lot, only the two found in the Guilford level, Zone VI, were sufficiently complete to make the identification accurate. The other five specimens shown in table 5 may have been fragments of some other large chipped implement, although at the time of the analysis of these axes it was thought that they might have been axe fragments.

Chipped Stone Scrapers

A total of 206 chipped stone scrapers was found, but only eighty-four of these were found in the undisturbed excavated levels. Their distribution is shown in table 4, but since a detailed description of these scraper types is given in Part Two it will not be repeated here. It is significant, however, that seventy-two out of the total of eighty-four scrapers were found in Zones IX and XI and associated with the Morrow Mountain I and the Stanly components. If this is a true picture, it would indicate that the chipped stone scraper had already been largely replaced by the bone scraper before Guilford times. In the Piedmont, at least, the chipped stone scraper became virtually extinct with the close of the Archaic period.

Chipped Stone Drills

Only twenty-two specimens of this type were found at the Doerschuk Site and twelve of those were found on

TABLE 4

PERCENTAGE DISTRIBUTION OF CHIPPED STONE SCRAPER TYPES BY ZONES AT THE DOERSCHUK SITE

Zone	Count*	End Scrapers		Side Scrapers			Oval Scrapers	
		Type II	Type III	Type I	Type II	Type III	Type I	Type II
I	3		66.7					33.3
II								
IIIa	1				100.0			
IIIb								
IV	----	----	---	---	– Sterile –	---	---	---
V	2			50.0	50.0			
VI	2				100.0			
VII	4				66.7		33.3	
VIII	----	---	---	---	– Sterile –	---	---	---
IX	39		69.2		20.5		10.3	
X				---	– Sterile –	---	---	---
XI	33	3.0	57.6	6.1	30.3	3.0		

* Total scrapers: 84.

TABLE 5

DISTRIBUTION OF OTHER MISCELLANEOUS STONE ARTIFACTS

Zone	Hammerstones					Quartz Abraders	Mortars	Chipped Axes	Atlatl Blanks	Engraved Slate
	Type I	Type III	Type IV	Type VI	Type VII					
I	1	2	1	9	3	1		2		2
II	1			2	1					
IIIa	3			1				1		1
IIIb	1			1			1	1		1
IV						---- Sterile ----				
V			1	2	1					4
VI	1						1	2		
VII			1							1
VIII						---- Sterile ----				
IX	4						1	1		
X						---- Sterile ----				
XI	4		2	1	1	1	1		7	1

the surface. Six of the remaining ten were found in Zone I and the other four were found in Zone XI. The four found in Zone XI were clearly part of the Stanly Complex. Three of these appeared to have been reworked projectile points while one had a simple rounded base for hafting (fig. 32 A). One of the six found in Zone I was of the Stanly type, but the other five were different. Instead of being carefully chipped with a prepared base for hafting, the Caraway drills were made from thin flakes with only the point being shaped. Since none of the specimens of this type have been altered at the base, it is presumed that they were hand held.

Hammerstones

As would be expected at a site where stone work was the primary occupation, hammerstones were found in great numbers. Forty-four were recovered from the excavated area, and their distribution, by zones, is shown in table 5. On the surface, the number of hammerstones appeared to be unlimited, and 210 additional specimens were collected. These hammerstones have been divided into seven major types, and a more detailed description of these types is given in Part Two. At the Doerschuk Site only five of these types were found in the excavated levels. Type I was an elongated river boulder of quartz about fist size. These were usually worked at the narrow or pointed ends. Type III was also a quartz river boulder but rounded and flatter than Type I. This type was worked all around the edge, and the flat surfaces were pitted. Type IV was a long, narrow, bar-shaped stone that was worked along the edges. These specimens were usually made from argillite rather than the harder quartz or rhyolite. Type VI was a rough oval chipped from the local outcrop of rhyolite. It was worked along several edges, but usually most of the abrasion occurred at one end. Type VII was also chipped from rhyolite but in the shape

of a small disc that averaged about 6 cm. in diameter. These were worked all around the edge. Although these various hammerstone types are distinct, there was no specific cultural association evident at the Doerschuk Site.

Stone Mortars

Thirty-three shallow stone mortars were found at the Doerschuk Site. Thirty were collected from the surface, and three were found during the excavation as shown in table 5. These mortars were all rough slabs of stone with shallow depressions on one or both sides. Most of these stones used were chipped along the edges to produce either an oval or a rectangular shape. Some, however, were made from flat river boulders. Their average size was about 14 cm. wide, 20 cm. long, and 6 cm. thick. The depressions were circular and measured from 10 to 14 cm. in diameter and 1 to 2 cm. deep. These depressions appeared to be as much the result of pecking as grinding, and, in this sense, they may have been more of an anvil than a mortar. Hammerstones, types II and III, usually had one or both surfaces flattened and abraded and probably served as a companion piece for these mortars. Although their distribution at the Doerschuk Site was weak and inconclusive, they most certainly belonged to the Archaic period.

Atlatl Weights

No finished specimens of this category, either whole or as fragments, were found at the Doerschuk Site. Three unfinished atlatl blanks and four other unfinished fragments, however, were found in the Stanly level, Zone XI (fig. 45). These specimens clearly illustrated the first steps in the manufacture of this product. The blank was first roughed out by chipping, then shaped in final form by pecking. The actual polishing was done with a quartz abrader. None of the specimens from this site were drilled, but an examination of similar specimens from the Hardaway Site indicated that the shaft hole was drilled after the atlatl weight was roughed into shape by pecking, but before it was given its final polishing. All of the Stanly type atlatl weights were semilunar or pick-shaped and round in section. All seven specimens from this site were made from argillite.

Polished Stone Celts

Twelve celt fragments were found on the surface of the site and one was excavated from Zone I. The shape of the fragments suggested that they were large specimens, averaging about 7 cm. in diameter and about 20 cm. in length. They all were oval or elliptical in section, and their entire surface was shaped by pecking. Only the bit or cutting edge, however, was actually polished smooth. These specimens were, undoubtedly, discarded by individuals during the Pee Dee or Caraway occupations.

Polished Stone Gorget

One whole but unfinished specimen of this type was found during the excavation of Zone IIIa. It was a crudely shaped, expanding center bar gorget that was elliptical in section. It had holes drilled from both sides, but one hole, however, was not finished. It had been started from both sides, but the holes were about one-quarter of an inch off center and this was never corrected. This specimen was made from a soft gray-green micaceous schist, and probably was associated with the Yadkin occupation.

Smoking Pipes

Only three small fragments of pipes were found at the Doerschuk Site, and they all were in Zone I. Two of them were made of clay and the third was made from stone. All three were Caraway in style and not Pee Dee. Both the stone pipe fragment and one of the clay pipe fragments were originally from long-stemmed tubular pipes with the bowl set at about a forty-five degree angle. The other clay pipe fragment was probably from the same type of pipe, but the stem had been squared. This was a common characteristic of the late Siouan pipes in this area.

Engraved Slate

Forty-nine specimens of soft argillite (slate) with engraved lines were found at this site. Thirty-nine were found on the surface and ten were found in the excavated levels as shown in table 5. These specimens were distributed from the top to the bottom of the deposit and appeared not to be characteristic of any one occupation. The exact purpose that these slate fragments could have served is also not clear. Many

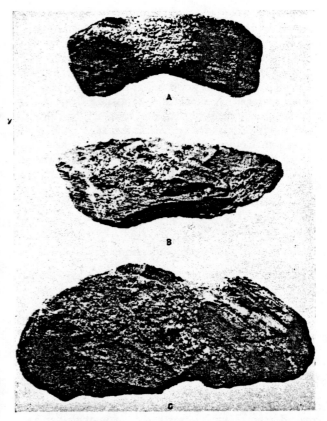

FIG. 45. Unfinished Stanly atlatl weights from the Doerschuk Site. A. Sq. 0L20, Zone XI. B. Sq. –5L15, Zone XI. C. Sq. 0L25, Zone XI. (½ natural size.)

of these specimens have random scratches across their surface, and it has been thought that these may have served as a lap board for the cutting of leather or other work that would require some sort of back support. This suggestion seemed most valid with specimens that also had signs of pecking, or smoothing and polishing, on one or both sides. Many of the other specimens, however, do not seem to have been the result of such use. They had deliberate designs which ranged from simple crisscrossed lines that extended across and down the edges to very fine and intricate geometric designs. Other specimens even suggest a drawing.[45] This practice of cutting designs on slate is not widespread in the Piedmont, and, therefore, it is surprising to find specimens of this type occurring in six separate zones of occupation. It is unlikely that this many different people could have received the same inspiration at the same spot through these several millennia.

IV. SUMMARY

This site contained the superimposed and stratigraphically separated remains of eight distinct cultural complexes and the suggestion of at least four others.

[45] Coe, 1952: fig. 163, s, w.

These eight primary occupations clearly illustrate the direction of cultural change within this area and establish, without doubt, the relative age of certain specific styles. It should be emphasized, however, that this evidence represents only a few events isolated from the continuum of life and preserved at this one spot on the earth's surface. It should not be assumed that these data are in any sense a complete inventory of cultural changes within this area or even at this site. It is quite probable that other levels of occupations have been destroyed by flood erosion in the past. The significance of this excavation lies in the fact that the remains of some of the prehistoric cultures of this area have now been found relatively free of later intrusive materials and can be viewed in their proper perspective.

A. FIRST OCCUPATIONS

There is substantial evidence that people lived in the vicinity of the Doerschuk Site long before the remains of the Stanly Complex were left in Zone XI. Throughout the underlying sands and gravel in every area that was tested stone chips and other fragmentary evidence of human occupation were found. Stone chips, scrapers, and crude "choppers" were found embedded in the very base of the talus slope at the foot of Wolf Den Mountain on the northern edge of the site. Furthermore, a number of fragments of chipped stone were recovered from Zone XI that had been in the river and water worn before they were recovered and reworked by someone during the Stanly occupation.

The evidence for cultural activity at this site before the beginning of the Stanly occupation is not meager, but, unfortunately, no projectile points or other diagnostic artifacts were found in these earlier deposits. Four Kirk Serrated projectile points, however, were found in the Stanly level, Zone XI, and since these have been demonstrated to be earlier than Stanly at the Hardaway Site (Part Two) there is a strong possibility that an earlier Kirk occupation did exist somewhere beyond the extent of our limited excavation.

A second type of projectile point that very closely resembles the Lake Mohave type of the California-Nevada area was found on the surface and also redeposited in Zone VIII (fig. 32 c). These points might have belonged to an occupation earlier than Stanly but all that can be safely concluded is that they were older than the age of Zone VIII in which they were redeposited.

B. STANLY OCCUPATION

The first occupation of the Doerschuk Site that could be clearly documented occurred on top of a long, low sand ridge that paralleled the river, and this was designated Zone XI in figure 13. A total of thirty-five projectile points, thirty-three scrapers, fifty-eight quarry blades, nine hammerstones, one mortar, seven atlatl blanks, and several hundred other fragments of chipped and worked stone were found in this zone. It is significant that thirty-one of these projectile points fit well within the defined limits of variability for the Stanly Stemmed type. The other four were the Kirk type previously mentioned. The association of these projectile points with a weighted atlatl was established by the presence of seven unfinished semilunar weights. The estimated date for this occupation is 5000 B.C. and, if this is correct, then it is one of the earliest identified occurrences of polished stone artifacts of this type in this eastern area.

C. MORROW MOUNTAIN OCCUPATION

Following the abandonment of this site and the deposition of the flood sands that formed Zone X, the Doerschuk Site was reoccupied by people with a different cultural orientation. The projectile points were quite different in style and appeared to be completely unrelated to the styles of the earlier occupations. With the exception of this projectile point style the artifactual inventory was essentially the same as that for the Stanly occupation. No atlatl weight fragments were found, however, and it is not known whether these people used that type of implement.

The first period of the Morrow Mountain occupation was ended abruptly by flooding and the deposition of nearly two feet of sand over the whole area. Following this flood, however, the site was again occupied by the same people. A thin layer of their refuse accumulated on the top of the sand, and this was identified in this excavation as Zone VII. There was no noticeable change in the artifact types.

D. GUILFORD OCCUPATION

Once again the cultural orientation changed and the new occupants of the site appeared to have shared none of the cultural heritage of the preceding Stanly and Morrow Mountain cultures. Their remains, however, are widespread throughout the Piedmont and the nature of their culture is now fairly well known. It was characterized primarily by a slender lanceolate point and a chipped stone axe. A Guilford occupation occurred at the Hardaway Site (Part Two) and two miles down river, at the Lowder's Ferry Site, a Guilford camp site was extensively excavated. At the Gaston Site on the Roanoke River the remains of a Guilford occupation was found to underlie the Halifax component which had a C-14 date of around 3500 B.C. (table 15).

E. SAVANNAH RIVER OCCUPATION

This was the most intensive occupation of all in terms of refuse accumulation. Sixty-seven projectile points and thirty-one quarry blades were recovered from the excavated area of Zone V, but surprisingly little else was found in spite of the large quantities of stone chips and partially worked specimens. It would appear that the primary purpose of the Savannah River occupation at this site was the quarrying and working of stone to be transported to other locations. No hearth or evidence of food refuse was found either in this zone or in any of the other earlier zones. This, however, would probably not be true if a larger area of the site could have been excavated. The projectile point style of this Savannah River period is basically similar to the earlier Stanly and Kirk types, and it appears to be a re-emergence of the same tradition after an absence from this site of over 2,000 years. The estimated date of the Savannah River occupation is around 2000 B.C.[46]

F. BADIN OCCUPATION

The Savannah River occupation was also followed by a flood which deposited a layer of sand, Zone IV, over most of the site. Following this flooding, at some unknown date, there appeared on the site the first people to manufacture pottery. It was a hard, sandy ware with cord and fabric-marked exterior surfaces, and their projectile points were large, crude, and triangular. · There seems to be little evidence for any degree of continuity between the Savannah River Archaic and the Badin ceramic period. The date of this occupation is estimated to be around the beginning of the Christian Era.

---

[46] A Savannah River hearth at the Gaston Site was dated 1944 ± 350 B.C. See table 15.

G. YADKIN OCCUPATION

This culture is an obvious continuation of the earlier Badin type, probably after an absence of several hundred years from this site. During that time the pottery styles changed slightly and the projectile points became better made, but there were no major innovations. It was during this period that most of the influence from the lower Pee Dee Valley was observed. A few specimens of dentate and linear check stamped pottery of local ware were found in Zone IIIa. Although these traits occurred earlier in the Georgia area, there seems little basis for estimating a date earlier than A.D. 500 for this occupation.

H. PEE DEE OCCUPATION

The Pee Dee occupation of the area south of the Narrows was extensive, but their use of the Doerschuk Site appeared to be that of a small hunting and fishing camp. Although 241 Pee Dee type sherds and 13 Pee Dee type projectile points were found during the excavation, they represent only a trace compared to the size of the average Pee Dee village located farther downstream.

I. CARAWAY OCCUPATION

This was the last recognizable aboriginal group to occupy this site, and, like the Pee Dee before them, this occupation was by small groups camping near the river while they hunted and fished in the area. Their main villages were located in the Uwharrie hills to the northeast. The date for these remains would have to be between A.D. 1700 and A.D. 1725.

PART TWO

THE HARDAWAY SITE

St^v4

I. THE NATURAL SETTING

A. LOCATION

The Hardaway Site is situated high above the Yadkin River on the top of a hill that forms the western bank of the Narrows (figs. 46, 47). From this commanding position, there is an excellent view of the valley to the north as well as the approaches to the Narrows proper. The elevation of the river as it entered the mouth of the Narrows before it was closed by the construction of the Badin Lake Dam was approximately 370 feet above mean sea level. The crest of the ridge upon which the site is situated is 650 feet above sea level or 280 feet above the bed of the river that flows below it. Four miles down the river, at the foot of the Narrows and on the opposite bank is the location of the Doerschuk Site which was described in Part One.

B. DESCRIPTION

The land that lies along the western bank of the Narrows rises steeply to form a long ridge that runs roughly north and south. To the west of this ridge there lies a shallow basin that drains to the northeast and enters the Narrows from the opposite direction of the Yadkin River. When the Badin Lake or Narrows Dam was constructed, this ridge became a peninsula surrounded on three sides by the impounded waters of the lake which emphasized its general topography (fig. 6).

FIG. 46. View of the Narrows looking south. This photograph was taken about 1890 and contained the following caption: "View of the Narrows of the Yadkin River from Palmer Mountain, Whitney, N. C. Width of river above the Narrows is 1,800 ft., at the Narrows, 60 ft. Buerbaum's Bookstore, Salisbury, N. C." The Hardaway Site is situated on the top of the hill to the right of the Narrows. The Narrows Dam was built across the rapids at the second projecting ridge to form the Badin Lake which now covers most of the area shown in this photograph.

FIG. 47. View of the Hardaway Site looking north. Palmer Mountain may be seen in the right background. This photograph was taken by the author in 1937 and the large boulders subsequently used for bench marks may be seen at the crest of the hill.

At the northern end of this ridge, the sides are steep, but not abrupt, and they rise almost conelike to a height of 280 feet above the river before they level off to form a small truncated area of about one acre. It is upon this flattened area that the Hardaway Site is situated. To the south of the site, the ground slopes downward for about 100 yards to a point twenty feet below the site. Back of this, however, the larger land mass continues to rise until it reaches a maximum elevation of 725 feet above mean sea level and an elevation of seventy-five feet above the Hardaway Site.

At the present time, the low saddle between the site and the higher hills to the south is not well drained, and it tends to stay damp and muddy for long periods of time. It has been reported by local people that this area was actually a small lake prior to being graded for a railroad by the Hardaway Construction Company. This certainly was an exaggeration, and the only time it could have appeared as a "lake" was after a very heavy rain. On the other hand, there may have been one or more springs in this area that were destroyed by the extensive grading that occurred during the period of dam construction. One reason for assuming this is the presence of the ruins of an early farm house just south of the site and west of the lowest part of the saddle area. Any attempt to have dug a well by hand would have been unsuccessful and the farmer who built this house nearly a hundred years ago would hardly have located there if his only source of water lay 280 feet below. The presence of such a source of water at the junction of these two hills would help to account for the extensive occupation of this relatively small area over a period of 8,000 years. Other hilltops along the Narrows were occupied at various times during this period, but none so intensively as the Hardaway Site.

The major rock mass that forms the ridge at Hardaway Point is greenstone. It is a hard, igneous rock that originated as part of the extensive volcanic action that uplifted large areas of the slate beds, and it is one of the contributing factors to the present topography of the Uwharrie Mountains. At various places, this older magma is cut by dikes of rhyolite and quartz, and the tops of the hills and ridges are covered with the remains of the uplifted and highly silicified slates. The large boulders that outcrop in and around the site are greenstone, and the surface of the whole ridge is covered with weathered boulders of rhyolite, quartz, and slate. This great abundance of dense siliceous rock occurring naturally on the surface was certainly another factor that induced the repeated occupation of the Hardaway Site.

The surface of the ridge is covered with a thin mantle of red, clayey soil that has developed from the decomposed underlying rocks. In the neighborhood of the Hardaway Site, this mantle has a thickness of from two to ten feet except in the few areas where there is still rock projecting above the surface (fig. 48). Since at least Triassic times, this land form has remained essentially unchanged, and in its natural state the processes of soil formation have proceeded at a slightly faster rate than those of erosion.[1] In both cases, however, the rate of change must be measured in terms of millennia rather than in years, and the crown of the hill that forms the base of the Hardaway Site has not changed significantly during the past 10,000 years.

The history of the site, in so far as it can be determined by the archaeological record, indicates that the first people to live on it found the area covered by a thin layer of humic soil that was only two to three inches thick (fig. 49). They built a number of stone-lined hearths on this surface and through the years many of their artifacts and general refuse became embedded in it. This soil zone has been labeled Zone IV, and the culture type found associated with it was called Hardaway after the name of the site.

In time, the Hardaway culture type disappeared from the area, and it was replaced by a different complex of traits. Stone-lined hearths continued to be made at random, but the relatively greater accumulation of refuse on the surface suggests the activities of a larger group of people and a longer period of occupancy. A deposit of soil and cultural debris from five to six inches thick accumulated on the surface of the site

during this period. It was designated Zone III and the cultural remains associated with it were named Palmer for Palmer Mountain which stands to the north of the site.

The third soil zone to develop on this site appears to have accumulated at a still faster rate. It reflects the concentrated activities of a group of people engaged in intensive production of large quantities of chipped stone artifacts rather than the casual occupation of a favored area by small groups of hunters and gatherers. The present depth of this layer of debris varies from one to one and one-half feet in the center of the site and originally must have been considerably deeper, since this land has been under cultivation and subjected to accelerated erosion for nearly a hundred years. This level was designated Zone II and its affiliated culture complex was called Kirk after a colonial homestead that was located nearby.

Zone I is the plowed soil. It varies from eight to ten inches in thickness and contains the remains of all subsequent occupations from Stanly to the historic Caraway. At the Doerschuk Site the Stanly complex was found at the lowest level (fig. 13), and it was estimated to have an antiquity of nearly 7,000 years. Since the Kirk, Palmer, and Hardaway artifacts all underlie those of the Stanly Complex, then it must be assumed that the Hardaway Site was first occupied at a considerably earlier date, perhaps as early as 10,000 years ago (figs. 116 and 117).

II. THE EXCAVATIONS

The Hardaway Site was first visited by the author in the spring of 1937 (fig. 47). At that time, the site and most of the surrounding area along the top of the ridge were in cultivation. A collection was made from the surface then and at various other times during the following eleven years, but no attempt was made to excavate on the site. In the summer of 1948, however, a five-foot square was dug into what appeared to be the center of the site to test the depth of the underlying midden deposit.[2] It was discovered at that time that this midden extended to a depth of twenty-eight inches below the surface and that it rested upon a thin layer of original topsoil only two inches thick. It was also discovered that about forty per cent of this midden was composed of fragments of worked stone and that only about sixty per cent was composed of soil. The only burial yet discovered at the site was found in this initial test pit. It was a fully flexed burial in a poor state of preservation, and it was found lying in a shallow pit just below the bottom of the plowed soil.

Three years later, on March 3, 1951, a second five-foot square was excavated to the south of the previous one.[3] This excavation showed a midden deposit that

[1] Bowman, 1954.

[2] This excavation was designated Square A (acc. no. 303), and it was located at -8L18 on the present grid.

[3] This excavation was designated Square B (acc. no. 323), and it was located at -13L15 on the present grid.

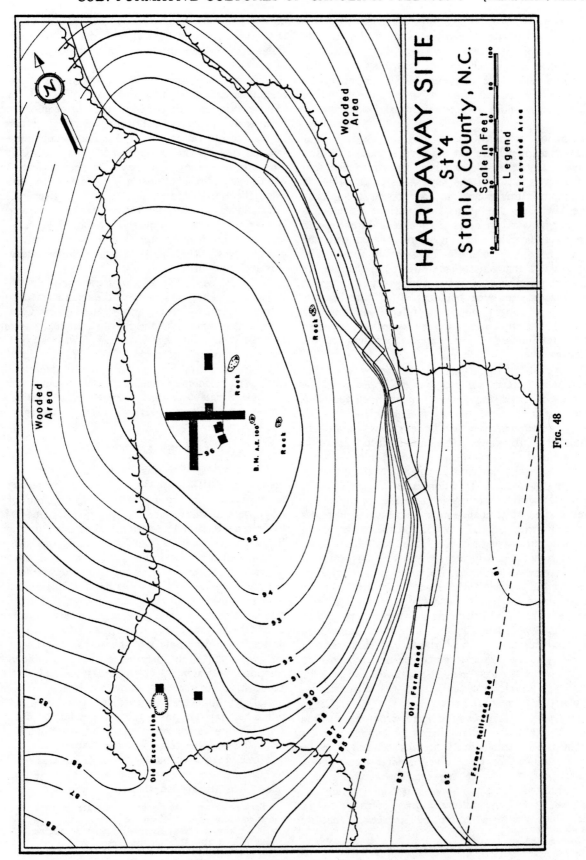

HARDAWAY SITE
St⌄4
Stanly County, N.C.
Scale in Feet

Legend
■ Excavated Area

Fig. 48

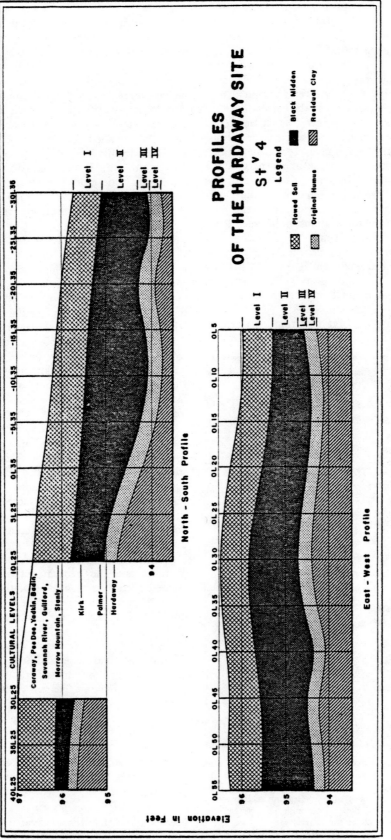

FIG. 49

also extended to a depth of twenty-eight inches below the surface. In both of these test pits, the procedure of excavation was simply to remove the undisturbed soil in six-inch levels, separating the material until the subsoil of residual clay was reached. In working this way, intrusions and natural zones in the midden could not be detected and only the thin layer of original topsoil was identified as the last level in the excavation.

The number of specimens recovered from these two squares was astounding. Over 1,500 artifacts of various types were collected and catalogued. It was noted that most of the pottery occurred in the upper part of the midden and in the plowed soil, and that most of the projectile point types, previously observed at the Doerschuk Site, were also found in the upper levels. An attempt to show a meaningful relationship between those and the new types that were being found at this site, unfortunately, was unsuccessful on the basis of their segregation by artificial six-inch levels. All types seemed to occur at all levels, and if the work had stopped at this point it might have been assumed that this was another "homogeneous" site.

In June, 1954, a lease was obtained from the Carolina

FIG. 50. View of the 1958 excavation at the Hardaway Site. This photograph shows workers preparing a profile on the west side of Squares –5L35, –10L35, and –15L35. The worker at the base of the profile is cleaning a Hardaway hearth in Zone IV. Soil Zones I through IV may be seen indicated on the profile above the hearth.

Aluminum Company for the purpose of conducting extensive excavations on this site. In August, 1955, the site was surveyed and a grid system was established using a point on a large boulder near the center of the area as a bench mark (fig. 48). A five-foot-wide trench was laid out for fifty feet to the west and excavations were begun first in squares OL5 and OL50. Unfortunately, this work could not be continued on a sustained basis and each square was excavated as a unit, then refilled. Although a large section of the east-west profile (fig. 49) was observed and recorded unit by unit, it still was impossible under those working conditions to do more than remove the soil by the same method of arbitrary levels, which, in general, continued to produce the same arbitrary results.

By August, 1957, a total of twenty-three five-footsquare units or 575 square feet had been excavated. It was becoming increasingly clear that all of the previously defined cultural units, from Caraway to Stanly, had occupied the site at a level higher than the base of the present plowed soil. Still all efforts at "across the board" comparison of artifacts by excavated levels failed to show any clear-cut separation of cultural units. For example, if figure 55 was taken at face value, it would suggest that many of the projectile point types were in use at the same time or were otherwise related. For this reason, it is not amiss to emphasize the obvious. Under natural conditions, soil is not deposited on a hilltop site—it is eroded away.

There was not enough activity at this site during the Hardaway or, perhaps, an even earlier period for soil or debris to accumulate through human use. Instead, erosion continued and the hearths and other signs of their scattered camps remained exposed on the surface. During the succeeding Palmer period, there was sufficient debris brought in to reverse the normal rate of erosion and actually to build up the soil over part of the site to a depth of five to six inches. Yet, this build-up took place over such a long period of time, and the general activity around the camps created such disturbances, that there never existed any sharp demarcation between the two periods. It was not until the Kirk period that any substantial accumulations of debris took place, and even this must be considered in terms of many generations and not as a single catastrophic avalanche. When those "Kirkers" were chipping their stones most furiously, they were still digging holes, making hearths, and otherwise living a normal existence for their time without a single care for the problems of some latter-day archaeologist. Thus, in light of the information that had been gained from the site by the fall of 1957, it was concluded that any further excavation by arbitrary levels and in single isolated units was a waste of time and a destruction of potential data.

In July, 1958, a camp was set up on the site and the area was intensively excavated for a period of six weeks. This time, however, a different and more satisfactory method of excavation was employed. A section of the former excavation from 0L35 to -20L35 was cleared, and the exposed north-south profile (fig. 49) was examined as a unit for the purpose of gaining a better understanding of the nature of those deposits (fig. 50). Zones I through IV were defined more precisely and a keener awareness of the ever-present intrusions was developed. The excavations during this period were controlled by the natural zones and every observed intrusion was separated from the zone area. Furthermore, every concentration of rocks or stone chips was cleaned and examined as a unit, and many of these turned out to be well defined hearths that could be identified with a specific culture group (figs. 51, 52, and

FIG. 52. Two hearths of the Kirk period in Sq. -40, Hardaway Site. Both of these hearths lay at the bottom of shallow pits intrusive through the lower midden and into the top of Zone III. A close-up of the hearth on the left is shown in figure 53.

FIG. 51. This cluster of rock in Sq. -20, Zone III Hardaway Site, is the remains of a hearth of the Palmer period. A small end scraper (Type I) may be seen in the side of the earth column supporting the rock in the center of the photograph and a side scraper (Type II) may be seen at the right of the picture.

53). Finally, by the end of the 1958 season, an additional 450 square feet had been excavated and seventeen hearths had been separated from the general matrix. The relative order of the Hardaway, Palmer, and Kirk components was well established and most of the later intrusive materials were isolated and identified.

III. THE ANALYSIS OF ARTIFACTS

Although the Hardaway Site proper does not cover an area much larger than an acre, a very large number of artifacts have been collected from the surface and along the eroding hillsides. A total of 22,015 catalogued specimens are at present in the Research Laboratories of Anthropology at the University of North Carolina, and they served as the basis for this analysis. The first collection of 255 specimens was made by the

author in 1937 (acc. no. 75), and a second collection of 539 specimens was made in 1940 (acc. no. 81). The first excavated material consisted of 1,607 specimens collected from Square A in 1948 (acc. no. 303). A second lot of 775 specimens was collected from the excavation of Square B in 1951 (acc. no. 323). The largest group (acc. no. 492), however, was donated to the University of North Carolina in 1953 by Mr. H. M. Doerschuk of Badin, North Carolina. This collection of 9,433 specimens represented only a part of the material which he had collected from this site over a

FIG. 53. Close-up view of a Kirk hearth at the Hardaway Site. This photograph illustrates a typical hearth situation formed by a cluster of rocks surrounded by flakes, blades, scrapers, projectile points, bone fragments, and flakes of charcoal. Note the Type I side scraper in the Hardaway zone to the left of the Kirk hearth.

period of nearly twenty-five years. He donated about 2,000 additional specimens to the American Museum of Natural History in 1942 and his present collection (now in California) consists of about 5,000 of the better made and more complete artifacts. During the 1955–1957 explorations, an additional 3,406 specimens were collected (acc. no. 690), and, finally, approximately 6,000 artifacts were recovered from the excavations made during the 1958 season (acc. no. 1010). All 22,015 of these artifacts have been examined, as well as the specimens in Mr. Doerschuk's private collection. For the purpose of illustrating the range and distribution of the artifact types, however, only two lots were used (tables 6–9). The tabulation of the range of types found on the surface was based on the 9,433 artifacts in accession number 492, and the distribution of types as they were found in the arbitrary levels was based upon the 3,406 specimens in accession number 690. These two groups of materials seemed to have every known type represented in adequate numbers to indicate their relative frequency of occurrence at the Hardaway Site. It should be emphasized that the levels referred to in this analysis are the arbitrary excavated levels and they can only be roughly correlated with the natural zones of deposition. This is a preliminary anal-

Fig. 54. A restored vessel of the Yadkin Fabric-Marked pottery type at the Hardaway Site (height: 25 cm.). Sq. –68L1, Zone I pit.

ysis of a representative sample from the Hardaway Site. It does not include data recovered in 1958 and subsequent years.

A. POTTERY

Almost every known pottery type in the Uwharrie area was found to be represented at the Hardaway Site. The tabulation shown in table 6 lists five separate pottery series that contain a total of fourteen separate types. Yet, the total pottery collection from this unit of excavation (575 sq. ft.) consisted of only 222 specimens or about six per cent of the total collection. Furthermore, the number of specimens present of each type varied from one for the Yadkin Linear Check Stamped to sixty-six for the Badin Fabric-Marked. This would indicate that after the Archaic the site continued to be occupied by the various succeeding culture groups, but never as extensively as during the preceramic period.

Table 6 shows that this pottery was found in each of the arbitrarily excavated levels, though occurring in diminishing amounts from top to bottom. It would be a mistake, however, to assume that any of this pottery was associated with the original occupation of any of the lower levels. What this distribution really shows is the depth of the various pits or other disturbances that have allowed this pottery to become embedded below the surface. During the 1958 excavation, almost every sherd was actually traced to a disturbance from the surface. Table 6 therefore, illustrates the difficulty that may arise when too much faith is placed upon the

TABLE 6

DISTRIBUTION OF POTTERY TYPES BY LEVELS AT THE HARDAWAY SITE*

Type	Levels				Total
	I	II	III	IV	
Caraway Series	25	5	6		36
Plain	21		2		23
Brushed	1	2			3
Corncob Impressed	1				1
Simple Stamped	2	3	4		9
Uwharrie Series	10	12	10	2	34
Net-Impressed	6	7	10	2	25
Brushed	4	5			9
Pee Dee Series	5	1			6
Plain	2				2
Simple Stamped	2				2
Complicated Stamped	1	1			2
Yadkin Series	20	14	3		37
Cord-Marked	18	13	1		32
Fabric-Marked	2	1	1		4
Linear Check Stamped			1		1
Badin Series	48	47	11	3	109
Cord-Marked	24	10	8	1	43
Fabric-Marked	24	37	3	2	66
Total	108	79	30	5	222

* This pottery is from acc. no. 690 only. This tabulation does not include pottery found on the surface or in other excavated units.

distribution of materials obtained through the mechanical excavation of arbitrary levels, especially in a shallow deposit.

All of the pottery types found at the Hardaway Site have previously been described in Part One and will not be repeated here.

B. PROJECTILE POINTS

Chipped stone projectile points were one of the prime commodities produced at the Hardaway Site during all of its periods of occupations. It is estimated that over 6,000 identifiable specimens of this kind have been collected from the Hardaway Site in recent years and most of them have been examined by the author. The present tabulation of 2,135 projectile points, however, is an adequate sample to show the relative proportions of the types as they were found on the surface and as they occurred in the arbitrarily excavated levels (table 7). Of this lot, 1,828 specimens were found on the surface (acc. no. 492) and the remaining 307 specimens were recovered during the 1955–1957 excavation (acc. no. 690).

The projectile points, like the pottery, were not neatly segregated at the Hardaway Site into relatively undisturbed zones by the rapid deposition of soil during conditions of flood as was the case at the Doerschuk Site. Instead, the deposit grew slowly, and it has been continually disturbed by one generation of people after another. In spite of all this, however, there was a definite separation of types. Figure 55 gives a reasonably clear picture of the primary association of the

TABLE 7

DISTRIBUTION OF PROJECTILE POINT TYPES BY LEVELS AT THE HARDAWAY SITE*

Type	Surface	Levels				Total
		I	II	III	IV	
Caraway Triangular	121	16	5			142
Pee Dee Triangular	42					42
Yadkin Triangular	64	2	2			68
Badin Triangular	78					78
Savannah River Stemmed	342	17	3			362
Guilford Lanceolate	58					58
Morrow Mountain II	178	12	4	1		195
Morrow Mountain I	141	10	8	1		160
Stanly	325	13	15	2		355
Kirk Stemmed	67	5	4			76
Kirk Serrated	243	18	29	8		298
Kirk Corner-Notched	88	2	37	9		136
Palmer Corner-Notched	40	5	13	19		77
Hardaway Side-Notched	10		3	6	8	27
Hardaway Blade	23			4	14	41
Hardaway-Dalton	8				12	20
Total	1,828	100	123	50	34	2,135

* Only projectile points from acc. no. 492 were tabulated for the surface, and the excavated specimens are all from acc. no. 690.

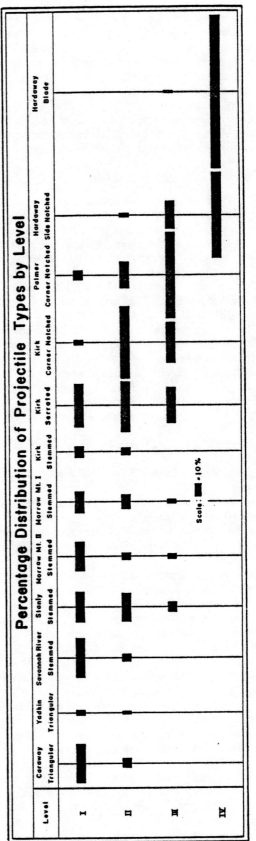

Percentage Distribution of Projectile Types by Level

FIG. 55

Hardaway types with Level IV, the Palmer type with Level III, and the Kirk types with Level II. All other types had their point of origin in Level I. This was confirmed during the 1958 excavation when several pits and hearths, identified with the Stanly period, were traced to the base of the plowed soil. Since the other types were demonstrated to be chronologically later than Stanly at the Doerschuk Site, it follows that they, too, were intrusive into Level II even where specific evidence for the intrusion could not be detected.

1. *Hardaway Blade* (fig. 56)

Summary description: A broad, thin blade with a concave and thinned base.

Form: (1) Blade: Broad and thin with rounded sides. Most specimens had their greatest width at the base, but a few appeared to be roughly pentagonal and had their greatest width about halfway between the base and the point. All of the blades had dull or rounded points. The ratio of width to length averaged about 1:1.8.

(2) Base: Usually concave, but occasionally straight. The bases of some specimens were deeply concave and the corners of the base tended to flare outward. All of the bases were thinned and the flake scars occasionally extended well down the face of the blade. Basal grinding was rare.

Size: (1) Length: Range, 50 mm.–80 mm.; average, 70 mm.

(2) Width: Range, 23 mm.–50 mm.; average, 40 mm.

(3) Thickness: Range, 5 mm.–12 mm.; average, 8 mm.

Material: The majority of the specimens were made from rhyolite and andesite with an occasional fine-grain porphyritic texture. Other specimens were made from argillite and novaculite of the Carolina Slate series.

Technique of manufacture: All specimens were characterized by broad, shallow flakes that extended well into the center of the blade, and they appeared to have been made by direct percussion. Very little retouching or secondary chipping occurred.

Comment: As a type, this group of artifacts is poorly defined. The nine points illustrated in figure 56 show considerable variation and may represent something more than mere variation of a single type. What these forms do have in common, however, is the depth at which most of them were found. Ten of the fourteen specimens recovered from Level IV were found embedded in the residual clay to a depth of four to six inches. There is no clear explanation for this, but they must have worked into a crack or some other opening in the clay before there was much humus on the ground, since there was no evidence of an intrusion.

There is little comparative data for this type in the Southeast, but the flaring of the base as illustrated in figure 56 B does occur in northern Alabama (Quad), central Tennessee, and across the Mississippi in Missouri on blades that generally are narrower and that tend to merge with the "Dalton" form. This also seems to be the case at this site. In any event, this type is the earliest to be excavated in the Piedmont and should date close to 10,000 B.C.

2. *Hardaway-Dalton* (fig. 57)

Summary description: A broad, thin blade with deeply concave bases and shallow side-notches. Bases and side-notches were ground and edges were frequently serrated.

Form: (1) Blade: Broad and thin with rounded sides which converged to a sharp point. On the variety that most closely resembled the western "Dalton" type, the edges were straight or slightly concave and were lined with fine serration (fig. 57 A). The average ratio of width to length was about 1:2.

(2) Base: Deeply concave and frequently recurved, also ground and smooth.

(3) Side-notches: Broad, shallow and roughly parallel. They averaged about 20 mm. in length and were ground smooth. Some specimens (fig. 57 C) appeared to be only slightly altered forms of the Hardaway Blade type.

Size: (1) Length: Range, 50 mm.–80 mm.; average, 60 mm.

(2) Width: Range, 30 mm.–40 m.; average 35 mm.

(3) Thickness: Range, 5 mm.–8 mm.; average, 7 mm.

Material: Same as for Hardaway Blade.

Technique of manufacture: Generally, the same as for the Hardaway Blade type except the edges were more finely retouched and frequently finished with fine serrations. Bases and side-notches were thoroughly ground.

Comment: There appears to be a definite connection between the Dalton or Meserve type in Missouri and the Hardaway type in the Carolina Piedmont. The Hardaway points, while falling far short of the excellence of some of the best examples of the Dalton type, nevertheless, still reflect the style and technique of the type with its own regional adaptation. Furthermore, the coarse grain stone available in the Piedmont was a definite factor that limited the quality of the product and handicapped the craftsman. Beveled blades were rare, but two of the twenty tabulated specimens were beveled on alternate sides. This appears to have been the result of resharpening rather than an initial intent. A brief survey of the published illustrations of the Dalton type also suggests that beveling was not a primary diagnostic trait. In general, the Hardaway variety appears to fit within the rather broad range of variations that have been described for the type, and it is presumed that it must also

FIG. 56.   The Hardaway Blade projectile point type at the Hardaway Site.   A. Sq. 0L35, Zone III; Sq. –15L35, Zone IV;
Sq. 0L20, Zone IV.   B. The two specimens on the right are considered to be "typical Quad" points.   Surface;
Sq. –40, Zone IV; Sq. 0L15, Zone IV.   C. Surface; Sq. 0L20, Zone IV; Sq. –20L35, Zone IV.   (Natural size.)

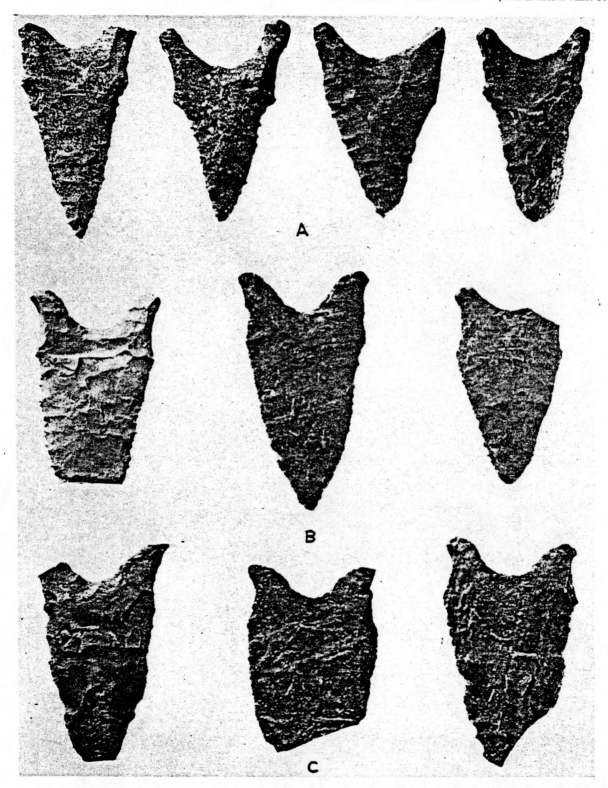

Fig. 57. The Hardaway-Dalton projectile point type at the Hardaway Site. *A*. Sq. −15L30, Zone IV; Surface; Sq. −25L30, Zone IV; Sq. −10L35, Zone IV. *B*. Sq. −50L15, Zone IV; Sq. −73, Zone IV; Sq. −50R25, Zone IV. *C*. Sq. −68L1, Zone IV; Sq. −20L30, Zone IV; Sq. −30L30, Zone IV. (Natural size.)

have existed at about the same period of time—roughly between 6000 and 8000 B.C.[4]

3. *Hardaway Side-Notched* (fig. 58)

Summary description: A small, broad, thin blade with narrow side-notches and a recurved, concave base.

Form: (1) Blade: Broad and very thin. The sides were usually straight, but also rounded occasionally. A typical blade had the shape of an equilateral triangle below the notch. A few specimens, however, had a blade that was larger and more rounded and resembled the characteristic form and size of the Hardaway-Dalton type (fig. 58 C). A few others were slender with a width to length ratio of 1:2.

(2) Base: Concave, recurved, and ground. On many specimens the base was deeply concave to the extent of being notchlike. All bases were thinned by broad, shallow flakes that frequently extended a third of the distance down their face.

(3) Side-notches: Narrow, deep, and U-shaped. The average notch was about 4 mm. deep and 5 mm. wide. On many specimens the notch was also ground.

Size: (1) Length: Range, 28 mm.–50 mm.; average, 35 mm.

(2) Width: Range, 23 mm.–35 mm.; average, 25 mm.

(3) Thickness: Range, 3 mm.–6 mm.; average, 4 mm.

Material: Same as for the Hardaway Blade with a selection of rocks with a higher degree of silicification.

Technique of manufacture: Initially the same as for the Hardaway Blade type; however, all edges were carefully reworked to produce a light delicate point in contrast to the general grossness of the Hardaway Blade. The primary flakes were usually broad and shallow, while the secondary flakes were long and narrow, but never completely removed the evidence of the former.

Comment: The Hardaway Blade, the Hardaway-Dalton, and the Hardaway Side-Notched all appear to be related types. Their form and technique blend together, making it difficult to place all of the specimens into mutually exclusive categories. At the Hardaway Site all three types were part of the Zone IV occupation and were frequently found embedded in the residual clay; so it must be assumed, until other evidence is available, that these three types did occur as variations during a relative long period of time prior to the beginning of the Archaic. The more specialized form (Hardaway Side-Notched)

developed later and lasted longer than the other two varieties. So far as the author knows, this specialized type with its horned appearance has not been reported elsewhere in the Southeast.

4. *Palmer Corner-Notched* (fig. 59)

Summary description: A small corner-notched blade with a straight, ground base and pronounced serrations.

Form: (1) Blade: Small and triangular. The ratio of width to length varied from 1:1 to 1:2.5 with the average being about 1:1.5. The sides were occasionally rounded or concave, but usually straight. Most specimens were serrated, some quite deeply.

(2) Base: Straight and ground. One of the most characteristic traits of this type was the thorough grinding of the base.

(3) Corner-notches: The typical point had a small, narrow, U-shaped corner-notch that averaged about 3 mm. in width and 5 to 7 mm. in length when measured on the stem. These notches were precisely made in the corner of the triangular blade in such a way that the bottom of the notch formed projecting barbs. The width of these barbs usually exceeded the width of the base.

Size: (1) Length: Range, 28 mm.–60 mm.; average, 35 mm.

(2) Width: Range, 15 mm.–25 mm.; average, 20 mm.

(3) Thickness: Range, 5 mm.–12 mm.; average, 8 mm.

Material: Most specimens were made from argillite, novaculite, or some other variety of the silicified slates. About ten per cent of the group was made from white vein quartz and two specimens were made from blue "Tennessee" chert which occurs locally in the Triassic gravel beds.

Technique of manufacture: These points were made by pressure flaking upon a prismatic flake of the proper proportions. The serrations, apparently, were made at the time the point was finished, since the flake scars produced by the serrations were long and overlapped toward the center of the blade. The bases were ground until they were straight.

Comment: On the basis of the excavated data, this type must have an antiquity of nearly 8,000 years. This is considerably older than any other comparable type so far reported. Points of this type do occur in Georgia, the Carolinas, Tennessee, and along the Atlantic Seaboard, however, in relatively greater numbers than the Hardaway types. Lewis and Kneberg illustrated a number of points similar to this type in their Camp Creek Site report, but, unfortunately, included them along with a series of Hardaway-like

---

[4] Suhm and Krieger, 1954: pl. 104; Davis, 1953: fig. 133 (Davis suggested a relationship to the Plainview type). Fowler, 1959: fig. 2; Lewis and Kneberg, 1958: 66; Logan, 1952: pl. 4.

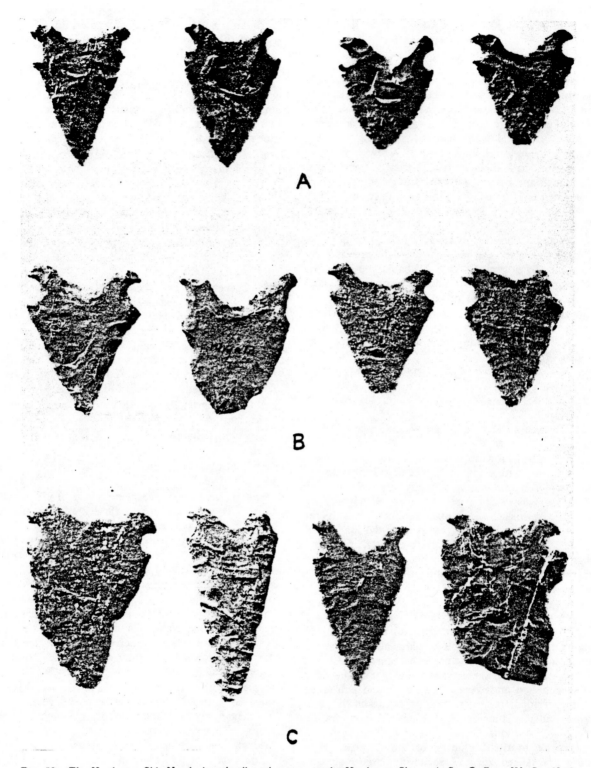

FIG. 58. The Hardaway Side-Notched projectile point type at the Hardaway Site. *A*. Sq. C, Zone IV; Sq. 0L10, Zone IV; Sq. 0L30, Zone IV; Sq. –5L35, Zone IV. *B*. Sq. –73, Zone IV; Sq. –40, Zone IV; Sq. –40, Zone IV; Sq. 0L35, Zone IV. *C*. Sq. 0L20, Zone IV; Sq. –15L35, Zone III; Sq. 0L40, Zone IV; Surface. (Natural size.)

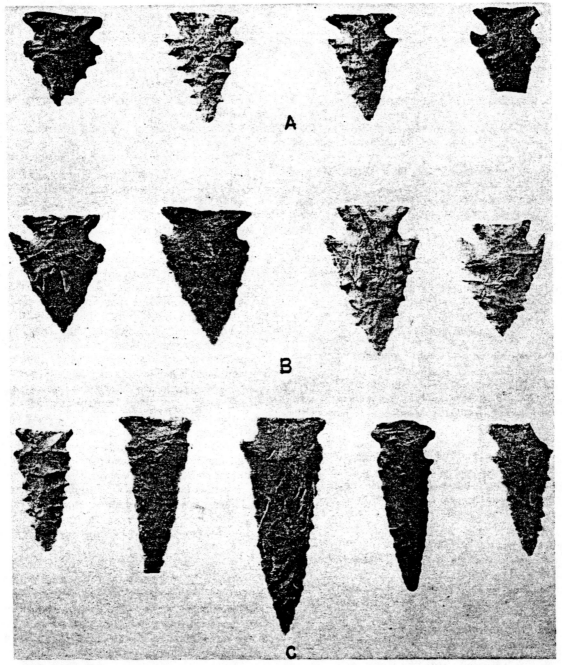

FIG. 59. The Palmer Corner-Notched projectile point type at the Hardaway Site.   *A.* Sq. 0L20, Zone III; Sq.
    –15L35, Zone III; Sq. 0L10, Zone III; Sq. 0L35, Zone III.   *B.* Sq. 0L20, Zone III; Sq. –30L35, Zone III;
    Sq. –5L35, Zone III; Sq. 0L50, Zone III.   *C.* Sq. 0L45, Zone III; Sq. –10L35, Zone III; Sq. –25L30, Zone III;
    Sq. 0L35, Zone III; Sq. 0L10, Zone III.   (Natural size.)

points in their Early Woodland ceramic complex.[5]
This type, however, does not appear to extend very
deep into the South, but does have much stronger
ties to the Northeast.[6]

---

[5] Lewis and Kneberg, 1957: fig. 20.
[6] Ritchie, 1944, 1958.

5. *Kirk Corner-Notched* (fig. 60 *A* and *B*)

Summary description: A large triangular blade with a
    straight base, corner-notches, and serrated edges.
Form: (1) Blade: Similar to Palmer Corner-Notched,
    but considerably larger. Edges were frequently
    serrated and occasionally beveled.

(1) Base: Generally straight or slightly rounded, but not ground or smoothed.

Size: (1) Length: Range, 40 mm.–100 mm.; average, 60 mm.

(2) Width: Range, 20 mm.–45 mm.; average, 30 mm.

(3) Thickness: Range, 6 mm.–12 mm.; average, 8 mm.

Materials: Most specimens were made from argillite and novaculite. Igneous rocks were seldom used and quartz, not at all.

Technique of manufacture: The basic blade appeared to have been made with broad, shallow percussion flakes. The edges were then shaped by pressure flaking, and the serrations were made as a final step.

Comment: This type appears to have evolved from the earlier Palmer type. The overall size about doubled, and the bases ceased to be ground. Percussion techniques appeared to have been used more extensively with only the final shaping of the edges, notches, and serrations being done by pressure flaking.

6. Kirk Stemmed (fig. 60 C)

Summary description: A long daggerlike blade with deep serrations and a broad stem.

Form: (1) Blade: Long, narrow, and thick. The edges were concave toward the base but recurved toward the point. Serrations were deep, especially in the concave area.

(2) Base: Straight or slightly rounded.

(3) Corner-notches: Broad notches that produced a stem that expanded slightly toward the base and shoulders that projected slightly backward.

Size: (1) Length: Range, 70 mm.–150 mm.; average, 100 mm.

(2) Width: Range, 30 mm.–50 mm.; average, 35 mm.

(3) Thickness: Range, 8 mm.–15 mm.; average, 10 mm.

Material: Same as for Kirk Corner-Notched.

Technique of manufacture: Same as for Kirk Corner-Notched.

Comment: From the standpoint of style, this type might be considered midway between the Kirk Corner-Notched and the Kirk Serrated types.

7. Kirk Serrated (fig. 61)

Summary description: A long narrow blade with deep serrations and a broad square stem.

Form: (1) Blade: Long, narrow, and relatively thick. The sides were always straight or nearly straight and deeply serrated. The short flake scars produced by the serrations again indicated that this was done after the basic blade had been shaped.

(2) Base: Usually straight and blunt but occasionally thinned and concave. Specimen B in figure 61

was unfinished. The base still shows the flat striking platform from which the original blade was struck.

(3) Stem: Always broad and nearly square. The width of the stem was usually about two-thirds of the width of the blade.

(4) Shoulders: Very narrow but squared with the stem.

Size: (1) Length: Range, 45 mm.–120 mm.; average, 70 mm.

(2) Width: Range, 25 mm.–35 mm.; average, 30 mm.

(3) Thickness: Range, 8 mm.–12 mm.; average, 9 mm.

Material: Same as for Kirk Corner-Notched.

Technique of manufacture: Same as for Kirk Corner-Notched.

Comment: The three varieties of Kirk projectile points were made during the period when the major part of the midden (Level II) was being accumulated at the Hardaway Site. These types overlie the earlier Palmer and Hardaway forms, but underlie the Stanly and later styles. This indicates that they were probably made between 5000 B.C. and 6000 B.C. Although these three types may have overlapped during this period, there is evidence to show that the Kirk Corner-Notched type appeared first and was most numerous in the lower level, while the Kirk Serrated type was most plentiful in the upper level. Furthermore, there is a strong suggestion of continuity of style which developed from the Palmer Corner-Notched into the Kirk Corner-Notched, thence into the Kirk Stemmed and the Kirk Serrated and, subsequently, into the Stanly Stemmed, to finally terminate in the Savannah River Stemmed projectile point type.[7]

C. OTHER MISCELLANEOUS ARTIFACTS

Quarry Blades

A total of 2,506 specimens of this category, as defined in Part One, was tabulated in table 8. Of this group, 2,506 specimens were found on the surface and 420 were recovered from the excavated levels. Very few blades were found in Levels III and IV, and most of those appear to have been intrusive. It seems fairly certain that the Hardaway and Palmer components made little use of quarry blades, and that they preferred to work directly on the basic flakes. In the Kirk zone (Level II), however, 163 quarry blades of various types were found and sixty-two of these were of type I which was associated with the Stanly level in the Doerschuk Site. While some of these were certainly intrusive along with other Stanly material, they may also suggest that the production of quarry blades began during the Kirk period and developed more extensively

---

[7] A description of the Stanly and Savannah River types appears on pages 35 and 44.

FIG. 60. The Kirk Corner-Notched and Stemmed projectile point types at the Hardaway Site. *A*. Kirk Corner-Notched. Sq. −15L35, Zone II; Sq. 0L30, dist. soil; Sq. 0L50, Zone II; Sq. −10L35, Zone II. *B*. Kirk Corner-Notched. Sq. −15L35, Zone II; Sq. −10L35, Zone II; Sq. −10L35, Zone II. *C*. Kirk Stemmed. Sq. A, Zone I; Sq. −5L35, dist. soil; Sq. B, Zone II; Sq. 0L25, Zone II. (Natural size.)

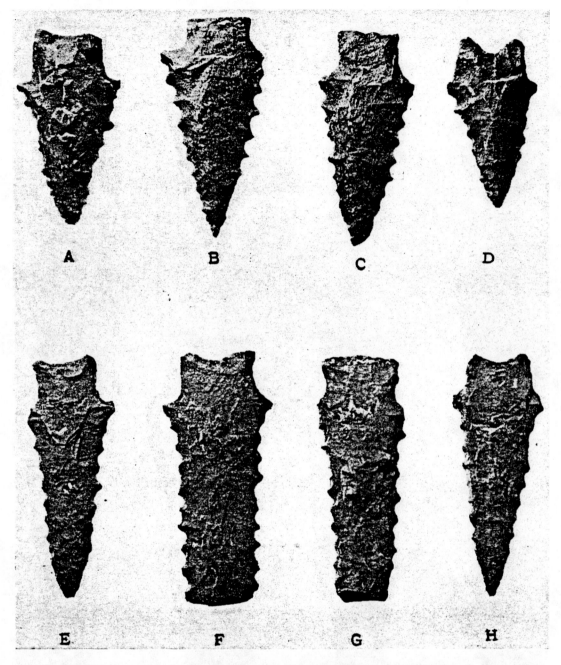

FIG. 61. The Kirk Serrated projectile point type at the Hardaway Site. *A*. Sq. 35L25, Zone I. *B*. Sq. 0L25, Zone II. *C*. Sq. A, Zone II. *D*. Sq. B, Zone III. *E*. Sq. 0L15, dist. soil. *F*. Sq. B, Zone III. *G*. Sq. A, Z   I. *H*. Sq. 0L15, dist. soil. (Natural size.)

in the later periods. A comparison of the proportion of Kirk points found on the surface to those excavated from Level II with the proportion of quarry blades found on the surface to those excavated in Level II shows a ratio of about four to one. This certainly indicates that the major part of the quarry blade production occurred after the Kirk period.

Chipped Stone Drills

Artifacts of this category were not common. Only twenty-two were recovered from the excavated levels and forty-eight were found in the surface collections. The two drills shown at the left in figure 62 *C* were found embedded in the clay at the base of Zone IV, and, without doubt, they were associated with the

Hardaway Complex. They were worn smooth on all of their surfaces, and this suggests that they were hand held and used on soft material only. The two illustrated at the right in figure 62 *C* were found higher in the deposit and appeared to have been reworked Palmer points. The specimens illustrated in figure 62 *A* and *B* were found in the Kirk level and were made with the characteristic Kirk stems. A few specimens of this type were extremely long and narrow. The

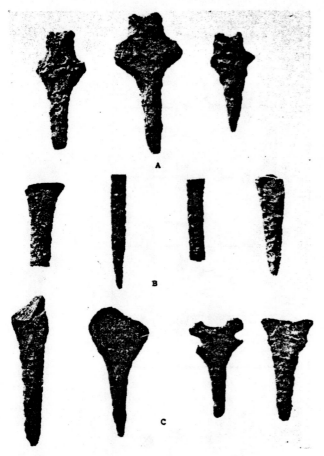

FIG. 62. Drills from the Hardaway Site. *A.* Kirk drills. Sq. 0L30, dist. soil; Sq. A, Zone II; Sq. 0L20, Zone II. *B.* Drill fragments. Sq. 15L15, Zone I; Sq. –15L35, Zone II; Sq. 0L25, Zone III; Sq. 15L15, Zone I. *C.* Hardaway and Palmer (right) drills. Sq. A, Zone IV; Sq. A, Zone IV; Sq. –50L15, Zone IV; Sq. –45L25, Zone II. (½ natural size.)

blade portion of the drill would measure less than 10 mm. in width, but would extend to a length of nearly 70 mm.

Chipped Stone Scrapers

The Hardaway Site is the first site excavated in the Piedmont where chipped stone scrapers were found in great abundance. A total of 1,930 are represented in the tabulation shown in table 9. As was true with the

TABLE 8

DISTRIBUTION OF QUARRY BLADE TYPES BY LEVELS AT THE HARDAWAY SITE*

Type	Surface	Levels				Total
		I	II	III	IV	
Quarry Blade Type I	1,016	67	62	19	14	1,178
Quarry Blade Type II	919	46	44	10	8	1,027
Quarry Blade Type III	294	29	29	9	6	367
Quarry Blade Type IV	105	8	10	5	4	132
Quarry Blade Type V	99	25	16	2		142
Quarry Blade Type VII	73	5	2			80
Total	2,506	180	163	45	32	2,926

* All surface specimens are from acc. no. 492 and all excavated specimens are from acc. no. 690.

other categories of artifacts collected from this site, the greatest number was found on the surface, but 387 of these were recovered from excavated levels. This amounted to eighty more than the total number of projectile points collected from the same excavated area.

End scraper, type I (fig. 64):

This type has long been associated with Paleo-Indian sites in the east, but its terminal period has not been known. In the Plains area it is thought that they were used from Folsom to historic times, but in the Piedmont they were not used much after 5000 B.C. At the Hardaway Site, they appeared to have a primary association with the Palmer period, although some may have been made along with the earlier Hardaway points, and some

TABLE 9

DISTRIBUTION OF CHIPPED STONE SCRAPER TYPES BY LEVELS AT THE HARDAWAY SITE*

Type	Surface	Levels				Total
		I	II	III	IV	
End Scrapers	503	23	71	46	18	661
Type I	154	9	42	31	8	244
Type II	303	14	27	13	8	365
Type III	46	0	2	2	2	52
Side Scrapers	827	11	48	76	48	1,010
Type I	356	4	16	16	17	409
Type II	340	3	7	38	21	409
Type III	131	4	25	22	10	192
Oval Scrapers	163	9	6	5	4	187
Pointed Scrapers	50	3	9	8	2	72
Total	1,543	46	134	135	72	1,930

* The surface artifacts are from acc. no. 492 and the excavated artifacts are from acc. no. 690.

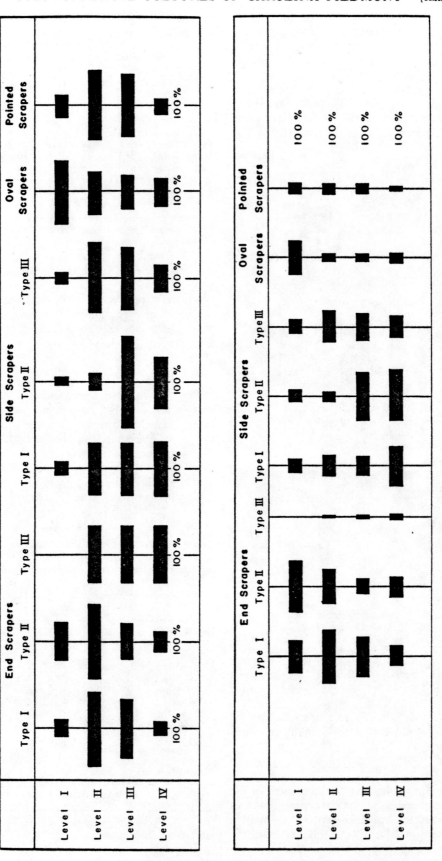

FIG. 63. Distribution of chipped stone scraper types by arbitrary levels at the Hardaway Site.

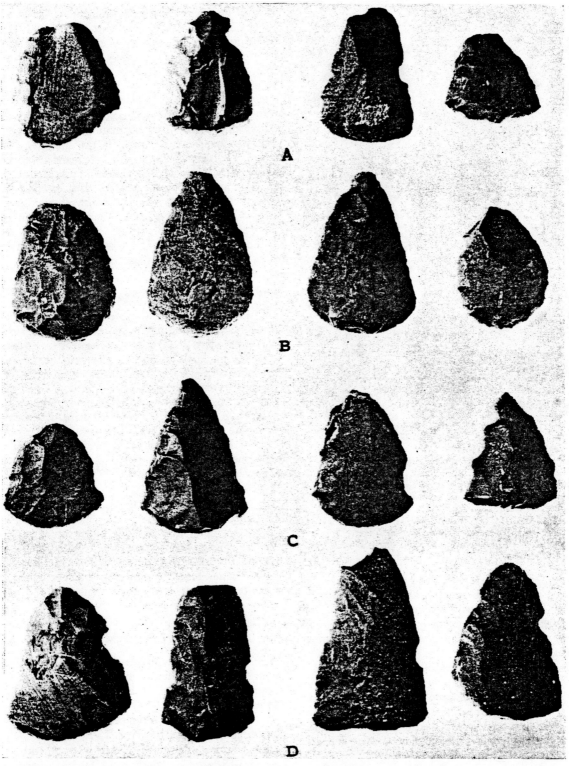

Fig. 64. Chipped stone end scrapers, Type I, from the Hardaway Site. *A*. Flat prismatic flakes trimmed along the sides. Sq. A, Zone I; Sq. 0L40, Zone III; Sq. 0L15, Zone II; Sq. –15L35, Zone II. *B*. "Tear drop" form with over-all flaking on the top surface. Sq. 0L45, Zone II; Sq. 0L50, Zone II; Sq. 0L35, dist. soil; Sq. 0L25, Zone III. *C.* Scrapers with graver points on one side. Second and fourth specimens are thick and triangular in cross section. Sq. –5L35, Zone IV; Sq. A, Zone II; Sq. 0L20, Zone III; Sq. 0L45, Zone II. *D.* Scrapers showing hafting notches. Sq. –20L30, Zone III; Sq. –30L30, Zone III; Sq. B, Zone II; Sq. 0L30, dist. soil.   (Natural size.)

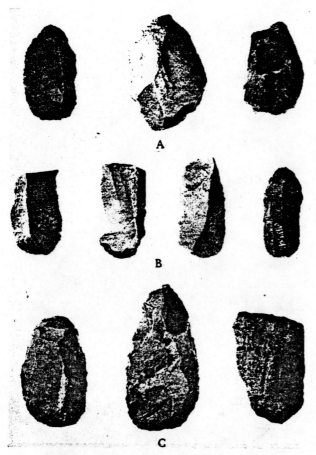

FIG. 65. Chipped stone end scrapers from the Hardaway Site. *A.* Type II end scraper. Thick, heavy, irregular flake variety. Sq. 0L10, Zone III; Sq. B, Zone II; Sq. 0L35, Zone IV. *B.* Type II end scraper. Thin, prismatic flake variety. Sq. −15L35, Zone III; Sq. 0L35, Zone IV; Sq. 0L50, Zone III; Sq. 0L50, Zone II. *C.* Type III end scraper. Thick ovals, shaped along the sides. Sq. 0L40, Zone III; Sq. 0L30, Zone III; Sq. 0L50, Zone II. (½ natural size.)

may have continued to be used through the Kirk occupation. They did not, however, continue into the Stanly period. Eighty-one specimens of this type were found in Levels II through IV as compared to nine in the plowed soil.

This type varies little from the description given of similar specimens found at the Lindenmeier, Quad, Williamson, Shoop, and Bull Brook sites.[8] They are basically triangular or trapezoidal in form and they were made from a thick prismatic flake. Many of the specimens retained the bulb of percussion on their underside and nearly all of them have been used until their cutting edge has worn smooth.

Figure 64 illustrates the major varieties that occurred

---

[8] Byers, 1954; McCary, 1951; Roberts, 1935; Soday, 1954; Witthoft, 1952.

at the Hardaway Site. So far as it is known, these variations have no distributional significance. Row *A* shows the basic scraper type that has been shaped along both sides, across the working end, but not across the face. Row *B* is similar, but these scrapers have been carefully worked across the face to give the whole upper surface a smooth rounded contour. Row *C* illustrates four specimens with graver spurs at the end of the cutting edge. This adaptation, however, occurred only on about five per cent of the specimens of this type. The second and fourth specimens from the left are very thick and are triangular in cross section. Row *D* illustrates the presence of hafting notches on the side of the specimens (see also the two center specimens in Row *A*). These notches occurred on about twenty per cent of these specimens, and they were usually found on just one side. A few specimens, however, were notched on both sides.

End scraper, type II (fig. 65 *A* and *B*) :

These specimens were made from flakes of random shapes and sizes and they were retouched only along the narrowest part to form a scraping edge. In general, this type may be divided into two varieties. The most common form was a large, thick, irregular flake that was rather casually shaped at one end. The cutting edge of this type was always irregular and sharp and must have been used for working hard materials, such as wood or bone. Their distribution was mainly in Level II and the plowed soil at the Hardaway Site, and only one specimen occurred in the Stanly level at the Doerschuk Site.

The second variety of this type was made from a thin, narrow, prismatic flake. The scraping edge was retouched along the narrow end which was opposite the bulb of percussion or striking platform. Only thirty-one specimens of this variety were found and they did not differ in their distribution from the former. These two varieties together, however, numbered 365 specimens or over half of the total number of end scrapers recovered from the Hardaway Site.

End scraper, type III (fig. 65 *C*) :

Scrapers of this type were large and rough duplications of the more finely made type I variety. They averaged about 70 mm. in length, 45 mm. in width, and 15 mm. in thickness. They were roughly chipped along the edges into an oval shape and worked across the broad end. Unlike the type I end scrapers, though, these working edges were never worn smooth. They remained irregular and sharp. Only six specimens of this type occurred in the excavated levels at the Hardaway Site, but they constituted the majority scraper type in the Stanly and Morrow Mountain levels at the Doerschuk Site.

Side scraper, type I (fig. 66 *A*):

A total of 409 specimens of this type were tabulated in table 9. Fifty-three of these were excavated and the remaining 356 were collected from the surface. Those specimens from the excavation, however, occurred in almost equal proportions in Levels II, III, and IV. All specimens of this type were made from

large, wedgeshaped flakes that were struck from a flat or prepared striking platform. Most of these specimens retained a considerable portion of this platform, as well as the bulb of percussion, in their finished form. The working edge of this type was rounded or crescent shaped and either one or both ends were rounded and curved back. The working edge remained sharp and irregular.

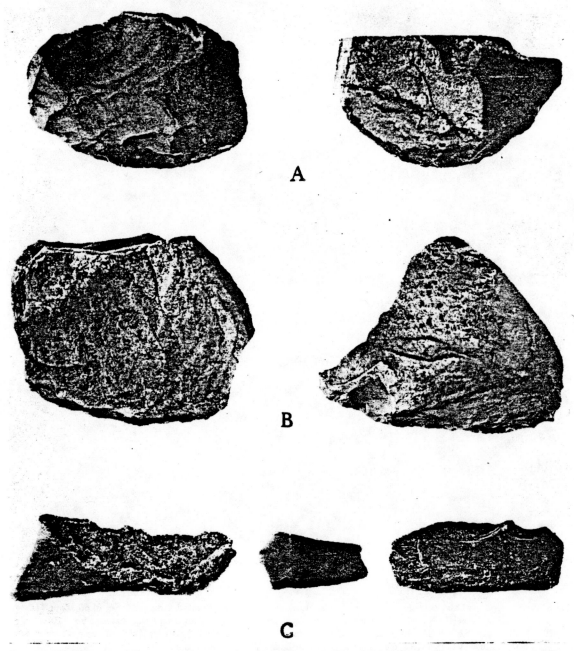

FIG. 66. Chipped stone side scrapers from the Hardaway Site. *A*. Type I side scraper. Heavy, wedge-shaped flakes. Sq. 0L15, Zone III; Sq. –25L35, Zone III. *B*. Type II side scraper. Large, irregular flakes. Sq. 0L50, Zone II; Sq. 0L40, Zone IV. *C*. Type III side scraper. Thin, narrow flakes. Sq. –20L35, Zone II; Sq. 0L25. Zone IV; Sq. –20L35, Zone II. (⅝ Natural size.)

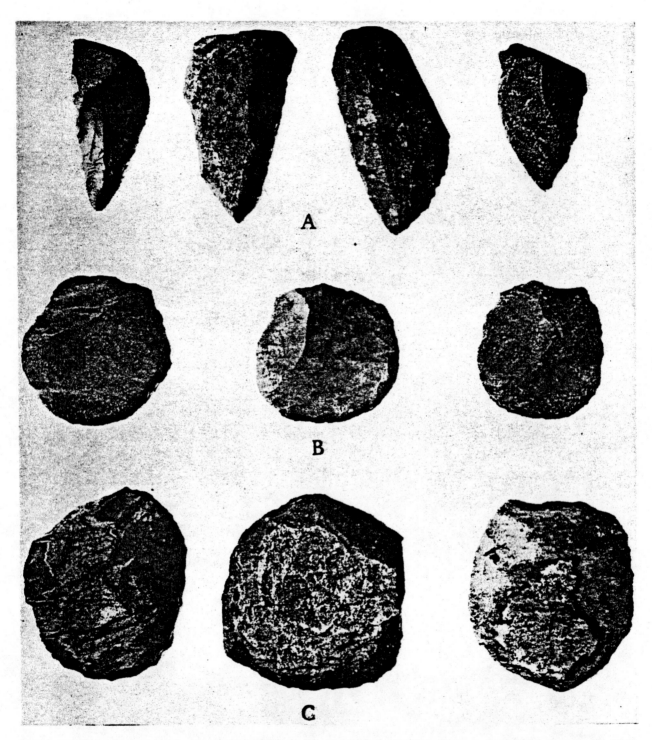

FIG. 67. Chipped stone oval and pointed scrapers from the Hardaway Site. *A*. Pointed scrapers. Sq. 0L50, Zone II; Sq. 0L50, Zone II; Sq. 0L50, Zone III; Sq. –25L35, Zone III. *B*. Oval scrapers made from broad thin flakes. Sq. –10L35, Zone III; Sq. –20L35, Zone III; Sq. –20L35, dist. soil. *C*. Oval scrapers made from thick flakes struck from the exterior of weathered boulders. Sq. A, Zone IV; Sq. 15L15, dist. soil; Sq. –15L35, Zone IV.   (⅞ Natural size.)

Side scraper, type II (fig. 66 *B*):

A total of 409 specimens of this type was also found at the Hardaway Site. Of the sixty-nine specimens excavated, fifty-nine were found in Levels III and IV in association with the Palmer and Hardaway components. Although only seven specimens of this type occurred in the Kirk level at this site, they were found in Stanly and Morrow Mountain levels at the Doerschuk Site. This type of scraper was made from a large irregular flake, and unlike the type I side scraper, there was no attempt to shape the working edge into any other form than what existed. These large flakes were simply picked up, sharpened, and used. Occasionally, more than one edge on the same flake would be used.

Side scraper, type III (fig. 66 *C*):

This type is very similar to type II and differed only in the selection of a relatively thin and narrow flake. Surface finds of this type consisted of 131 specimens, and sixty-one specimens were excavated. It may be of some significance that twenty-five specimens of this type were found in Level II as contrasted to only seven of the type II variety.

Pointed scrapers (fig. 67 *A*):

This type appears to be an adaptation of the type II side scraper. It was made from a thick flake with two sides shaped to form a definite point. Only twenty-two of these specimens were excavated and fifty others were collected from the surface. No particular associations were indicated.

Oval scrapers (fig. 67 *B* and *C*):

Although 163 specimens of this type were collected from the surface, only twenty-four were found in the excavated levels. These oval scrapers may be divided into two somewhat different varieties. One was made from a relatively thin flake and the other was made from a thick exterior spall that retained large areas of the original weathered surface. Although the distribution figures fail to indicate any particular relationship, two of the three specimens illustrated in figure 67 *C* were found embedded in the clay at the base of Level IV and must be associated with the Hardaway occupation.

Hammerstones

Although hammerstones were common on the surface (536 specimens), they were disappointingly scarce in the excavated levels. Only thirty specimens of types I, V, and VI were found, and their distribution failed to show any significant relationship. A brief description of the hammerstone types, however, is given below.

Type I (fig. 68 *B*):

A water-worn boulder of quartz or rhyolite, roughly eggshaped, was used in its natural condition. Continued use gradually abraded and wore down the ends and eventually the sides were worn also. Forty-seven specimens of this type were found on the surface and twenty-four from the excavated levels. These specimens varied in weight from 6 to 40 oz.

Type II:

A water-worn boulder, usually of quartz or quartzite, was used and abraded around all the edge and across one or both faces. The abrasion on the faces suggests that these specimens were also used as manos in association with the numerous shallow mortars that were also present at the site. These specimens varied in weight from 20 to 60 oz. A total of 101 specimens of this type was collected from the surface, but none were found in the excavation.

Type III (fig. 68 *A*):

This type is similar to type II, but it was pitted on one or both faces. Fifty-six specimens of this type were found on the surface. None were found in the excavation.

Type IV (fig. 68 *C*):

This type of hammerstone was made from a bar-shaped fragment of rock that varied from 12 to 20 cm. in length and weighed from 16 to 50 oz. No specimens were found in the excavation and only thirteen specimens were found on the surface.

Type V (fig. 69 *A, B, C,* and *E*):

Hammerstones of this type were round and, frequently, were completely spherical in shape. Most of these specimens were made from greenstone or quartz, and they were abraded over their whole surface. A total of 272 examples of this type was found on the surface and six more specimens were recovered from the excavations. They varied in size from 30 to 120 mm. in diameter and in weight from 4 to 48 oz.

Type VI (fig. 69 *D* and *F*):

This type of hammerstone was similar to type V, but differed in that it was almost invariably made by chipping a block of porphyritic rhyolite into a rough sphere and then using the two polar ends. Eventually, some of these specimens would be partially worked over the whole surface like the specimens in type V. Only twenty specimens of this type were found on the surface at the site. None were found in the excavation.

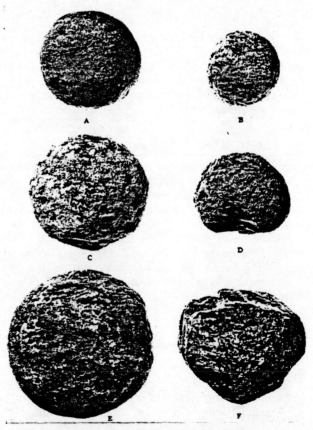

These mortars were made from rough slabs of igneous rock, usually greenstone or rhyolite, and they averaged about 25 cm. in diameter. Their ground depressions were always shallow (1 to 2 cm. deep) and they covered most of the surface of the stone. Frequently, these depressions occurred on both sides of the stone while in other cases a series of small hemispherical depressions (nut-stones) were made on the side opposite the shallow mortar depression.

Atlatl Weights

There were 172 examples of unfinished atlatl weights (fig. 70 E and G) and a total of sixty-five finished specimens found on the surface (fig. 70 C). Fifty-eight of the sixty-five finished specimens, however, were broken. Only one atlatl specimen was found in the excavated area. It was a half of a finished specimen, and it was found in the bottom of an intrusive pit of the Stanly period. Ground stone atlatl weights, apparently, first appeared in this area in association with the Stanly Complex.

Although several different types of atlatls were represented in the surface collection, the only type clearly associated with a particular component was the semi-

FIG. 68. Hammerstones from the surface of the Hardaway Site. *A.* Type III hammerstone (left). Type VII hammerstone (right). *B.* Type I hammerstones. *C.* Type IV hammerstone. (½ natural size.)

These specimens varied in size from 60 to 90 mm. in diameter and from 8 to 24 oz. in weight.

Type VII (fig. 68 A):

These hammerstones were thick discs, chipped from porphyritic rhyolite, and used only along the edges. Their average size was about 70 mm. in diameter and 25 mm. in thickness. The total collection of this type consisted of twenty-seven specimens found on the surface.

Stone Mortars

A total of seventy-eight shallow mortars was found on the surface, but not a single specimen in the excavations. It is possible that artifacts of this type were more characteristic of the later Archaic and, therefore, should not be expected in the early levels at the Hardaway Site. One specimen was found in the Stanly level, however, at the Doerschuk Site.

FIG. 69. Hammerstones from the surface of the Hardaway Site. *A, B, C,* and *E.* Type V hammerstones. *D* and *F.* Type VI hammerstones. (½ natural size.)

lunar "pick" type. Unfinished specimens of this type were found in the Stanly level at the Doerschuk Site and the broken specimen, mentioned above, was found in a Stanly period pit at the Hardaway Site. Twelve of the other specimens found on the surface were of the "notched ovate" type as described by Knoblock, and six other specimens might be assigned to his "concave humped" group.[9] These types, however, were unquestionably used by the later Archaic people. A single atlatl hook (fig. 70 *A*) made from antler was found in Feature 22, but, unfortunately, there were no associated projectile points.

Engraved Slate

A total of 213 engraved fragments of slate and forty-six engraved water-worn pebbles were found on the surface (fig. 71). In the excavated area, sixteen engraved slate fragments and five engraved pebbles were found at various levels, but their cultural association remains as much an enigma at the Hardaway Site as was true at the Doerschuk Site (see page 53).

IV. SUMMARY

This site is considered to be especially significant for the record it contains of the transition from the Paleo-Indian to the early stages of the Archaic. The demonstration that the Kirk, Palmer, and Hardaway components underlie the whole sequence previously found at the Doerschuk Site has extended the concept and perspective of the early Archaic in the Piedmont area. The repeated occupation of this site, however, by later groups has resulted in extensive disturbances to the earlier deposits, but it is believed that the basic form of these early cultures has been identified and that subsequent work at the Hardaway Site may still find the answer to many of the present questions of association.

A. HARDAWAY OCCUPATION

Very close to 8000 B.C. a small group of people climbed the hill at the mouth of the Narrows to camp and there built the first of a series of fires in a rude hearth lined with scattered stones. They made and used spears tipped with broad, thin, chipped stone points (Hardaway Blade) that were occasionally formed with broad, shallow side-notches (Hardaway-Dalton). They also used a small hafted end-scraper of stone (type I) for dressing hides and several other forms of large flake side-scrapers (types I and II) for their work on wood and bone. The archaeological evidence suggests that this site was occupied intermittently by these people for a relatively long period of time and that toward the end of this period there evolved a specialized form of projectile point (Hardaway Side-Notched) that seems to be limited to the Piedmont area.

[9] Knoblock, 1939: pls. 111, 172.

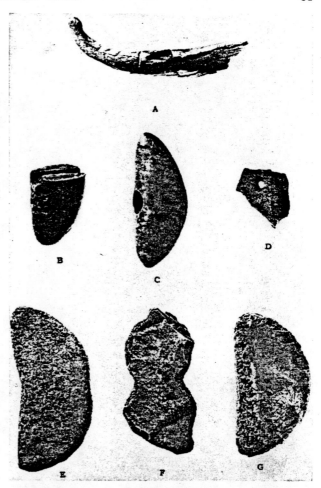

FIG. 70. Stone atlatl weights and antler atlatl hook from the Hardaway Site. *A*. Antler atlatl hook. Sq. –35, Fea. 22. *B*. Broken and partially redrilled Stanly type atlatl weight. Sq. –25, intrusive, Zone III. *C*. Stanly type atlatl weight. Surface. *D*. Fragment of "notched ovate" type atlatl weight (Savannah River period?). Surface. *E*. Unfinished atlatl weight. Surface. *F*. Notched bolas weight. Surface. *G*. Unfinished atlatl weight. Surface. (½ natural size.)

B. PALMER OCCUPATION

At some later date, perhaps before 6000 B.C. the site was occupied more extensively by a group of people whose culture type may be a direct lineal descendant of the Hardaway. There was considerable change in the style of their projectile points. The large, broad, but thin projectile point of the earlier period was replaced by a small corner-notched and serrated point (Palmer Corner-Notched). The use of hafted end-scrapers (type I) increased considerably while the large heavy side-scrapers (types I and II) were used less frequently, but very little else remains of their culture. They continued to camp around small rock-lined hearths and by the end of this period a shallow layer of occupational refuse had accumulated over the site.

FIG. 71. Engraved slate from the surface of the Hardaway Site (¾ Natural size).

C. KIRK OCCUPATION

The beginning of the Kirk period of occupation at the Hardaway Site is identified with a change in projectile point style. The small, ground base, corner-notched points developed into a larger form without basal grinding and, ultimately, into a square stemmed, serrated style. The population was also larger at this time, and there was a greater concentration of activities at the site proper. This resulted in the accumulation of a refuse deposit that at the present time averages about eighteen inches deep and was certainly much deeper before the present cycle of plowing and erosion began.

These people, apparently, continued to use the various scraper types that were known for the earlier periods, but there was a definite shift in emphasis to the cruder forms of end scrapers (type II) and the thin blade type of side scrapers (type III). A large number (51) of the small, finely-made, hafted end-scrapers (type I) were recovered from the upper midden, but, in view of the general disturbance in the deposit, there was no convincing evidence that they were actually associated with the Kirk period. Stone-lined hearths continued to be used, but there was now a tendency to prepare them in shallow pits rather than flat upon the surfaces as was true of the earlier periods.

D. STANLY OCCUPATION

There is little doubt that the Stanly occupation was a continuation of the Kirk horizon. The projectile point styles changed only slightly and the major difference was the appearance of the polished stone atlatl weights.

At the Hardaway Site, the Stanly occupation occurred in the upper part of the original midden which has either been lost or exists now as the plowed zone. At the Doerschuk Site, however, this connection is also suggested as four Kirk Serrated points were found in the Stanly level.

E. LATER OCCUPATION

After the close of the Stanly occupation, this site was occupied by at least eight other culture groups, with the Caraway component occurring after A.D. 1700. Of these groups, the Morrow Mountain and Savannah River complexes were most strongly represented by the artifacts recovered from the surface. The Guilford and Pee Dee complexes were least well represented, but there were sufficient numbers of their artifacts recovered to indicate that these people did occupy the site, even if in small numbers or for short periods of time.

PART THREE

THE GASTON SITE[1]

Hx[v]7

I. THE NATURAL SETTING

A. LOCATION

The Gaston Site is situated on the south bank of the Roanoke River about six miles above the present town of Roanoke Rapids in Halifax County, North Carolina. From this point the river flows one hundred and forty miles to the southeast and enters Albemarle Sound near the town of Plymouth. Eighty miles farther to the east and across the sound lies Roanoke Island and Oregon Inlet to the Atlantic Ocean. For most of this distance, to and from the sea, navigation is easy. Small commercial boats still ply the river as far inland as the town of Weldon, twelve miles below the site. From this point on for a distance of seventeen miles the river rises rapidly at a rate of almost ten feet per mile. At Weldon the low water stand in the river is only twenty feet above sea level, but twelve miles up the river at the Gaston Site it has risen to one hundred and five feet. Five miles farther upstream at the Halifax and Warren County line the elevation of the river at normal stage is one hundred and fifty feet. Here the river levels off but continues its rise gradually until it reaches the height of two hundred feet forty miles to the west where the present Buggs Island Dam is located.

B. DESCRIPTION

The valley of the Roanoke above Weldon is narrow, rough, and rocky. It is braided by hundreds of small islands which are interspaced with seven others that are over one mile in length. The largest is Vincent Island which begins opposite Hx[v]7 and extends downstream for a distance of four miles. The narrow, rock-walled valley and the fall of the river have prevented the formation of a definite meander pattern. In general, the main course of the river alternates from north to south through the gorge area with secondary channels following the opposite route. At the head of the rapids the two courses of the river are nearly equal as it surrounds Clements Island.

The rapid fall of the river through the narrows tends to maintain a low and somewhat constant water level throughout most of the year. Since over 8,000 square miles of hinterland are drained through this channel,

however, the flow of the river may increase with sudden intensity. During most of the year the river flows at an average rate of 8,000 cubic feet per second. In 1912 this increased to the highest recorded rate of 210,000 cubic feet per second. During periods of drought the other extreme exists. In the month of October, 1930, for nine consecutive days the flow of the river did not exceed 700 cubic feet per second.[2] Thus, during flood stage the high water sweeps the valley from wall to wall and during dry periods one may walk and wade across the channels at will.

Both sides of the valley are steep and irregular. In many places the bedrock is exposed and at intervals it juts out to the river's edge like the teeth of a giant saw. In between these rocky promontories are a series of shallow basins where the former meandering of the river has eroded away the softer rocks at a somewhat greater rate. Most of these covelike areas were once scoured to bedrock like the present channel, but have been filled subsequently by alluvial deposition. These projecting ledges of rock tend to break the force of the water as it floods past and cause eddies to form behind them. It is in these eddies that the largest amount of material is dropped from the water and it is also where the natural levee formations are protected from subsequent erosion for longer periods of time. Since these areas were higher and semi-protected they were invariably chosen for habitation sites.

For all practical purposes navigation stops at the foot of the rapids at Weldon. In 1815, however, a canal and a series of locks were completed around the rapids and between then and 1900 a yearly average of $6,000,000 in goods was transported on the river between Weldon, North Carolina, and Clarksville, Virginia.[3] The remains of these locks and part of the canal system are still visible (figs. 75, 76). In 1895 the canal and locks at Weldon and Roanoke Rapids were converted to the production of hydroelectric power by the Roanoke Rapids Electric Company. This Company was subsequently bought by the Virginia Electric and Power Company which replaced these small stations with a major dam at Roanoke Rapids in 1955.

The Gaston Site (fig. 77) is situated just downstream from a high rock outcrop that extends from the south

---

[1] The Gaston Site is one of seventy-four located by the University of North Carolina field party in 1955 while surveying the Roanoke Rapids Basin. This study is concerned primarily with this one site. A detailed report of the whole project is being prepared by Mr. Stanley South under the author's direction.

[2] United States Army Corps of Engineers, 1935: 22. The Virginia Electric and Power Company in a 1954 report gives the maximum flow as 261,000 cu. ft. per sec. in 1940, and the minimum flow as 458 cu. ft. per sec. in 1932. The source of this information is apparently their own power station at Roanoke Rapids.

[3] United States Army Corps of Engineers, 1935: 30.

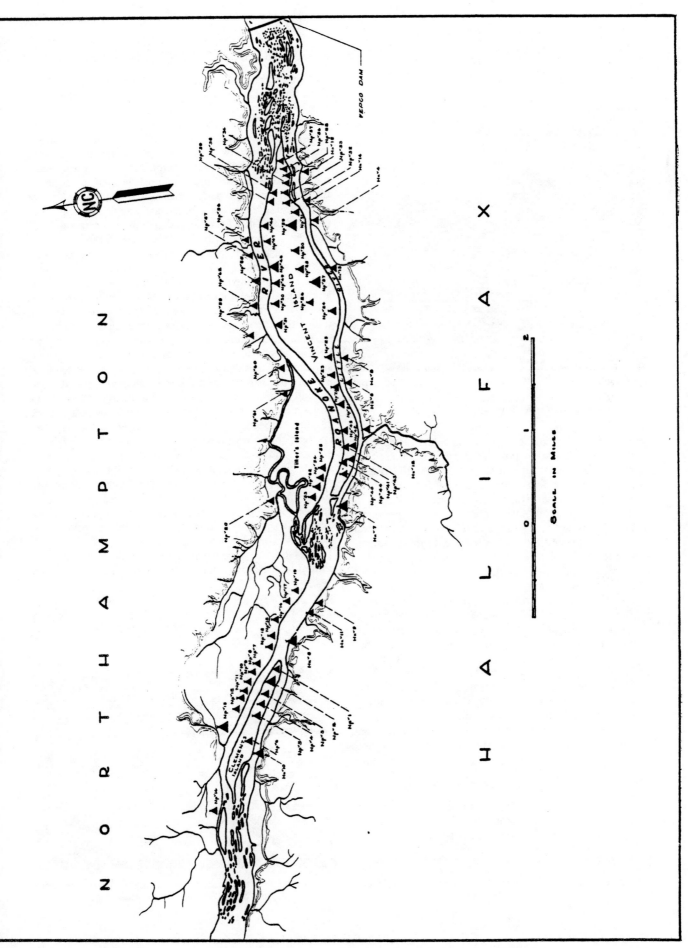

Fig. 72. The Roanoke Rapids Reservoir Basin.

FIG. 73. A view of the Gaston Site looking to the west or upstream. Note the rock outcrop that extends to the river along the western edge of the site.

wall of the valley to the edge of the river. Below this barrier the river has deposited, at various times, thick layers of clay, sand, and small gravel. At the present time this natural levee stands fifteen feet above the normal flow of the river.[4] Its surface is nearly flat over an area of about three acres; then it slopes gradually downstream to the east and toward the valley wall 200 feet to the south. At this point a series of springs originates in the rocks at the base of the slope and drains around the eastern end of this sand ridge to the river, 300 yards downstream from the center of the site.

The only known structure on this site was a small building erected in 1815 to house the personnel tending the locks. This was situated at the northwest corner of the site near the canal, and a few nails, bricks, and bottle fragments still indicate its former location. In 1858 the Weldon to Gaston railroad was completed and traffic on the river virtually ceased. On February 7, 1882, the lands of the Roanoke Navigation Company were sold at public auction and the canals above Roanoke Rapids were abandoned.[5] The locks and house were destroyed and the land was put into cultivation.

C. PHYSIOGRAPHY

The Gaston Site is located at the fall line where the Roanoke River descends from the Piedmont Plateau to the Atlantic Coastal Plain. This is slightly east of the

[4] In 1955, before the area was flooded by the Roanoke Rapids Dam.

[5] Notice, Clerk of the Court, Northampton County, North Carolina.

Carolina Slate Belt which was described in detail in Part One. The Piedmont surface, in which the Slate Belt lies, slopes gradually and continuously from the base of the Blue Ridge Front toward the Coastal Plain. This surface has been eroded to a rolling, mature stage, interrupted only by local areas of differential erosion. In general, it is an area composed of volcanic-sedimentary rocks which include subaerial and subaqueous tuffs, tuff breccias, and devitrified lava flows. Quartz veins and greenstone masses are intruded into these deposits and late Triassic diabase dikes cut through all of them. On the hilltops, overlying the base rocks, are deposits of loosely consolidated sands and gravels which are the remains of Tertiary fluvial terraces. These terraces lie along the eastern edge of the Piedmont Plateau at an elevation of about two hundred and fifty feet above sea level. Farther to the east these deposits disappear under the Pleistocene deposits of the Coastal Plain.

An understanding of the depositional history at this site is of considerable importance in interpreting the sequence of cultural events that transpired there. The absence of charcoal in the lower levels and the absence of pollen throughout the aerated sands and clays makes any estimate of the age for the early deposits a matter of pure conjecture. The present order of the deposits is clear, but the amount lost during the intervals of erosion and unconformity is not known.

The first stage, as it is now known for the site, was when the main course of the river flowed along the southern edge of the valley and scoured the area to bedrock leaving only pebbles and large boulders lying loose in its path. This stage must have an antiquity in excess of 10,000 years.

The second stage began when the flow of the river shifted to the north edge of the valley. This resulted in

FIG. 74. View of the Roanoke River from the north side of the Gaston Site. The river is at normal stage.

FIG. 75. The remains of the old Weldon to Clarksville canal locks at the western edge of the Gaston Site.

its former route filling in gradually with fine clay sediments which settled from the relatively still water that occasionally overflowed into this now cut-off and swampy area. As the levees built up along the main course of the river the swamp also built up in the area of the site. This situation continued until the clay sediments of the swamp had built to a height of two feet above the present normal level of the river or altogether about five feet above the bedrock at the site (fig. 78).

The third stage is represented by a deposit of fine white sand nearly five feet thick. At this time the main force of the river apparently broke through the old levee systems that had built up along its northern course and flowed toward the south. This new channel was sufficiently close to the site for the velocity of the overflow to carry this fine sand, but not close enough to transport gravel or pebbles to the deposit. This level appears to have built up rapidly. There is no trace of banding or erosion. It is possible that the total deposit could have been dropped during one major flood period. In any event, no long period of time elapsed between floods, if more than one was responsible for this deposition. The absence of clay, as part of the deposit itself or in the form of seepage veins, suggests that this sand zone was now well above the swamp level for the valley as a whole and that there was no standing water on the site. There was also no evidence of vegetation and the surface of this area must still be considered as relatively unstable.

The fourth and final stage of deposition began with the break-through of the river along the very edge of the site itself. This initial flooding deposited along the river's new bank a heavy load of coarse sand and gravel. At the site this deposit was nearly two feet thick at the river, but it tapered rapidly and finally disappeared one

hundred feet to the south. The river at that time was flowing very nearly along its present course which approximates that of stage one. The main difference is that the river is now flowing in a more easterly direction and the old deposits are protected by the rock outcrop immediately to the west.

After this last deposit of sand and gravel the surface of this area had reached a height of eight and a half feet above the normal river level. Upon this there then accumulated an additional deposit of sand about two and a half feet thick. This last deposit appears to have accumulated slowly and in a somewhat irregular manner. Although there are clay streaks and seepage lines running throughout the upper part of this zone, there is still no evidence of vegetation or organic matter in the sand, and it must have been subjected to periods of wind and water erosion and redeposition. Of major importance, however, was the finding of stone-lined hearths in this loose sand that have given a C-14 date of 3484 ± 350 B.C. (M-523) for those highest in the sand. Others lying deeper in the sand are estimated to be at least 6,000 years old. The top of this sand zone, on the other hand, did remain stable long enough for a humus zone of six to eight inches in thickness to develop over most of the area examined. A number of hearths were found originating in this zone and extending slightly below it. Charcoal from three of these, when combined, gave a C-14 date of 1944 ± 250 B.C. (M-524).[6] If these dates accurately reflect the site history, then less than one foot of soil accumulated on this site during a period of 1,000 years. There is, of course, the possibility that part of the depositional sequence was lost to erosion, but there is no evidence

[6] Crane and Griffith, 1958b: 1122–1123.

FIG. 76. Old locks and canal section three miles to the east of the Gaston Site. Note the rock outcrop extending to the river and the Virginia Electric and Power Company Dam in the background.

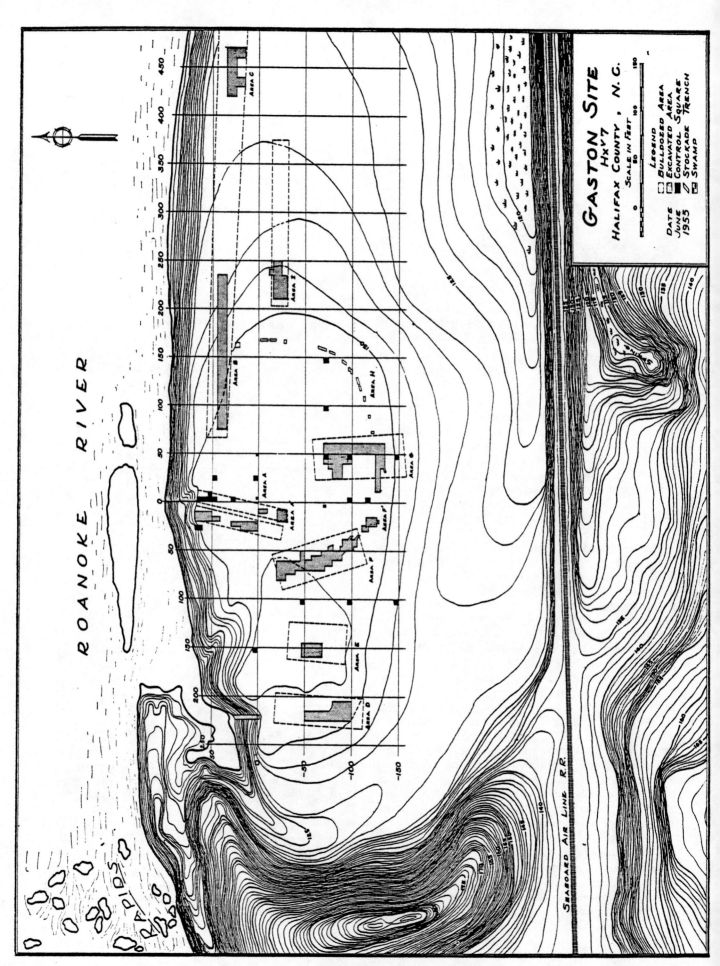

ROANOKE RIVER

AREA C

AREA B

AREA A

AREA H

AREA I

AREA G

AREA F

AREA E

AREA D

GASTON SITE
Hx V7
HALIFAX COUNTY, N. C.
SCALE IN FEET
0   50   100   150

LEGEND
☐ BULLDOZED AREA
▨ EXCAVATED AREA
■ CONTROL SQUARE
◿ STOCKADE TRENCH
▦ SWAMP

DATE
JUNE
1955

SEABOARD AIR LINE R.R.

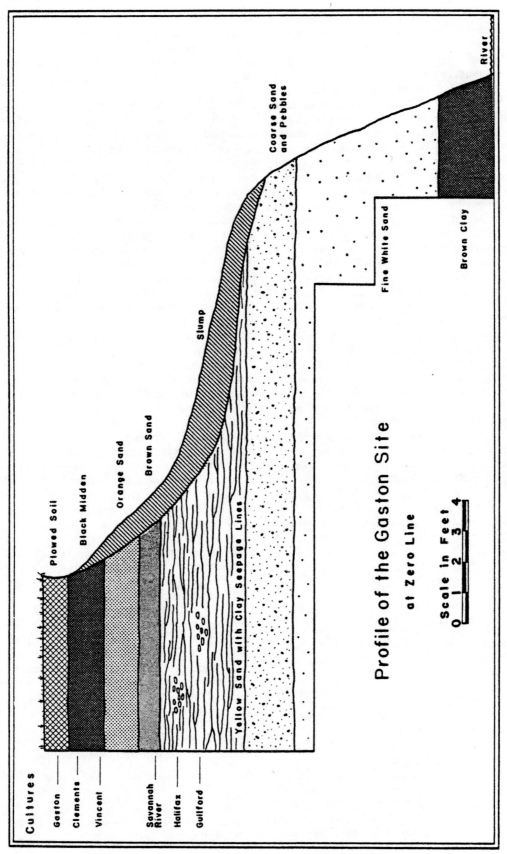

Profile of the Gaston Site

at Zero Line

Scale in Feet

FIG. 78

for this. The humus develops directly on the sand surface and there is no indication of an unconformity at this point. On the other hand, it is obvious that, as the deposits are built higher above the river, the magnitude of the flood must be greater in order to cover them.

Following this period of relative stability the site was covered with a final mantle of flood-deposited sand which varied from twelve to fourteen inches in depth. Immediately upon this developed the midden deposit of the later prehistoric occupants. The maximum depth of this accumulated debris was twenty inches along the river, and it thinned out toward the southern edge of the site. This, in turn, was overlaid by a plowed zone averaging ten inches in depth. There is no evidence of recent flood deposits and the plowed zone must have developed out of the top part of the midden. The earliest date for the lower part of the midden was A.D. 916 ± 200 (table 15). This date, unfortunately, was obtained from the combined charcoal samples from four pits. Subsequently, one of these pits was found to contain specimens that were typologically later than those found in the others. It is estimated, therefore, that the date A.D. 500 would be more nearly correct for the beginning of this later occupation. If this is true, then the rate of soil accumulation had slowed down still more. Only fourteen inches of soil separate the C-14 samples of 1944 B.C. and the estimated date of A.D. 500. This gives, in round numbers, a rate of one foot in two thousand years or about half of that for the preceding period. It is not suggested that these are constant rates or that they might ever be applicable in another situation. It is, however, an excellent example of a geomorphological type—the mature river levee, a land form that builds up at a progressively slower rate and, if protected, will be preserved as a remnant in an eroding valley system. This is exactly the same situation as that described in Part One.

II. THE EXCAVATIONS

A. PROBLEMS AND METHODS OF EXCAVATIONS

In the spring of 1953 a United States Supreme Court decision authorized the Virginia Electric and Power Company to begin the construction of a $34,000,000 dam across the Roanoke River just above the town of Roanoke Rapids, North Carolina. This dam, when completed, was to flood the relatively small area of 4,400 acres. The basin would be nine miles in length and have a shore line of forty-seven miles. In April, 1955, two years later, no effort had been made by anyone to attempt a salvage program in the area to be flooded. This was due, partly, to the lack of federal funds for archaeological salvage work at the time and the rather poor relations the Department of the Interior was having with private power developments. It was also due, in part, to the fact that it had been dismissed

as an inconsequential archaeological area. Since it was apparent that no federal support would be available for salvage work, and in view of the fact that the dam was being completed nearly a year ahead of schedule, it was felt that the University of North Carolina should at least look into the matter. On April 10, 1955, the author wrote to Mr. J. G. Holtzclaw, President of the Virginia Power and Electric Company and suggested a meeting to discuss ways and means for conducting a salvage program in the time that remained before the completion of the dam. On April 19 a meeting was held at the Company's office in Roanoke Rapids. As a result of this meeting, the Virginia Electric and Power Company agreed to finance the field work through a contribution to the University. Actual field work began on the day of the meeting and continued on an extended weekend schedule until the end of the Spring Semester at the University of North Carolina. On May 29 a permanent camp was set up in the basin and work was continued from sunrise to sunset until the area was flooded on June 29. As a result of this brief survey, seventy-four sites were located, five were given exploratory excavations, and one, the Gaston Site, was excavated in depth.[7]

The major problem involved in this project was the limiting time factor. The first six weeks of surveying and testing were handicapped by the fact that all of the personnel involved had to continue to meet classes and finish the Spring Semester to which they were already committed. By the end of May, however, the content of the basin was fairly well known, and a site was selected with some confidence upon which work should be concentrated for the remaining four weeks. The Gaston Site was selected because, in the author's judgment, it contained a better represented cultural sequence than any of the other seventy-three sites. It also contained a greater concentration of protohistoric or historic Indian remains, and it was so situated that we could expect to find, with a high degree of certainty, true stratigraphic levels. In all these things we were not disappointed.

As a first step, preparatory to the actual excavation, a one-foot contour map was made of the area, and a control grid was established over the site at fifty-foot intervals (fig. 77). For some reason, unknown at the present time, the point of origin for the grid was located in the north central part of the site. This resulted in the use of both left and right, as well as plus and minus, coordinates. All locations were designated in terms of feet, left or right, plus or minus, from the point of origin. The square or unit designation was the measurement of the coordinates to its southeast corner.[8] As

[7] Credit for this rather remarkable performance is due entirely to the ability and enthusiasm of Mr. Stanley South and the assistance given him by Mr. Lewis Binford.

[8] The standard method of the Research Laboratories of Anthropology, University of North Carolina—a modified version of the University of Chicago system.

the plan of operation developed four rather distinct types of exploration were used. These categories were: control squares, bulldozing for features, stockade trench, and stratigraphic levels.

B. THE CONTROL SQUARES

An approach trench, five feet wide, was begun at the edge of the river bank. It was excavated to a depth of three feet and carried south along the zero line for a distance of fifteen feet. Twenty-one other five-foot squares were excavated at random throughout the site in an effort to secure as accurate a picture of this upper midden deposit as possible (fig. 77). The excavation of all of these units followed the same pattern. The top soil was removed as a level, then the remaining undisturbed midden was removed in six-inch levels down to the first sterile sand zone. When the sand subsoil was reached, it was troweled and the various pits and postholes observed were recorded and excavated. All of the soil removed from these control squares was sifted.

The profiles exposed in the control squares showed a plowed zone of about ten inches in depth covering the whole site. Immediately below this was a black midden deposit which was thickest along the river bank near the center of the grid system and tapered to the east, west, and south. Its maximum depth was twenty inches in square 55R5 of the original approach trench.

All of the material recovered from these units was analyzed with considerable care since it was felt that it would contain evidence supporting the change in early pottery styles already suggested by other sites and by the material collected from the surface at this site. In the final analysis all squares that showed major disturbances were eliminated as well as all squares that

FIG. 80. Bulldozer from the Stone and Webster Construction Company removing overburden in preparation for the excavation of the preceramic levels at the Gaston Site.

had less than three levels (eighteen inches) of midden deposits. Only eight of the original twenty-five seemed to offer a reasonably true and undisturbed depositional picture. These squares showed that the Vincent, Clements, and Gaston Series specimens were superimposed in that order. This confirmed the seriation of surface collections from the basin as a whole as well as that of the features at the Gaston Site itself (fig. 94).

C BULLDOZING FOR FEATURES

After the excavation of the control squares was completed, the next major concern was for a better understanding of the areal distribution of features, burials, and other aspects of the site. This could best be achieved in the time available by using powered earthmoving equipment to strip off the midden deposit and expose the pits and disturbances that extended below the midden into the sand subsoil. On June 1, twenty-three days before the closing of the dam gates, two motor graders were borrowed from the State Highway Department, and they removed two strips of midden on the eastern side of the site paralleling the river. These strips are designated areas B, C, and I in figure 77. The largest of these two strips was approximately twenty-five feet wide and five hundred feet long.

The drivers of the graders were instructed to strip the soil off in relatively thin layers and as they proceeded with this task they were followed and all objects visible were picked up (fig. 79, 80). When the sand subsoil was reached the graders made one last run over the area cleaning it of all the loose dirt that may have been missed before. All pits or postholes that

FIG. 79. Motor graders from the North Carolina Highway Department removing the upper midden level over selected areas of the Gaston Site.

FIG. 81. Features exposed by bulldozing Area *D* at the Gaston Site. The plowed soil and midden has been removed exposing the top of the underlying orange sand. The dark areas indicating features or other disturbances are marked with a stake and incised.

were observed at this time were marked with sticks or circled so that they might be readily located after the soil had dried out (figs. 81, 82).

There is no doubt that this procedure destroys a great deal of archaeological evidence, and it is no substitute for traditional methods when the circumstances permit. In the case where time is the prime consideration, this combination of excavating control units for vertical data and grading for horizontal data is much more satisfactory than either would be alone. The archaeologist should keep in mind, however, that his grading operations have reduced all of the pits to the same level, the tops of those which originated higher in the deposit are lost, and the relative age and cultural association now must be determined by their content rather than their position.

On June 13 a bulldozer was borrowed from Stone-Webster Construction Company and the areas *D, E, F,* and *G* were graded to the bottom of the midden level. It was found that a bulldozer is a far more satisfactory machine for moving sand in large quantities than a motor grader. The wheels of the latter lose traction and dig into the sand. The wheels also concentrate the weight of the machine more than the treads of a bulldozer. This was illustrated by the fact that burials recovered from the bulldozed areas were damaged less than those recovered from the area cleaned by the motor grader. On the other hand, the graders give a much cleaner floor when they are not required to push heavy loads of dirt. The moral seems to be that any well-equipped archaeological expedition should have on hand both a motor grader and bulldozer.

After the midden deposit was stripped from these areas of the site, work was concentrated on excavating the exposed features. The unit of work was usually a ten-foot square laid out along the grid coordinates. These units were then troweled and the disturbances that were visible were plotted and photographed. The pits were excavated and the soil sifted. When concentrations of rock, bone, pottery, or other materials were found they were cleaned as a unit before removal. The work on features was stopped when an even two hundred were excavated. In addition to these features, fourteen human burials and eight dog burials were found.

1. *Garbage Pits*

Regardless of the original intent of the aborigine, these holes appeared to the archaeologist as pits containing general village refuse composed of animal bone, shell, charcoal, pottery fragments, and, occasionally, a bone or stone artifact. Regardless of how one might look at them from a functional point of view, they still contained garbage. They were seen as dark areas in the yellow sand at the base of the midden deposit and they varied from two to seven feet across and from six to fifty-four inches deep. The soil in which they were dug was loose sand, and most of them had clean, even-cut sides. They appear to have been dug for immediate use and refilled soon afterwards. If this had not been the case, the sides would have sloughed off or caved in as they did after they were excavated.

Of some interest were four features that contained fragments of human bones as well as a general run of garbage. Feature 2 contained six human teeth, Feature 71 contained one human tooth and several other bone fragments, Feature 72 contained a fragment of a human skull and jaw, and Feature 199 had lying on its

FIG. 82. Features exposed by bulldozing Sq. 35R185 at the Gaston Site. This square has been laid out along the grid coordinates and the surface has been troweled to clean the surface of the features and postholes preparatory to mapping.

bottom twelve human finger bones and four teeth. This may suggest that the species *Homo sapiens* had been added to their diet, but it is more probable that earlier burials had been disturbed in this area. Feature 2 dates back to the Vincent period while the other three appear to belong to the later Clements horizon.

Only twelve of the two hundred features appear to have been used extensively for fires. Eight of these pits were lined with small boulders and the bottom was covered with wood charcoal. Many of the rocks were cracked or otherwise showed signs of having been burned. Four others had thick layers of charcoal in their bottom, but did not contain rocks. Of these twelve pits, six definitely belonged to the Vincent period and two others contained steatite sherds. None of these relatively deep fire pits contained Gaston sherds, and, apparently, were used by the earlier inhabitants of the site.

Another type of pit that contained garbage and also some remains of fire was that with small postholes on the edge of the pit. Four of these pits were between a single pair of postholes and three others had four postholes quartered around them. Perhaps these were the remains of a primitive rotisserie. In any event, they were used primarily during the Vincent period.

2. Dog Burials

Eight fully articulated dog skeletons were found in their own individual burial pits. Most of these contained deer bones that may have represented an offering since they were found on the flood of the pit next to the skeleton rather than loose in the pit fill. In one instance, a dog was buried over a human fetus.

3. Human Burials

Fourteen human burials were excavated at the site. Thirteen of these were tightly flexed and buried in round or oval pits which extended below the black midden into the yellow sand. Several of these were partially damaged by the bulldozing operation but the rest were buried a foot or more below the midden level. Burial 9, however, was a bundle burial with the mandible and pelvis located at one end of the bone pile and the skull at the other. With one exception these burials contained nothing visible in the way of grave offerings. The exception was Burial 7 which contained a fine example of an alate-stemmed engraved stone pipe (fig. 114 *D*).

The cultural period to which these burials belong cannot be determined with any great degree of accuracy; however, it appears that at least five belong to the Gaston period since the pit fill contains sherds of that type. Five of the other burial pits contained sherds of the Clements type and are certainly no older. The remaining five burials had no pottery in the fill of the pits and, therefore, nothing to indicate their cultural affinity.

It would seem that the majority of the burials, if not all of them, belong to the Clements or Gaston periods and not to the earlier Vincent period. This is further indicated by the following analysis of the skeletal material prepared by Dr. Newman in which he compared five specimens from the Gaston Site (Hx⁷7) with four from the Thelma Site (Hx⁷8).[9] Feature 2, on the other hand, was used during the Vincent period and, since it contained human bones, there must have been some burials of this earlier period at the site.

Thelma Site
Hx⁷8

Ossuary Burial—Vincent Period

Bu 1—Posterior calva and mandible lacking condyles; Sex —?, possibly male; age—?–30; maximum breadth 139; low occiput; type—probably Neumann's Lenapid.

Bu 2a—Restored calva and most of mandible; sex—male; age—40–50; glabello-occipital length—192; maximum breadth—131 ? (warping and incompleteness); auricular height—115 ?; low pinched occiput; type—Neumann's Lenapid.

Bu 2b—Warped calva and right half of mandible; sex—male; age—20–25; minimal frontal diameter—93; unmeasurable but patently long-headed; small parietal losses; flat temporals; type—Neumann's Lenapid.

Skull #3—Part of frontal and anterior parietals; sex— ?; age—35–?. No other data.

Gaston Site
Hx⁷7

Individual Pit Burials—Clements and Gaston Periods

Bu 1 (Clements)—Complete restored calvarium (skull and mandible); sex—male; age—40–45; glabello-occipital length 178, maximum breadth 139, ba-bregma height 144, min. frontal diameter 92, total facial height 120*, upper facial height 70, bizygomatic diameter 144, nasal height 51, nasal breadth 26; type—Neumann's Lenapid.

Bu 2 (Gaston)—Fragmentary incomplete calva and mandible; sex—female; age—35–45 or more; maximum breadth 139 ?, bigonial breadth 75; low slightly pinched occiput; type—probably Neumann's Lenapid.

Bu 4 (?)—Fragmentary incomplete calva and mandible: sex—female; age—adult (young?); glabello-occipital length (approx.) 195; low pinched occiput; type—probably Neumann's Lenapid.

Bu 6 (Gaston)—Very fragmentary and incomplete calva; sex—?; age—30 or more; type—indistinguishable; pathology—small perforations in tabla interna of frontal and parietals, in one case penetrating completely through diploe and tabla externa.

Bu 9 (Clements)—Very incomplete calva; sex—female?; age 35 or more; min. frontal diameter 90, vault appears rather broad; type—indistinguishable.

Comparison of Hx⁷7 and Hx⁷8 Skulls

There is no decided contrast between the two groups of skulls. If there were, the samples are so small it would be a matter of sheer conjecture whether the differences extended to the parent populations.

---

[9] Dr. Marshall T. Newman, Smithsonian Institution, 1957, personal communication. The primary occupation at the Thelma Site was during the Vincent period.

* 4 mm. added for tooth wear.

As near as I can tell, all skulls are Neumann's Lenapid (or Hrdlička's Algonkin) variety. The only possible difference may be that the Hx^{v}7 skulls are somewhat rounder —and the Hx^{v}8 skulls somewhat longer-headed. This is the same situation, still within one variety, that pertained at the N. Alabama Archaic site of Lu°25. There the upper stratum skulls were rounder-headed than those of the lower stratum. The dividing line between strata was roughly preceramic—early ceramic.[10]

D. STOCKADE TRENCH

When square 35R165 was cleaned, a row of postholes was observed crossing it from north to south with no obvious curvature. A check was made by excavating cross trenches at fifteen and thirty-five feet toward the south which confirmed this to be a stockade wall, and it was traced throughout most of its length. While time did not permit the complete excavation of the stockade, its course was estimated and excavations were made at frequent intervals to check its position (fig. 77). Finally, Area F (fig. 83) was bulldozed to expedite the tracing of its course. It was originally estimated that the overall length of the stockade was about five hundred feet, that it originated at the river bank, ran southward, and then circled back to the river to a point two hundred and fifty feet from where it began, enclosing a roughly circular area of about one acre. A closer inspection of the field notes and photographs in the laboratory, however, showed that halves of two stockades had been excavated rather than one as originally described in the field. The evidence indicated that the eastern half of one stockade overlapped the western half of another stockade in the southern part of Area G. There was some uncertainty about the direction of the stockade at this point even during the excavation, but, when the other stockade was found a little farther to the west, it was mistaken for a continuation of the original one that had been traced from the east. The only difference that this makes is that there were two stockades instead of one and that the area that they enclosed was somewhat larger. Both stockades were built during the Gaston period. This was indicated by the presence of Gaston sherds in five postholes in the eastern section and the intrusion of the western stockade into two pits that were dated at A.D. 1586 ± 200 (table 15).

E. STRATIGRAPHIC LEVELS

On June 21, a bulldozer was borrowed from Stone-Webster Construction Company and Area A' was graded down to within a foot of the older humus zone which contained the preceramic Savannah River cultural material. Work was now concentrated on clearing these lower levels, and finally eight separate units were dug to the Guilford level in various parts of the

[10] Dr. Marshall T. Newman, Smithsonian Institution, 1957, personal communication.

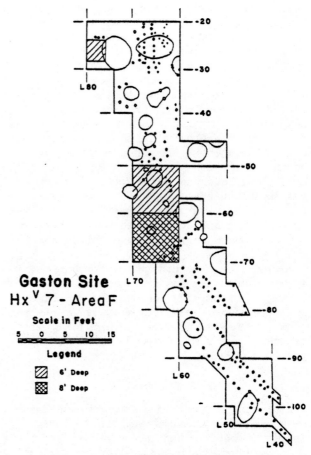

Gaston Site
Hx^v 7 - Area F

Scale in Feet
5 0 5 10 15

Legend
▨ 6' Deep
▩ 8' Deep

FIG. 83

site. These excavations exposed a total of seven hundred square feet. On June 23, one day before the gates of the dam were to be closed, Mr. Holtzclaw, President of the Virginia Power and Electric Company, offered to delay this closing date, if it were felt that more time was needed. Since it was originally agreed not to delay the project and since we had secured a reasonable sample from the site, the author declined this thoughtful offer and the gates were closed the next day. Five days later the site was under water.

The procedure used in excavating these deeper levels differed somewhat from that used in the initial work with the control squares. As each of the eight units was selected, its surface was carefully cleaned to remove all traces of the later midden or intrusive pits (fig. 90). A narrow trench was then dug along one side of the square in order to obtain a visual profile and a control surface from which to work. This trench was usually taken down in three-foot intervals. After this preparation, the unit was excavated in six-inch levels with all the dirt being sifted and *all* objects that did not pass through the screen were saved for later analysis.

The sand zone which separated the midden from the earlier humus line was completely sterile of cultural material. The old soil surface, however, contained the Savannah River artifacts, and it was taken off as a unit. Below this level the remaining soil was removed in approximately two-inch levels. As soon as the Halifax level was reached and an artifact found, its actual horizontal location was plotted and its vertical position located by means of a transit. This placed all finds in absolute relationship to the vertical control datum. A detailed description of squares -60L60 and -70L60 is given below. The other six units contained essentially the same information and were located as follows: Area A, 5 × 10' excavation at 60R5; Area A', 10 × 10' ex-

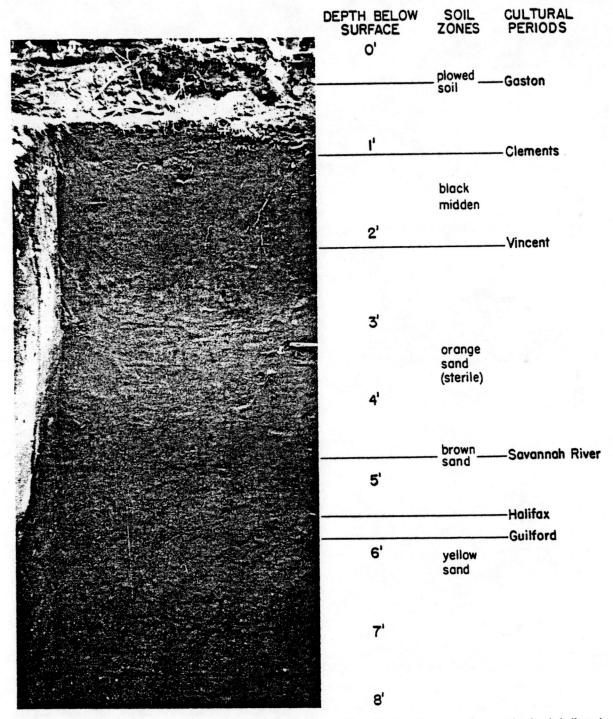

DEPTH BELOW SURFACE	SOIL ZONES	CULTURAL PERIODS
0'		
	plowed soil	Gaston
1'		Clements
	black midden	
2'		Vincent
3'	orange sand (sterile)	
4'		
	brown sand	Savannah River
5'		
		Halifax
		Guilford
6'	yellow sand	
7'		
8'		

FIG. 84. Photograph of the south profile of Sq. 55L25 at the Gaston Site with the soil zones and occupation levels indicated.

FIG. 85. Halifax Hearth No. 1 at the Gaston Site, located 10″ below the Savannah River level and 66″ below the surface in Sq. 55L25.

FIG. 87. Close-up view of Halifax Hearth No. 2 at the south edge of Sq. 10L20 at the Gaston Site. The large stone in the background has been pitted and ground as the result of use as a shallow mortar.

cavation at 60L10, 5 × 10′ excavation at 55L25, and 10 × 10′ excavation 10L20; Area F, 5 × 5′ excavation at -28L76; Area G, 10 × 12.5′ excavation at -105R50. All of these excavations were carried to a minimum depth of six and one-half feet and spot checks were made from two to three feet deeper.

FIG. 86. Halifax Hearth No. 2 at the Gaston Site, located directly below Number 1 in Sq. 55L25 and separated by two inches of sand. Charcoal from the two hearths has been dated at 2324 ± 350 B.C.

FIG. 88. View of hearths 1 and 3 in the Halifax level at the northeastern corner of Sq. 10L20 at the Gaston Site. The excavated level shown in this photograph was fifty-eight inches below the surface of the site, and the charcoal taken from these hearths was dated at 3484 ± 350 B.C.

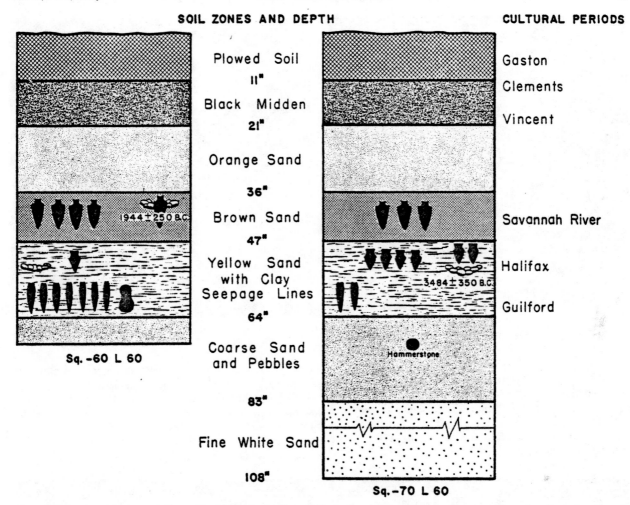

FIG. 89. Profile of Squares –60L60 and –70L60 at the Gaston Site. Symbols indicate the actual number of artifacts found and their respective levels for each Square.

1. *Excavation of Square -60L60*

This unit is located in Area F and was found to contain, after bulldozing, a segment of the stockade wall and Feature 111, 112, 114 (fig. 83). These features were excavated and found to contain very little material. Feature 111 had nine potsherds of the Clements Series; Feature 112 contained a small amount of burned deer bones; and Feature 114 was sterile. After these features were excavated the postholes were removed together with all other traces of intrusion.

The approach to the lower levels was begun by digging a trench along the east side of the square. This vertical profile exposed the old humus zone, which lay between thirty-six and forty-seven inches below the surface at this point. When the excavation of this level reached the western side of the square a stone hearth was uncovered that contained fifty-nine rocks in a tight cluster and the base of a Savannah River projectile point (fig. 93). A small amount of charcoal was collected from this hearth and it was combined with two

other hearths in this level for the C-14 date of 1944 ± 250 B.C. (table 15). Four other Savannah River type points were found near the hearth as well as seven hammerstones.

After the excavation passed the fifty-one inch level the amount of chips in the sand decreased sharply for about six inches; then at fifty-seven inches from the surface the per cent of slate chips increased rapidly and at the sixty-three-inch level one Halifax type point was found at the northern edge of the square. At this same level but clustered more toward the southern and central part of the square were found seven Guilford type projectile points, one Guilford type chipped axe, and one lump of red ochre that had been scraped. The square was excavated to a depth of seventy-two inches but no artifacts or chips were recovered in the last six inches.

2. *Excavation of Square -70L60*

This unit adjoined the preceding square on the south side and is a continuation of the same situation de-

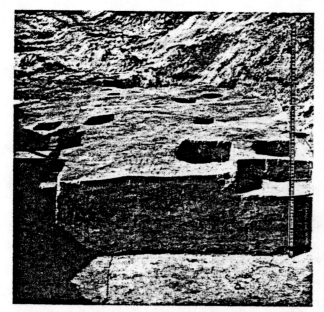

FIG. 90. Preparation of Sq. –70L60 at the Gaston Site after the removal of the overburden by bulldozers. All traces of disturbed soil were removed.

FIG. 92. A closer view of the Halifax hearth in square –70L60 (fig. 91) showing two Halifax points *in situ*.

scribed above. The surface, after the bulldozer had removed the midden, also contained a segment of the stockade and a few small pits. These were all removed with care to eliminate any possibility of intrusive materials being found in the lower levels (fig. 90). Since this square was approached from the preceding one, it

was not necessary to cut an entrance trench to allow the levels to be worked off from the side and top.

The old humus line was again traced through the square at a depth of thirty-six to forty-seven inches below the surface. No hearths were found at this level but three Savannah River projectile points and one small oval blade were found.

FIG. 91. A Halifax hearth exposed at the 54″ level of Sq. –70L60 at the Gaston Site.

FIG. 93. Savannah River hearth found in Square –60L60 at the Gaston Site. Charcoal from this hearth combined with that from two others in square 60L10 has been dated at 1944 ± 250 B.C.

Fifty-four inches below the surface, in the yellow sand underlying the old humus, a stone-lined hearth of the Halifax period was found. This hearth had thirty-seven fist-size rocks surrounding the area in which the fire had been built. The charcoal from this pit was combined with that from three other similar hearths in square 10L20 (figs. 87, 88) for a C-14 date of 3484 ± 350 B.C. Lying close to the rocks of this hearth were two Halifax type points (fig. 92). Slightly below these and scattered toward the northwest were four more Halifax type points. Two of these four were found at a depth of sixty-three inches. Two Guilford type points were also found at this depth near the north edge of the square. This sometime association of Halifax and Guilford points at the same level is not surprising, since the soil is loose sand and the hearths of the two periods were not separated by more than ten inches of soil. The total picture, however, shows that the Guilford material is stratigraphically earlier (fig. 104).

After the Guilford level this square was carefully screened to a depth of nine feet for signs of an earlier occupation. Not a single chip was recovered. At seventy inches below the surface or fourteen inches below the Guilford level, however, a large hammerstone was found. This certainly suggests that the Guilford occupation was not the earliest in the basin.

III. THE ANALYSIS OF ARTIFACTS

A. POTTERY

There was a total of 33,483 fragments of pottery collected from the various sites within the basin. Of this total, 19,885 specimens were found at the Gaston Site. This seemed to be an adequate sample and there was no reason to doubt that they represented a true picture of the ceramic tradition in that area. As this material was being collected, it became obvious that there was little variation in style from site to site throughout the area. This apparent homogeneity could be interpreted as a large occupation for a relatively short period of time, or, with equal impunity, as a relatively small population over a long period of time during which

TABLE 10

PERCENTAGE DISTRIBUTION OF POTTERY SERIES FROM CONTROLLED LEVELS* AT THE GASTON SITE

Level	Vincent Series		Clements Series		Gaston Series		Total Count
	Count	Per Cent	Count	Per Cent	Count	Per Cent	
I 0–10″	166	17.9	137	27.7	300	67.6	603
II 10–16″	322	35.0	182	36.7	108	24.3	612
III 16–22″	435	47.1	176	35.6	36	8.1	647
Total	923	100.0	495	100.0	444	100.0	1,862

* Only squares 0L75, 0L150, 25R5, 45R25, 50R5, 53R10, 60R5, and −75R100 were used for this tabulation.

TABLE 11

PERCENTAGE DISTRIBUTION OF POTTERY SERIES FROM PITS CONTAINING 50 OR MORE SHERDS AT THE GASTON SITE

Feature Number	Sherd Count*	Vincent Series	Clements Series	Gaston Series	Other Types
2	168	54.8	33.3	4.2	7.7
7	82	58.5	37.8	1.3	2.4
8	56	67.9	26.7	3.6	1.8
18	83	36.1	60.2	0.0	3.7
36	51	64.7	19.6	7.8	7.9
38	119	6.7	65.6	8.4	19.3
43	143	47.6	43.4	5.5	3.5
45	67	64.2	29.8	1.5	4.5
55	138	13.3	84.8	0.0	2.9
57	84	35.7	57.2	0.0	7.1
59	196	14.4	76.0	1.5	9.1
61	139	12.2	74.8	1.4	11.6
63	106	40.5	58.6	0.0	0.9
64	113	24.7	70.8	0.0	4.5
66	219	40.7	28.3	10.5	20.5
67	188	33.5	63.8	0.0	2.7
71	71	91.6	5.6	2.8	0.0
73	71	70.4	18.3	4.2	7.1
95	206	89.3	0.0	2.9	7.8
102	61	98.4	0.0	0.0	1.6
103	53	56.6	16.0	7.5	18.9
105	238	60.0	38.4	0.8	0.8
106	78	85.8	14.2	0.0	0.0
107	158	86.7	10.2	1.3	1.8
113	98	87.6	7.4	1.0	4.0
121	72	38.2	50.0	9.7	1.2
124	343	7.6	11.6	75.9	4.9
125	229	12.2	11.1	74.3	2.4
148	1062	11.6	16.6	64.7	7.1
158	103	46.6	27.2	0.0	26.2
179	50	16.0	10.0	66.0	8.0
180	55	21.8	9.1	58.2	10.9
181	173	11.0	5.7	83.3	0.0
184	225	27.0	19.6	47.5	5.9
188	57	73.7	15.8	10.5	0.0
195	209	7.1	28.8	62.1	2.0
196	99	26.2	47.5	24.3	2.0

* Total sherds: 5,663.

there was little change in the basic styles. Previous experience with over two hundred other sites in the Roanoke Valley indicated that the latter interpretation would probably be correct. It was anticipated that the excavations at the Gaston Site would produce convincing evidence for this long-term point of view.

Prior to this work very little was known about the archaeology of the lower part of the Roanoke Valley, although collections have been studied from sites at the mouth of the Roanoke River and from sites along the adjacent shores of Albemarle Sound.[11] In 1938 the author collected from thirty-two sites in the area now flooded by the Buggs Island Reservoir, forty-five miles up river from the Gaston Site. At that time it was his observation that the pottery from those sites represented at least three distinct groups with significant time differences.[12] Subsequent work in the lower part of the

[11] Evans, 1955: 134; Haag, 1958: 46.
[12] Griffin, 1945: 323.

Buggs Island Basin in 1952 confirmed this opinion, and this present work in the Roanoke Rapids Basin demonstrates a parallel and interrelated development.

In the Buggs Island area the earliest pottery was found redeposited in water-laid sand on three of the four islands investigated. It lay under, and was separated stratigraphically from, the later cultural material. The pottery recovered from these early deposits was cord-marked and the paste was hard and compact. Fine sand was used for temper. This pottery has been referred to occasionally as Piedmont Cord-Marked; and it parallels the Vincent Series in the present study.[18]

The second ceramic period in the Buggs Island Basin has been called Roanoke, and it was characterized by both cord and fabric-marked bowls or simple jars. Its paste contained a larger per cent of sand and mica than the former type, and it had a sugary appearance in cross section. In 1938 it was obvious that the Roanoke Complex was distinct from the Clarksville type, since it had an areal distribution quite independent of the latter. On the basis of style and associated artifacts, it was also presumed to be earlier. This was demonstrated in 1952 when pottery of the Roanoke type was found separated by sterile flood sand eighteen inches below the later Clarksville type. This stratigraphy was found on site Va[v]33 located on the west bank of the Roanoke

[18] Witthoft, 1950: 11.

River four miles downstream from Clarksville. The pottery of the Roanoke period corresponds to the Clements Series at Roanoke Rapids, and their contemporaneity was indicated by the presence of Roanoke type sherds in pits of the Clements period at the Gaston Site.

The final period at Buggs Island was called Clarksville. The pottery consisted of bowls and flaring rim jars that were finished for the most part with a net-roughened surface. Cord-marked surfaces were rare and the wicker-type fabric so common during the earlier period was completely absent. Other pots were finished smooth, scraped, or stamped with either a simple or check design. These last variations, however, represented less than ten per cent of the pottery, but they foreshadowed the styles that would become more popular in this area a generation later.

The Clarksville jars were also characterized by the thickening of the rim, either by folding over the upper margin of the rim or by adding a strip and bonding it to the rim below the lip. The lips were occasionally notched along the outer corner, but even more commonly, the lower margin of the rim fold was incised or punched. This type of rim decoration also distinguished the Gaston type pottery. At the Gaston Site, however, net-impressed pottery was rare and the majority of the late pottery was simple stamped. Smooth pottery was more plentiful than at Clarksville and corn-

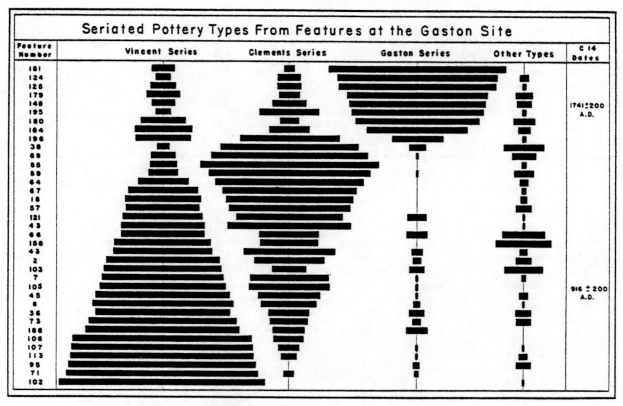

FIG. 94

cob-roughened surfaces were found in small quantities. The loss of net-roughened surfaces and the increased emphasis on simple stamping indicated a later date for the Gaston occupation than the approximate A.D. 1675 terminal date for the Clarksville period. Stylistically, the Gaston pottery suggested a post A.D. 1700 date and confirmation of this was indicated by the C-14 date of A.D. 1741 ± 200 based on charcoal obtained from a Gaston period pit, Feature 148. On the basis of this information it seemed apparent that the Clements styles lasted considerably longer in the Roanoke Rapids area than did their counterpart in the Buggs Island area.

1. *Vincent Series*

This pottery (figs. 95, 96, 97) was represented by two types: Vincent Cord-Marked and Vincent Fabric-Marked. The paste of this series was relatively hard, compact, and, in general, had a light brown or orange color. The clay had been tempered with a few stray pebbles and a large quantity of very fine sand. The texture was uniform, and slightly gritty to the touch. The vessels were simple in form and they varied from small conical bowls to large straight-sided jars. The rims were irregular and finger smoothed. They were not decorated.

These types were described on the basis of the material collected from the Roanoke Rapids Basin, but they had a much wider distribution. Specimens have been collected from Clarksville, Virginia, to the shores of Albemarle Sound. In Virginia similar material was collected to the northeast of this area and described by Evans as the Stoney Creek Series.[14] Unfortunately, he did not distinguish between the early and late forms of the cord- and fabric-marked pottery. They were all grouped, together with net-impressed and simple stamped pottery, into one unit using their "compact, sandy texture" as the most diagnostic feature.[15] The present types were named for Vincent Island in the Roanoke Rapids Basin where sites having the largest per cent of these types were found.

Vincent Cord-Marked (fig. 95):

Method of manufacture: Annular segments built upon a starting coil. Paddle-malleated on exterior surfaces. Fractures were usually along the junction of coils or segments.

Paste: (1) Temper: Very fine sand with an occasional small pebble. All particles were rounded and appeared to be river sand.
    (2) Hardness: 2.5 to 3.5.
    (3) Texture: Gritty and sandy to touch, although many of the interior surfaces had a clayey feel. The clay was compact, well kneaded, and hard. It was not porous or granular.

---

14 Evans, 1955: 69–74.
15 Evans, 1955: 69.

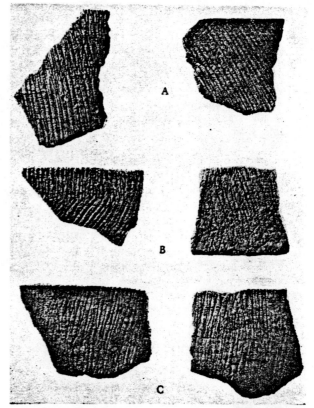

FIG. 95. The pottery type Vincent Cord-Marked from the Gaston and Thelma sites. *A.* Hxᵛ8, Sq. 65, pit; Sq. 35R225, Fea. 67. *B.* Sq. 35R115, Fea. 18; Sq. 35R215, Fea. 63. *C.* Sq. 35R115, Fea. 18; surface after grader.

    (4) Color: On the exterior the color varied from earth to medium brown, but the majority of the specimens were of the lighter shades. There was also a definite orange tone to many specimens. The interior surfaces were almost always the same color as the exterior surfaces. The core, on the other hand, was always darker and varied from gray to dark brown. The oxidized exterior and interior surfaces ranged from 0.5 to 2.0 mm. in thickness.

Firing: Fired upright in an open fire. All exposed surfaces were oxidized. Firing was even and well controlled, and there were very few traces of firing clouds.

Surface treatment:
    (1) Exterior: The whole exterior surface of the vessel was malleated with a cord-wrapped paddle. The impressions of the cords were clear, and, for the most part, were applied at right angles to the rim. A smaller per cent ran diagonally to the right. There was considerable overlapping but deliberate crisscrossing has not been observed. The shift in angle of the cord to the rim appeared to be incidental to the shift of the vessel in the maker's hand as it was being shaped with the paddle.

(2) Interior: The interior surfaces were smooth but irregular. There was no evidence of tooling and almost all specimens showed clearly that the hand was used for finishing and smoothing the interior of the vessel. This smoothing or "floating" process tended to cover most of the sand particles in the paste and gave the interior its clayey feel. On a small per cent of the specimens the cord-wrapped paddle was applied to the interior of the rim, but this seldom extended down into the vessel more than two or three centimeters and was frequently obscured by subsequent smoothing.

Decoration: None.

Form: (1) Lip: Usually rounded and finger smoothed. In some cases the tendency was to thin the lip and in other cases it was flattened. Occasionally, the cord-wrapped paddle was used to flatten the lip as well as to shape the inside of the rim. In every case the lip was irregular and undulated along the horizontal plane of the orifice.

(2) Rim: Straight and vertical. In a few instances the rims of deep jars tended to curve inward.

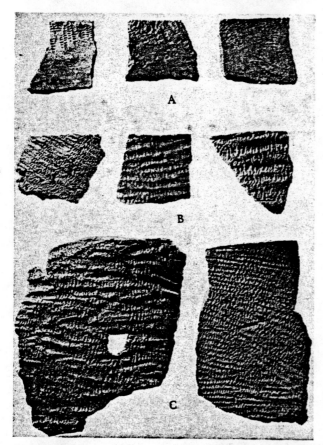

FIG. 96. The pottery type Vincent Fabric-Marked from the Gaston and Thelma sites. A. Sq. 35R185, Fea. 55; Sq. −60L140, Fea. 95; surface after grader. B. Sq. −30L70, Fea. 107; Sq. −70L140, Fea. 102; surface. C. Hx`8, Sq. 65R5, 12–18″; Hx`8, Sq. −5, (6–12″).

(3) Body: Bowls varied from conical to hemispherical in form. The conical types were more numerous. Jars are usually deep, straight-sided, and pointed toward the base. The whole range of form showed little variation.

(4) Base: Usually conical, but tended to be more rounded in the broader hemispherical bowls.

Vessel size: The majority of the vessels reconstructed for size ranged from 25 to 30 cm. in diameter. The conical bowls averaged about 30 cm. in height and the rounder bowls averaged about 15 cm. in height. The jars were usually larger. A few were estimated to be 45 cm. in diameter and 50 cm. in height. The thickness of the vessel walls were fairly uniform throughout any given vessel, but ranged from 0.5 to 1.0 cm. for the type. The average wall thickness was 0.8 cm.

Vincent Fabric-Marked (fig. 96):

Method of manufacture: Same as Vincent Cord-Marked.

Paste: Same as Vincent Cord-Marked.

Firing: Same as Vincent Cord-Marked.

Surface treatment:

(1) Exterior: The whole exterior surface was malleated with a wicker-type fabric. This fabric had a large stiff rodlike warp which varied from 0.6 to 1.1 cm. in diameter and averaged about 0.8 cm. The weft was usually a twisted cord with a diameter of 0.1 or 0.15 cm. The cord was platted over and under the warp and in most cases it was forced together so that it completely covered the warp. The surfaces that were malleated with this fabric indicated that it was folded along the line of the warp to form a paddle and was used very much as one would use a roll of newspaper.

(2) Interior: The interior surfaces were hand smoothed but irregular. Finger and hand swipings were usually visible over most of the surfaces. There was no evidence of scraping or tooling on the interior surfaces.

Decoration: None.

Form: Same as Vincent Cord-Marked.

Vessel size: Same as Vincent Cord-Marked.

2. Clements Series

The pottery of the Vincent and Clements Series represented one ceramic tradition for a long period of time. The Vincent types were made at the beginning and the Clements types persisted to the historic period. As would be expected, this pottery did not fall into mutually exclusive categories. The particular traits that identified the Vincent Series continued long after the newer techniques and styles of the Clements Series were introduced. This continuation of the old with the new existed for a long period of time and was reflected

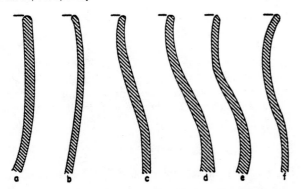

Rim Profiles of Clements Pottery

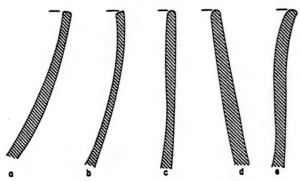

Rim Profiles of Vincent Pottery

Fig. 97

segments were well bonded together and fractures usually ran across the coil lines rather than with them.

Paste: (1) Temper: Medium fine to coarse sand. Coarse grains as large as 4–5 mm. occurred at random together with the predominantly finer sand that averaged about 1 mm. in diameter. There was also present a large per cent of very fine mica that apparently occurred naturally in the sand or clay.

(2) Hardness: 2.5 to 3.0.

(3) Texture: Compact, granular, and sandy. The large quantities of sand temper that were mixed with the clay gave it a sugary appearance in cross section.

(4) Color: The exterior color ranged from red earth to dark brown. In general, the color ran toward the darker shades. The interiors tended to be somewhat lighter than the exteriors. The core was frequently the same color from surface to surface, although in some cases the exterior portion tended to be more thoroughly oxidized. This was true even where the surface was relatively dark, and this suggested that the darkening may be the result of carbonization through use.

Firing: The vessels appeared to have been fired upright in a well-controlled open fire. The firing continued

in the pottery. Because of this gradual change, it was not always possible to determine the type with any degree of assurance. This is illustrated in figure 94 and table 11. The presence of the Vincent types in the later levels together with the premature appearance of the Clements styles in the earlier levels reflect, in part, the inability to type many sherds correctly that lacked specific identifying traits.

The pottery designated as the Clements Series (figs. 97, 98, 99) was well made, and it was considerably thinner than the earlier Vincent types. The interiors were scraped and tooled smooth. The rims on jars tended to flare, and they were occasionally decorated by notching along the lip. The exterior surfaces were malleated with cord and fabric as before, but the cord was finer and twisted tighter. The fabric, while still of the wicker type, had a much smaller warp. Finally, the most diagnostic feature was the paste. It was granular and tempered with large quantities of river sand. In cross section it had a sugary appearance.

Clements Cord-Marked (fig. 98):

Method of manufacture: Annular segments built upon a starting coil. In some cases a disc 4 to 6 cm. in diameter was used to start the coil. These coils or

Fig. 98. The pottery type Clements Cord-Marked from the Gaston Site. *A, B,* and *C.* Sq. 35R115, Fea. 20. *D.* Sq. 35R175, Fea. 48. *E.* Surface after grader.

FIG. 99. The pottery type Clements Fabric-Marked from the Gaston Site (height 50.5 cm.) Sq. 50R5, Fea. 199.

for a sufficiently long period to thoroughly oxidize the core. Firing clouds were rare and the darkening of the exterior surfaces appeared to have occurred after its manufacture.

Surface treatment:

(1) Exterior: The whole exterior surface was malleated with a cord-wrapped paddle. The cord impressions usually ran perpendicular to the rim with no attempt at crisscrossing. The cords used were relatively fine and made with a tight S-twist. They averaged about 1 mm. in diameter.

(2) Interior: Usually scraped or tooled with a smooth object. The rough particles of temper were pressed into the clay to give a smooth, even surface. In some cases the interior was also hand smoothed after scraping.

Decoration: Occasionally the lip was flattened or slightly notched by the paddle edge.

Form: (1) Lip: Usually rounded and finger smoothed. Occasionally flattened by the paddle. The line of the lip is straight and not irregular like those of the Vincent Cord-Marked type.

(2) Rim: Straight to slightly flaring.

(3) Body: Bowl forms were rounded and hemispherical. Jars were globular with the largest diameter at approximately two-thirds of its heights. The necks were slightly restricted and the rims projected vertically or flared slightly outward.

(4): Base: Bowls were rounded and jars were usually conical although some were semi-rounded.

Vessel size: The vessels ranged between 15 and 30 cm. in diameter and between 20 and 50 cm. in height. Bowl forms tended to be smaller than the jars. The wall thickness was very uniform and ranged between 0.4 and 0.8 cm. The average wall thickness was 0.6 cm.

Clements Fabric-Marked (fig. 99):

Method of manufacture: Same as Clements Cord-Marked.

Paste: Same as Clements Cord-Marked.

Firing: Same as Clements Cord-Marked.

Surface treatment:

(1) Exterior: The whole exterior surface was malleated with a wicker-type fabric. This fabric was similar to that used on the Vincent pottery, but it had a much finer weave. The warp elements averaged about 4 mm. in diameter and the weft was woven tighter than in the Vincent fabric. In general, the paddling was done so that the warp impressions lay parallel to the rim, but there was

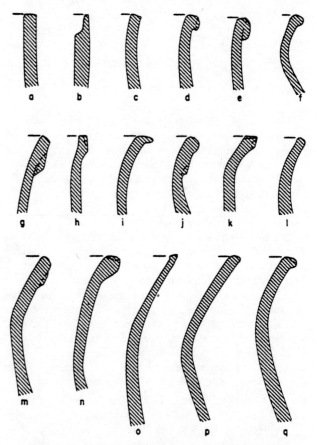

Rim Profiles of Gaston Pottery

FIG. 100

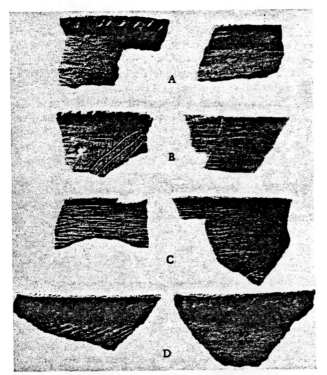

FIG. 101. The pottery type Gaston Simple Stamped from the Gaston Site. *A, B,* and *C.* Sq. 35R235, Fea. 148. *D.* Sq. -10L10, Fea. 195; Sq. 40L15, Fea. 184.

also considerable over-paddling which occasionally crisscrossed or lay at an angle to the rim. The excessive paddling resulted in the better bond between the coil segments and accounted for the fewer fractures along the coil lines.

(2) Interior: Same as Clements Cord-Marked.

Decoration: Lip notching occurred on a small per cent of the jar forms. This notching was usually done with the folded edge of the fabric struck across the lip.

Form: Same as Clements Cord-Marked.

Vessel Size: Same as Clements Cord-Marked.

3. *Gaston Series*

This pottery appeared to be something more than a mere continuation of the Vincent-Clements tradition. It is quite different in most respects and could very well represent a population change in the area at the historic period. In any event, the change from Clements to Gaston occurred abruptly at this site and an intermediate stage was not apparent in the data collected. The Gaston style had its closest relationship to the Clarksville and Hillsboro series to the west.[16]

This series was composed primarily of one type, Gaston Simple Stamped (figs. 100, 101, 102). A small amount of cord-marked, cob-marked, and check stamped pottery also belonged to this group, but they were not

[16] Coe, 1952: 311; Evans, 1955: 49–54.

found in sufficient quantity to warrant separate descriptions at this time. The Gaston pottery was distinguished primarily on the basis of its crushed quartz temper and its folded and decorated rims. It was the only pottery in the basin to be consistently decorated.

Gaston Simple Stamped (figs. 101, 102):

Method of manufacture: Coiling or annular segments. Bonding was good and fractures were usually across coil lines.

Paste: (1) Temper: Crushed quartz that ranged from 0.5 to 5.0 mm. in diameter. Only this prepared material was used for temper, rounded river sand was not used. The clay source also contained a high per cent of fine golden mica.

(2) Hardness: 2.5 to 3.5.

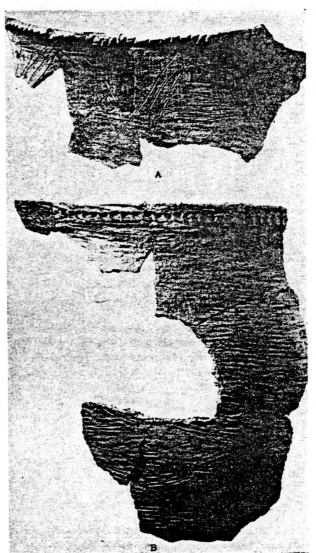

FIG. 102. The pottery type Gaston Simple Stamped from the Gaston Site. *A* and *B.* Sq. 35R235, Fea. 148.

(3) Texture: Porous, granular, and rough. It had a conglomerate appearance and temper particles frequently showed on the surface of the vessel.

(4) Color: The exterior color varied from dark brown to dark gray or black. The interior surfaces had the same range of color, but they were usually darker. The core was quite dark and varied from dark gray to black with the darkest portion toward the inside of the vessel.

Firing: The majority of the vessels were fired in a reducing atmosphere. The dark interior surface together with the lighter color of the exterior surface toward the base indicated that the pots were fired in an inverted position. Variation in color and in hardness on the same vessel suggested a poorly controlled method of firing.

Surface treatment:

(1) Exterior: The whole exterior surface was malleated with a grooved paddle. In most cases, a wooden paddle carved with parallel grooves of about 2 to 3 mm. in width was used for beating the surface. In other cases, the impressions are more rounded and may have been made with a paddle wrapped with some form of non-twisted thong.

(2) Interior: Usually scraped with a serrated tool or smoothed with a stone or bone tool. The large particles of temper were tooled into the clay to make an even surface. Hand smoothing frequently finished the surface after it had been scraped.

Decoration:

(1) Lip: Usually flattened with the same paddle used for malleating the surface. The parallel groove impression of the paddle usually ran across the lip. In most cases, the exterior edge of the lip was notched. Frequently, this was done with the finger, but in other cases the edge of the paddle was used.

(2) Rim: Pots without folded or thickened rims were decorated primarily by notching the lip. In some cases a decoration was placed on the outside of the rim just below the lip. This was made by incising, by circular punctation, or by pinching with the fingers. The most characteristic decoration, however, was the folded or thickened rim which averaged between 1.5 and 2 cm. in width. The lower edge of the fold was usually punched or incised. When it was incised, the impression continued a short distance below the fold on to the surface of the body of the pot.

(3) Neck: The neck area was frequently scraped, apparently with the same tool that had been used to scrape the interior surface. This scraping always followed the paddling of the surface, and it, in turn, was usually followed by an incised design. The most common design was a series of alternating oblique lines 4 to 8 cm. long. Another design consisted of triangles filled with horizontal lines. A few vessels had crude zoomorphic forms incised around the neck.

Form: (1) Lip: Usually flattened with a paddle. Some were rounded and finger smoothed.

(2) Rim: Moderate to pronounced flared rims on jar forms and straight to slightly incurved rims on bowl forms.

(3) Body: Round to globular, short-necked jars with side walls incurved to a constricted neck then flared to form a recurved rim.

(4) Base: Round to flat. A few were conical.

Vessel size: Mouth diameters ranged from 28 to 40 cm. Body diameter ranged from 30 to 52 cm., but averaged about 35 cm. The body wall thickness ranged from 4 to 7 mm.

B. DISTRIBUTION OF POTTERY TYPES

1. Control Squares

At the beginning of the work at the Gaston Site twenty-two units were excavated into the upper occupation zone for the purpose of determining the natural soil conditions and the superposition of artifacts, if any existed. It was unfortunate, for this purpose, that the occupation of the site resulted in the digging of many intrusive pits through these levels. The presence of most of these pits could not be detected until the midden deposit had been removed and their contents could not be kept separate from the normal deposits in the midden itself. Because of this situation fourteen of the twenty-two units were found to be useless for stratigraphic purposes. The remaining eight units were relatively free of discernible intrusive pits and they have been used to illustrate the percentage distribution of the pottery series by levels (table 10). As should be expected in such a shallow and partially disturbed deposit all levels contained all pottery types. On the other hand, the sample of 1,862 sherds from these eight units was sufficiently large to suggest the sequence of ceramic development that was later clarified by the seriation of the contents of the individual pits (fig. 94).

The priority of the Vincent Series was clearly illustrated by the presence of 47.1 per cent of this pottery in the bottom level. The Gaston Series, on the other hand, had 67.6 per cent of its pottery in the top level. The intermediate position of the Clements Series was less well illustrated. The largest number of sherds (36.7 per cent) to appear at any level, however, did occur in Level II.

2. Features

After the midden had been removed from the control squares, the bottoms of pits that extended on into the sand subsoil were excavated. Many more of these pits

were found and excavated in other areas where the
midden had been removed by grading. All together
two hundred of these pits were excavated. Nearly all
of these features contained pottery, but for the purpose
of the present analysis only those pits which contained
fifty or more sherds were used. This seriation, therefore, is based on thirty-seven refuse pits that contained
a total of 5,663 sherds.

During the process of typing the sherds, it was found
that each feature contained most of the types known
for the site. At the same time, the percentage of these
types differed. These differences were plotted and arranged to form the graph shown in figure 94. The
stratigraphic evidence obtained from the levels of the
control squares served as the basis for orienting the direction of change and the two C-14 dates (table 15)
confirmed it. The Vincent style began first and lasted
throughout most of the occupation of the site with a
gradual loss of popularity. The Clements Series, on
the other hand, began later and reached its greatest
popularity at the beginning of the historic period. Gaston pottery appeared after A.D. 1700 and replaced all
other types at this site. The fourth column in figure 94
labeled "Other Types" is composed of unidentified plain
sherds, net-impressed sherds, and a few shell-tempered
sherds described by Evans as Chickahominy Fabric
Impressed.[17] This last type was found only in Features
38 and 158.

Seriation, as a technique for ordering archaeological data, is theoretically simple and fundamentally
sound. Its application, however, is another matter.
Since Ford popularized this technique,[18] it has been
applied indiscriminately to many situations. In some
publications, a tabulation of percentages automatically
becomes a seriation graph. If such a graph is to have
meaning, it must be assumed that each bar represents
the relative degree of popularity, or use, of two or
more distinguishable types in free variation at one
point in time. The degree of validity of such an interpretation is directly proportional to the degree that
the collections reflect the above situation. A selected
or unrepresentative collection will give a distorted picture. A collection that contains specimens from two or
more cultural groups or a collection that represents a
long period of time is of little value for seriation purposes. While the trend of ceramic change at the Gaston Site is clearly shown by the seriation graph in figure
94, it also shows that many of the pits were contami-
nated by intrusive material. The presence of Gaston
type sherds in "early pits" and the presence of Vincent
and Clements sherds in the "late pits" are clear indi-
cations of the disturbance of early material by the activities of later people. This is what should be expected
and it would have been most unusual if this had not
been the case.

17 Evans, 1955: 44–46.
18 Ford, 1949: 31–57; 1952.

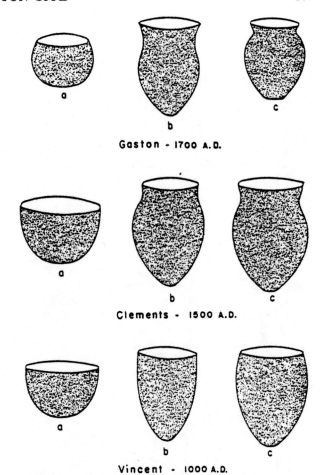

EVOLUTION OF VESSEL FORM

Fig. 103

C. PROJECTILE POINTS

All symetrically chipped stone artifacts that were
pointed at one end have been classified as projectile
points. While it is always possible that these objects
may have been used for purposes other than that for
which we think they were primarily intended, the size
and shape of most of these projectile points make them
ill suited for any other obvious function. The few
specimens that had been altered for use as a drill, as a
scraper, or as a knife were easily recognized as such
and those that had not been so altered remained, typologically, a projectile point regardless of its particular
life history.

There was a total of 1,512 projectile points collected
from the basin area. Of this total, 967 were from the
Gaston Site. One hundred and seventy-six of these
were found in the control levels (table 12, fig. 104) and
155 were found in pits that were used in the preparation of the pottery seriation graph (table 13). The
remaining 636 from the Gaston Site were found on the

TABLE 12

PERCENTAGE DISTRIBUTION OF PROJECTILE POINTS FROM
CONTROLLED LEVELS AT THE GASTON SITE

Level	Count*	Clarks-ville	Roanoke	Savannah River	Halifax	Guilford
I 0–11"	63	54.0	46.0	0.0	0.0	0.0
II 11–16"	45	21.3	78.7	0.0	0.0	0.0
III 16–20"	21	0.0	100.0	0.0	0.0	0.0
IV 20–24"	8	0.0	100.0	0.0	0.0	0.0
V 24–37"	0	----	----	Sterile	----	----
VI 37–47"	12	0.0	0.0	100.0	0.0	0.0
VII 47–52"	0	----	----	Sterile	----	----
VIII 52–58"	17	0.0	0.0	0.0	76.5	23.5
IX 58–68"	10	0.0	0.0	0.0	10.0	90.0

* Total points: 176.

surface, in disturbed soil, or in pits that could not be properly classified as to period of occupation. While these totals are not large, they are representative. Since these sites were all situated in the alluvial river bottoms, the earlier cultural occupations were buried and, therefore, the greater number of specimens collected belonged to the later occupations. The earlier specimens were either recovered from places where they had been disturbed by chance or from our excavations at the various sites.

The earliest type of projectile point found in the basin was a small contracting stem variety previously designated as Morrow Mountain II in Part One. This type has an estimated antiquity of over 6,000 years. Unfortunately, only a few specimens of this type were found on the surface and their significance in the Roanoke River Basin can only be guessed. The Guilford type points described in Part One, however, were found *in situ* in the lowest occupation level at the Gaston Site and they were followed, in turn, by Hali-

fax, Savannah River, Roanoke, and Clarksville types. The Guilford points were found in association with hearths, but not enough charcoal was recovered for dating. The hearths with which the Halifax points were associated were more plentiful and a charcoal sample from them gave a date of 3484 B.C. Charcoal from the hearths associated with Savannah River type points gave a date of 1944 B.C. The Roanoke points were associated with material which dated A.D. 916 and the Clarksville points have the final dates of A.D. 1586 and A.D. 1741 (table 15). These radiocarbon dates confirmed the stratigraphy shown in figures 84 and 104 and places the occurrence of these types in a framework of absolute dates.

1. *Guilford Lanceolate* (fig. 105)

For description of this type see page 43.

2. *Halifax Side-Notched* (fig. 105)

Summary description: Slender blade with slightly restricted base. Shallow side-notches. Base and side-notches were usually ground. The material most frequently used was vein quartz.

Form. (1) Blade: Usually long and narrow. The few short specimens appeared to be the result of resharpening since the width of all of the points of this type was fairly uniform. Most specimens had their maximum width at two-thirds of their length from the point. The sides of the blades were slightly convex except for the short resharpened points, where they were either straight or concave. All specimens were oval in cross section.

(2) Base: Usually straight and ground. All bases were broad, but slightly narrower than the maximum width of the blade.

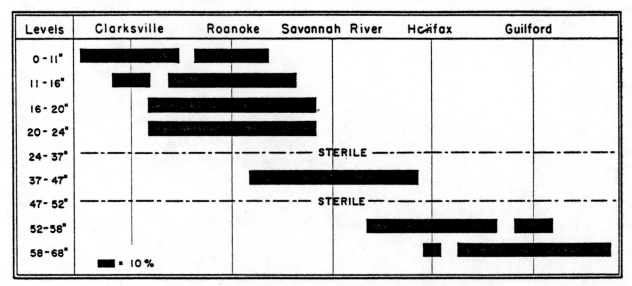

FIG. 104. Percentage distribution of projectile point types at the Gaston Site by levels.

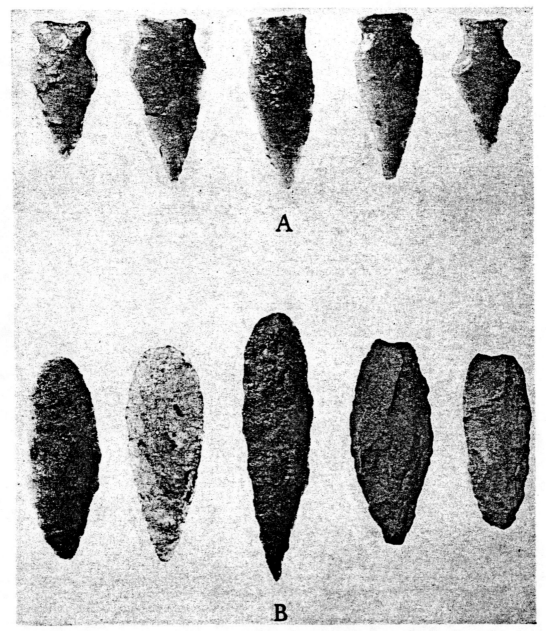

Fig. 105. Halifax and Guilford projectile point types from the Gaston Site. *A.* Halifax Side-Notched projectile point type. Sq. –70L60 (62″), Sq. –70L60 (54″), Sq. –70L60 (63″) Sq. –70L60 (54″), Sq. –70L60 (63″). *B.* Guilford Lanceolate projectile point type. Sq. –60L60 (63″), Sq. –28L76 (58″), Sq. –60L60 (63″), Sq. –70L60 (63″), Sq. –60L60 (63″). (Natural size.)

(3) Side-notch: Broad, shallow and frequently ground. The length of the notch was about one-third of the length of the blade. It began at the point of maximum width and continued to the base. In a few cases, the notch continued past the base giving the impression of a stem rather than a side-notch.

Size: (1) Length: Range, 29–56 mm.; average, 44 mm.

(2) Width: Range, 17–25 mm.; average, 20 mm.

Material: Usually vein quartz, occasionally argillite (Carolina Slate) or quartzite.

Technique of manufacture: Pressure flaked. The typical specimen was relatively thick and worked from a "core" rather than a thin flake. These cores, however, frequently originated as thick spalls struck from quartz or quartzite boulders common to this area of the Roanoke River.

Comments: In so far as it is known, this type has a greater distribution north and east of the Roanoke

River Basin than it does to the south or west. Points of this type are relatively common in eastern North Carolina and Virginia. The specimens that Holland illustrates as types I and M are apparently the same as this type.[19]

3. *Savannah River Stemmed* (fig. 106)

For description of this type see page 44.

4. *Roanoke Large Triangular* (fig. 108)

Summary description: Large, well-made, triangular point with slightly concave base and sides. Usually made from argillite, but also from vein quartz and quartzite.

Form: (1) Blade: Triangular in shape. Sides and base were usually concave, but may be straight. The base tended to have more concavity than the sides. In a few cases, there was a slight serration of the edges.

(2) Base: Usually concave but occasionally straight. In some cases, the bases were rather deeply concave.

---
[19] Holland, 1955: 169–171, pls. 28, 30.

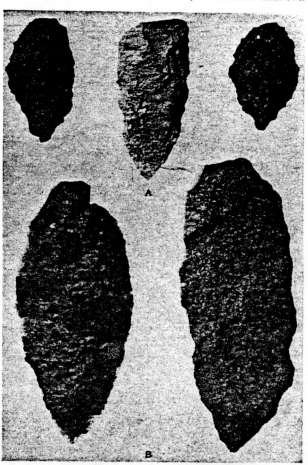

Fig. 107. Oval blade types from the Gaston Site. *A.* Small oval blades associated with Halifax projectile points. Sq. –70L60 (53″), Sq. –60L60 (63″), Sq. –70L60 (46–49″). *B.* Large oval blades associated with Savannah River projectile points. Sq. 60L10 (37″), after scraper. (½ natural size.)

Fig. 106. Savannah River projectile point type from the Gaston Site. *A.* Small variant of the Savannah River Stemmed type. Sq. –60L60 (42″); Sq. 35R235, Fea. 148; Sq. –30L70, side of Fea. 107; Sq. –70L60 (56″). *B.* Large variant of the Savannah River Stemmed type. Sq. –105R50 (47″); Sq. –70L60 (41″); Sq. 35R85, Fea. 2; Sq. –60L215, Fea. 74. (½ natural size.)

Size: (1) Length: Range, 20–60 mm.; average, 43 mm.
(2) Width: Range, 18–34 mm.; average, 29 mm.

Material: The majority of the specimens of this type were made from argillite (Carolina Slate). The remaining specimens were made from vein quartz or quartzite.

Technique of manufacture: Pressure flaked. The smaller points were made from broad thick flakes struck from a core with a hammerstone. The larger points were frequently roughed out by percussion, then finished with carefully controlled pressure flakes. The crude triangular points illustrated in figure 108 *D* are examples of these triangular blanks before they have been finished by pressure flaking.

Comments: This type was first recognized in association with the Roanoke component in the Clarksville area.[20] The Roanoke cord- and fabric-marked pot-

---
[20] Coe, 1939.

tery of the Clarksville area has been equated with the Clements period in the present report, and there is good evidence to show that the Roanoke point type is also associated with the Clements period (table 13). It should be noted, however, that the larger variety of this type is associated with the earlier Vincent period. The large forms (fig. 108 C), though repre-

senting less than 20 per cent of this type, occurred most frequently in association with the Vincent period material. There was a definite progression from the larger to the smaller forms. This type is similar to Holland's type C.[21]

[21] Holland, 1955: 167, pl. 25.

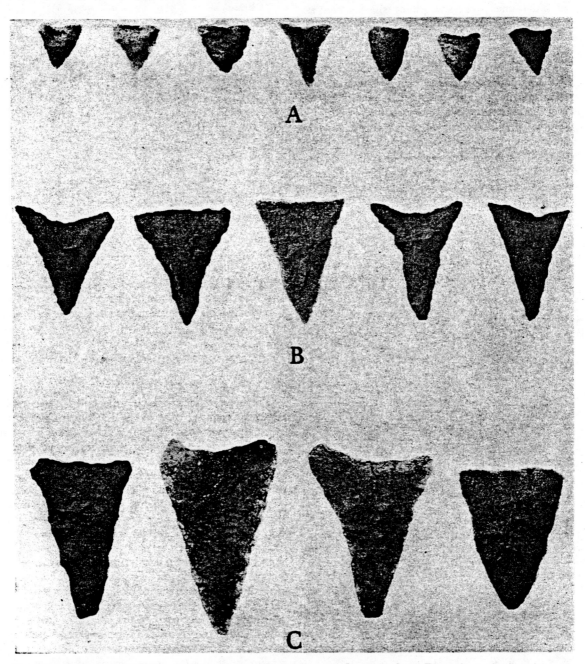

FIG. 108. Triangular projectile point types from the Gaston Site. *A*. Clarksville Small Triangular projectile point type. Sq. 50R5 (0–12″), Sq. 45R5 (12–15″), Sq. 45R5 (12–15″), surface, surface, surface, surface. *B*. Roanoke Large Triangular projectile point type. Sq. –70L140, Fea. 102; Sq. 0L150, Fea. 105; Sq. 45R5 (5–12″); Sq. 35R95, Fea. 7. *C*. Roanoke Large Triangular projectile point type. Sq. 35R85 (9–19″); surface; Sq. 40L15, Fea. 184, Sq. –25R230, Fea. 126. (Natural size.)

5. *Clarksville Small Triangular* (fig. 108)

Summary description: Very small triangular point, equilateral in shape and almost always made from vein quartz.

Form: (1) Blade: Small equilateral triangle. A few of the longer specimens were in the shape of isosceles triangles. On all of the equilateral triangular forms the sides were straight or slightly convex. On the few isosceles forms the sides varied from straight to concave.

Size: (1) Length: Range, 10–18 mm.; average, 14 mm.
(2) Width: Range, 10–16 mm.; average, 12 mm.

Material: Approximately 95 per cent of the specimens were made from white vein quartz. Quartz crystal and argillite (Carolina Slate) were rarely used.

Technique of manufacture: Fine pressure flakes on both surfaces. Well made and symmetrical.

Comments: This type was described in 1938 as being associated with the historic period in the Clarksville area and later it was shown to continue into the

FIG. 109. Steatite bowl fragments from the Gaston Site. *A.* Interior of steatite rim sherd showing cross-hatched design. Sq. —40L60, yellow sand. *B.* Exterior of steatite rim sherd showing rodent gnawed area. Surface.

TABLE 13

ANALYSIS OF ARTIFACTS FROM FEATURES AT THE GASTON SITE

Associated Artifacts	Vincent Period	Clements Period	Gaston Period
Objects of Stone			
Projectile Points			
Clarksville	0	0	22
Roanoke	42	68	15
Thelma	3	0	0
Celts	0	0	5
Atlatl Weights	6	1	0
Stone Drills	4	2	1
Drilled Pebbles	0	1	1
Grooved Stones	1	0	2
Hammerstones	36	14	21
Pitted Stones	8	1	1
Objects of Clay			
Pipes	0	4	11
Objects of Bone			
Awls	3	6	15
Needles	0	0	2
Beamers	0	2	2
Fish Hooks	0	0	1
Deer Toe Projectile Points	0	2	1
Worked Antler	2	1	4

eighteenth century.[22] In the Roanoke Rapids Basin it was also found associated with the historic Gaston period. This is apparently the same type as Holland's type A and B.[23]

D. OTHER MISCELLANEOUS ARTIFACTS

Steatite Vessels

There were sixty-two fragments of stone pots recovered from the Gaston Site. Thirty-five of these specimens were found during the excavation of pits. It is not believed, however, that this stone ware was associated with the ceramic period, but rather that these fragments were brought up from the lower levels by the digging of deep pits. Actually, several specimens were found in the undisturbed yellow sand subsoil as the sides of the pits were being cleaned. The distribution of these steatite vessel fragments in the pits also indicated that their inclusion was fortuitous. Of the thirteen pot fragments that were found in the pits used for the pottery seriation, five were found in three Vincent period pits and eight were found in four Gaston period pits. Of the twenty-seven remaining fragments, twenty-three were found in the excavated levels. Thirteen of these twenty-three specimens were found in the yellow sand underlying the midden deposit and the remaining ten were found scattered throughout the midden. The majority of the evidence, therefore, indi-

22 Coe, 1952: 311.
23 Holland, 1955: 166–167, pl. 24.

cated that the point of origin of these steatite pot fragments was the Savannah River level.

The specimens of steatite vessels recovered were relatively small fragments. The larger pieces, however, suggested an oval bowl with a rounded base, and occasionally lug handles. The diameters of the bowls appeared to have been between 20 and 30 cm. and the maximum depth was estimated to be 20 cm. The rim fragments were smooth and rounded with no decoration on the exterior surfaces or the lip. One specimen, however, had a series of cross-hatched lines engraved along the inside of the rim (fig. 109 *A*).

Chipped stone axes

Six axes of the Guilford type were recovered from the excavated levels. Two of these were found below the sixty-inch level and were in definite association with the Guilford hearths. The other four were found slightly higher in the deposit and at the level where Halifax material was usually found. They were not, however, associated with the Halifax hearths and, since four Guilford points were also found at this level, the association of the axes was undoubtedly still Guilford. Both the Guilford and the Halifax occupations were on loose sand and minor differences in ele-

FIG. 111. Savannah River grooved axes from the Gaston Site. *A*. Roughly chipped axe type with slight grooving. Surface. *B*. First stage of pecking and grinding of a full-grooved axe. Sq. 35R115 (40"). (½ natural size.)

vation from the present surface were not necessarily significant. The important consideration, however, is that in every specific situation the Halifax material was separate from, and stratigraphically higher than, the Guilford material.

The Guilford axes from the Gaston Site are identical to those previously described for the Piedmont area.[24] The length of these specimens varied from 8 to 12 cm. and their width varied from 5.5 to 7 cm. The width between notches ranged from 4 to 5.5 cm. Two of the six axes had their notches smoothed and one (fig. 110 *C*) had this smoothing continued around both faces. This suggests an early stage for the ground and grooved axes of later periods.

Polished Stone Axes

Only two specimens of this type were found during the excavation of the Gaston Site. Both of these were unfinished. One specimen (fig. 111 *B*) was a full-grooved axe in the first stage of manufacture. It was found in the sand subsoil after the excavation of Feature 19 and, without doubt, came from what was later dis-

FIG. 110. Guilford chipped axes from the Gaston Site. *A*. Sq. –28L76 (41"). *B*. Sq. –60L60 (61"). *C*. Sq. 55L25 (66"). (½ natural size.)

[24] Coe, 1952: 304.

covered to be the level of the Savannah River occupation. The other specimen was found in Level III of
Square 60R5, but, unfortunately, since it was not complete, it cannot be determined whether it was a three-
quarter or a full-grooved axe.

Polished Stone Celts

Two complete celts and fourteen fragments of celts
were found at the Gaston Site (fig. 112). Five of
these specimens were found in pits, nine were found on
the surface, and one each was found in Levels I and II.
The five specimens found in pits were all associated
with Gaston period pottery (table 13). These celts
ranged in size from 3 to 5 cm. in width and 8 to 13 cm.
in length. They were all carefully made and polished.
In form, however, there appears to be two types. The
larger specimens (fig. 112 C and D) are thick and
oval in cross section. The small specimens (fig. 112 B)
are relatively thin and rectangular in cross section.
Those specimens that were associated with the Gaston
period were of the latter type, therefore, the larger type

Fig. 113. Stone atlatl weights from the Gaston Site. A.
Grooved and pitted atlatl weights. Bottom view (left).
Top view (center and right). After scraper, Sq. 35R145,
Fea. 36, Sq. 35R85, Fea. 4. B. Grooved and pitted atlatl
weights split across the middle. Side view (left and center).
Top view (right). Sq. 0L150, Fea. 105, Sq. 35R85 (9–19″),
Sq. 35R95, Fea. 8. C. Unfinished, winged type atlatl weight.
After scraper. D. Steatite bolas weight. Sq. –75R100 (12–
16″). (½ natural size.)

must have been more common during the earlier
Clements period.

Atlatl Weights

One of the more unusual finds at the Gaston Site was
a series of small stone objects that resembled the half of
a large hickory nut. These objects were usually oval
in plan and hemispherical in section. Their length
varied from 2 to 5 cm., and their width varied from 1.5
to 4 cm. Their height was more uniform, varying only
from 1 to 2 cm. These objects were all hollowed
out on the flat or underneath side and a groove was
cut length way along the convex or top side (fig. 113
A and B). It has been assumed that these objects
represent a unique form of atlatl weight. They are
somewhat similar to the more conventional form of
boatstones, but they were not perforated for attachment.

There were seventeen of these weights found during
the excavation. Seven of these specimens were found in
pits, three were found in disturbed soil, and seven were
found in the excavated levels. Six of the seven found
in the fill of pits were associated with the Vincent

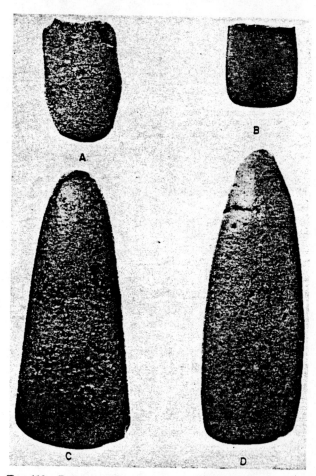

Fig. 112. Polished stone celts from the Gaston Site. A. Surface. B. Sq. –100R100 (9–20″). C. After grader. D.
After grader. (⅜ natural size.)

period pottery, and the seventh one was found in a Clements period pit. Of the seven found in the excavated levels, one was recovered from Level I, one from Level II, and the remaining five came from the bottom of the midden deposit. The distribution of these weights shows quite clearly that they were used primarily during the Vincent period.

Polished Stone Gorgets

There were five fragments of the two hole type of stone gorget found at the Gaston Site. All specimens appeared to be of the elliptical bar type with the holes drilled halfway from both faces. Only one of the five specimens was complete enough to be measured accurately, and it was 9 cm. long, 3 cm. wide, and 1 cm. thick. In every case, these fragments appeared to have been associated with the Gaston period; however, this evidence is not conclusive. This form of gorget has a wide distribution both in time and space.

Hammerstones

These specimens were numerous and occurred at all levels. During the excavation of pits, 148 hammerstones were found, 82 more were recovered from the excavated levels, and 108 additional specimens came from disturbed areas. All of these 388 specimens were originally small water-rounded boulders. A few of the larger weighed as much as three pounds. A few of the smaller weighed as little as three ounces. The great majority, however, were about 10 cm. across at their greatest diameter and weighed about one pound. Most of these specimens were hammered at the ends. Those that were used more extensively were hammered along the sides as well as the ends, and a few were also hammered on one or both faces. In the original analysis, an attempt was made to type these hammerstones and to look for some significant distribution. It was found later that both the typing and distribution showed only that all occupants of the site used hammerstones and picked them from the river as they were needed.

Pitted Stones

There were twenty-four other stones found that apparently were not used for hammering yet had one or more pits on their surface. Ten of these were found in pits (table 13), four came from the bottom of the midden deposit, four others were recovered from the preceramic levels, and the last six were found in the disturbed soil. These specimens were small water-rounded boulders that had a small depression usually pecked on two opposite sides. These depressions were fairly small in diameter but deep and did not appear to be the result of their use as hammerstones. There is a suggestion that these may have been used for stone boiling, and that the two holes made it easier to pick the stone from the fire. There were, however,

no obvious signs of burning on the specimens of this type that were recovered. In any event, this particular type of artifact saw little use after the Vincent period.

Stone Mortars

The only two specimens of this type found were associated with a hearth at the Halifax level in Square 10L20 (fig. 106 A). These were large flat slabs of stone that had a shallow depression ground on one side. It would appear that they had been used for grinding and that the grinding stone or mano was used with a circular motion.

Smoking Pipes

There were forty-one specimens of smoking pipes found at the Gaston Site. One specimen found in the slump of the river bank was the stem of a European trade pipe. Four other pipe specimens were made from stone and the remaining thirty-six pipe specimens were made from clay.

Two of the stone pipes were complete. One was found after the grading (fig. 114 C) and the other was found with Burial 7 (fig. 114 D). This first specimen is a local example of the Hopewell type platform pipe, but, unfortunately, it was disturbed by the motor grader and its actual association is unknown. It is believed, however, that it was associated with the Vincent period. The second pipe was recovered from a Gaston period burial and was of a type known to have been used during the historic period. This alate-stemmed type with engraved triangles and squares has been found in a number of other historic Piedmont sites.[25] The other two stone pipe specimens were fragments. One was too small to even suggest its original shape, but the other was part of the bowl of a large, short-stemmed pipe. This type has sometimes been called biconical because the stem and bowl were formed by large conical holes that met at right angles. This specimen was found near the bottom of the midden level and appears to have been used during the Vincent period.

The thirty-six clay pipe fragments had a wider distribution and represented at least three types. The earliest form was a large trumpet-shaped tube and it is illustrated by specimen B in figure 114. This particular pipe had two sets of seventeen lines incised crisscross fashion along the bowl, but the other pipes of this type had plain smoothed surfaces. There is little question but that this type was associated with the Clements period. The composition of the paste of these pipes was similar to that used in the manufacture of the Clements pottery and all five of these specimens were found associated with material of the Clements period.

The second type of clay pipe was smaller with long, round stems and a conical bowl set at a slight angle to the stem. The bowls were decorated with fine inter-

25 Coe, 1952: 311.

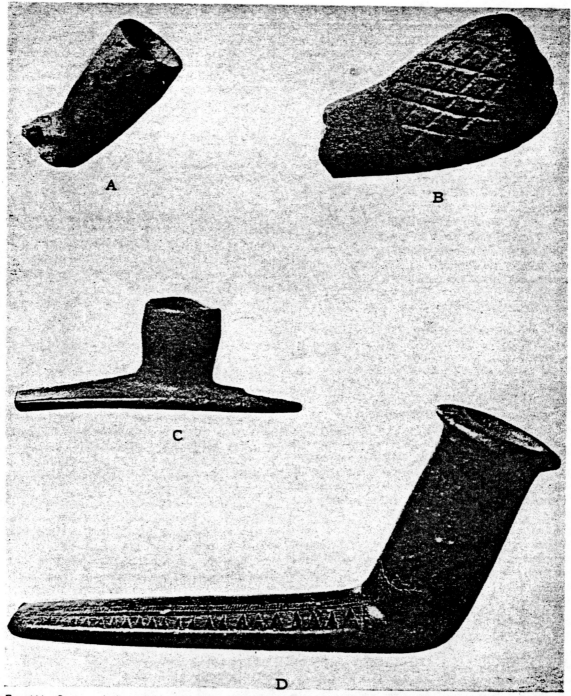

FIG. 114. Stone and clay smoking pipes from the Gaston Site. *A*. Clay pipe bowl. Sq. 25R440, Fea. 138. *B*. Incised clay pipe bowl. Sq. 53R10 (12–16″). *C*. Stone platform pipe. After scraper. *D*. Stone alate stemmed pipe. Burial 7. (Natural size.)

rupted lines (cord impressions?) in bands around the bowl. These pipes were made from a fine textured, compact clay, and they appear to be identical to the Potomac Cord Impressed pipe type described by Stephenson [26]

[26] Stephenson, 1959.

for the Potomac area. Four specimens of this type were found in the excavated levels: one in Level I, two in Level II, and one in Level III. In spite of this small sample, it is suggested that they were in use toward the end of the Clements period.

The third type of clay pipe was represented by twenty-seven specimens. Eleven of these were found in Gaston period pits and the remaining sixteen specimens were recovered from Levels I and II. This type had the form of a tube which expanded at one end to form the bowl. Some specimens had the bowl continuing in a direct line with the stem and others had it set at a slight angle (fig. 114 A). The stems were usually round, but in three cases it had been squared toward the bit end. There were also two cases where the bit was swollen or bulblike and one specimen had the bit formed by a narrow collar. This type is similar to those described for the A.D. 1700 Hillsboro Focus,[27] and seven of the eleven specimens found in pits of the Gaston period came from Feature 148 which had a C-14 date of A.D. 1741 (table 15).

Bone and Antler Artifacts

Bone and antler artifacts were also relatively scarce. Forty-two specimens, however, were recovered from the excavations at the Gaston Site. All of these specimens were found in pits with the exception of one specimen, and their distribution is shown in table 13. Twenty-five specimens came out of Gaston period pits, eleven specimens were found in Clements period pits, and five specimens were in pits of the Vincent period. This seems to indicate that bone was used more extensively for tools during the historic period, but it may also indicate that the older bone specimens have not been as well preserved. The largest number of bone specimens were split bone awls. Twenty-four of these were found and are illustrated in figure 115 B and C. There were also two needles (fig. 115 A), five beamers or hide scrapers, one unfinished fishhook (fig. 115 D), three projectile points made from deer toes (fig. 115 E), and seven antler flakers (fig. 115 B).

IV. SUBSISTENCE

The main source of food for all periods was the natural resources of the forests and streams. Large quantities of mammal, bird, and fish bones were recovered from the pits of all of the three last occupation periods, but not a single specimen was found in the preceramic levels. The greater age and soil conditions apparently resulted in their decay and loss. Dr. Fred S. Barkalow, Jr., of North Carolina State College of Agriculture and Engineering of the University of North Carolina, examined the bone collection and identified the specimens listed in table 14 . He did not, however, make a quantitative analysis, and this table simply indicates the presence or absence of bones in the three periods. Most of the animals were used as food through all three periods, but it is interesting to note that the elk, the fox squirrel, and the spotted skunk

[27] Coe, 1952: 311.

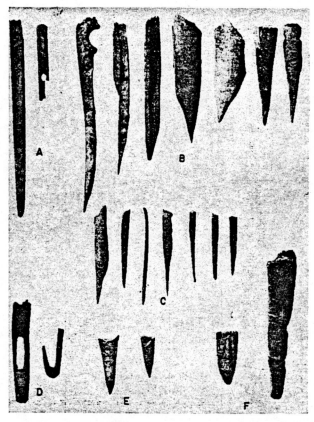

Fig. 115. Artifacts of bone and antler from the Gaston Site. A. Bone needles. Sq. 35R175, Fea. 48; Sq. 35R95, Fea. 8. B. Bone awls. Sq. 0L20, Fea. 180; Sq. -10L10, Fea. 195; Sq. 0L20, Fea. 180; Sq. 0L20, Fea. 180; Sq. -60L140, Fea. 95; Sq. -80L50, Fea. 116; Sq. 35R185, Fea. 53. C. Small bone awls. Sq. 35R135, Fea. 29; Sq. 35R95, Fea. 9; Sq. -10L10, Fea. 195; Sq. -25R230, Fea. 124; Sq. -10L10, Fea. 195; Sq. -25R230, Fea. 124; Sq. -10L10, Fea. 124; Sq. -10L10, Fea. 195; Sq. -25R230, Fea. 124; Npᵛ2, Sq. 1 (0-6"). D. Fishhook blank (left). Completed fishhook (right). Sq. 35R95, Fea. 9; Hxᵛ8, Sq. 0 (12-18"). E. Projectile points. Bone (left). Antler (right). Sq. -10L10, Fea. 195; Npᵛ2, Sq. 1 (0-6"). F. Antler flakers. Hxᵛ8, Sq. 60R30, Fea. 1; Sq. -60L140, Fea. 95. (½ natural size.)

were found only in the oldest period. It is equally interesting to note that the gray squirrel, the gray fox, the rabbit, and the striped skunk were found only in the latest period. This is at best only a suggestion, but it may indicate the direction in which the habitat has changed for some of these animals during the last one thousand years, assuming that the sample is adequate and that this difference is not the result of a change in food preference.

During the Vincent and Clements periods, at least, the dog was a definite part of the diet of these people. Dog-bones were found as food refuse in sixteen separate pits. This seems to be too large a sample to dismiss as accidental and these specimens of food refuse were

TABLE 14

ANALYSIS OF BONE REFUSE FROM FEATURES AT THE GASTON SITE

Type of Bone	Count*	Vincent Period	Clements Period	Gaston Period
Mammals				
Beaver	14	x	x	x
Deer	57	x	x	x
Dog	20	x	x	x
Elk	5	x		
Fox Squirrel	2	x		
Gray Fox	3			x
Gray Squirrel	5			x
Mole	2	x		
Muskrat	25	x	x	x
Opossum	12	x		x
Otter	11	x	x	x
Rabbit	5			x
Raccoon	23	x		
Spotted Skunk	5	x		
Striped Skunk	2			x
Woodchuck	4	x		x
Birds				
Turkey	25	x	x	x
Canada Goose	3		x	
Others	8	x	x	x
Fishes				
Catfish	2	x		
Garfish	1	x		
Others	22	x	x	x
Turtle				
Miscellaneous	38	x	x	x

* The count indicates the number of bones actually identified and not the total collection of bone material.

not confused with the dog burials which were described on page 93.

Seventy-two pits contained fragments of charcoal in considerable quantity. Most of this was identified as wood and probably was the ashes from fires. In six other pits, however, charred hickory nuts were found in quantity. One pit (Fea. 32) contained nearly a gallon of nut fragments. In spite of a careful search of all charcoal fragments, no other food item, domestic or wild, was found. It is well documented that all of the historic tribes in this area had a variety of agricultural products and several sherds of the Gaston type were found that had their surface roughened by corn-cobs. Nevertheless, no specimen of a domesticated plant was found.

V. SUMMARY

Six distinct cultural periods were found to have existed in the Roanoke Rapids Basin. Three of these were preceramic and existed before the Christian Era and three were ceramic and existed after the birth of Christ. All six of these periods were represented at the Gaston Site where their remains were found stratigraphically deposited one above the other.

Guilford Occupation

The Guilford culture had a wide distribution throughout the Piedmont and coastal areas, and its cultural relationship in another area has already been described in Parts One and Two. At the Gaston Site, it was represented by the remains of a few rock-lined hearths scattered along the top of the loose sand deposit on the bank of the river. Associated with these hearths were a few projectile points and chipped axes, together with a quantity of chips and hammerstones. This material was found at an average depth of sixty inches below the present surface. A small amount of charcoal was recovered from one hearth, but it was not sufficient for dating. These fires must have been extinguished, however, at least 6,000 years ago, since a C-14 date of 3484 B.C. was secured for the succeeding Halifax period.

Halifax Occupation

Around 3500 B.C. the Gaston Site was again occupied by small bands of hunters who camped along the river and built fires on the sand. They built them in shallow rock-lined pits which were very similar to those used earlier by the Guilford folk. Scattered around these hearths were also a number of side-notched projectile points, chips, and hammerstones. One major difference in their craft was the selection of quartz and quartzite as a raw material instead of the Carolina Slate

TABLE 15

RADIOCARBON DATES FROM THE GASTON SITE*

University of Michigan Number	University of North Carolina Number	Location		Cultural Association	Date B. P. (1956)
M-527	619eb1280	Sq. 35R235,	Fea. 148	Gaston	215 ± 200
M-525	619eb1176	Sq. −90L50,	Fea. 117	Clements	370 ± 200
	619eb1182	Sq. −80L50,	Fea. 119		
M-526**	619eb927	Sq. 35R185,	Fea. 55	Vincent	1040 ± 200
	619eb1104	Sq. −70L140,	Fea. 102		
	619eb1126	Sq. 0L150,	Fea. 105		
M-524	619eb180	Sq. 60L10,	Fea. 191	Savannah River	3900 ± 250
	619eb181	Sq. 60L10,	Fea. 192A		
	619eb183	Sq. −60L60, Hearth 1			
M-522***	619eb178	Sq. 55L25, Hearth 1		Halifax	4280 ± 350
	619eb179	Sq. 55L25, Hearth 2			
M-523	619eb175	Sq. 10L20, Hearth 1		Halifax	5440 ± 350
	619eb176	Sq. 10L20, Hearth 2			
	619eb177	Sq. 10L20, Hearth 3			
	619eb184	Sq. −70L60, Hearth 1			

* Crane and Griffin, 1958, pp. 1122–3.
** Feature 55 contained a large per cent of Clements type pottery, and since it was combined with the other two features, this date is probably later than it should be for the Vincent Period.
*** Hearth 1 appeared to be below the Savannah River zone, but there is some question as to its association with the Halifax level.

which was used so consistently by the earlier group. On an average the Halifax hearths were found about six inches higher than those of the Guilford period or about fifty-four inches below the present surface.

Savannah River Occupation

The third preceramic level of occupation was found separated from the former two by about six inches of flood sand. This level had remained stable long enough for it to have developed a recognizable humus content. At this level, the stone-lined hearths were again found as they had been before, but charcoal was more plentiful. Every indication suggested a larger group occupying the site over a longer continuous period than had been true of the earlier periods. In addition to the characteristic projectile points, a number of other traits of the late Archaic period were found, including steatite vessels and full-grooved axes. Charcoal combined from three of these hearths gave a date of approximately 2000 B.C.

Vincent Occupation

The last Archaic occupation of the Gaston Site was buried by subsequent flooding to the depth of about twelve inches. Upon this surface a new group of people settled around the year A.D. 500. These people lived in houses arranged in a small, compact village. They cooked in deep rock-lined pits and made extensive use of pottery. While they may have used the bow and arrow at this time, they also used the atlatl with shafts pointed with large triangular points. Polished stone celts were used as axe heads and stone pipes were used for smoking.

Clements Occupation

As the life and times of the people who have been labeled "Vincent" continued in the Roanoke area, they changed and acquired new characteristics. By A.D. 1200 these changes had become sufficiently obvious to be recognized in the archaeological material. The pottery style changed and clay smoking pipes became more numerous. The atlatl was completely abandoned in favor of the bow and arrow. This last change was reflected in the reduced size of the average projectile point which was also made occasionally from antler or the bone of a deer toe. Awls and hide scrapers made from bone were more numerous. The Vincent-Clements tradition must have lasted at least 1,000 years, during which time the midden deposit grew to an average depth of twenty inches. The closing date for the Clements period is approximately A.D. 1600.

Gaston Occupation

There was no great break between the culture complex called Clements and the subsequent one called Gaston. Yet there is no evidence for the transition in the Roanoke Rapids area. The innovating influences seem to have had their source in the Piedmont to the west, and it may be that the Clements Complex was displaced by the Gaston occupation rather than being its sire. The major differences seem to be in the pottery styles, smaller projectile points, celts, and considerably more emphasis on bone tools and smoking pipes. The Gaston village was also fortified by a series of stockades. This occupation was definitely post A.D. 1700 and the C-14 date of A.D. 1741 was close to the terminal date for all aboriginal occupation in that area.

SUMMARY

The primary purpose of this study was to identify and define the progression of cultural entities that developed in the Carolina Piedmont from the earliest beginnings to the historic period. Toward this end, three sites have been examined and reported in detail, and approximately 65,851 specimens were recovered, catalogued, and analyzed. While this study of three sites does not propose to treat this subject exhaustively, it does present an outline of cultural development that has not, heretofore, been known for the area. It also demonstrates that the Archaic, as a period, developed through a series of identifiable cultural units and no longer needs to be thought of as a great heterogeneous morass of traits that spread from the mountains to the sea.

I. PALEO-INDIAN CONSIDERATIONS

If what is meant by Paleo-Indian is an early Pan American horizon characterized by fluted projectile points and an economy oriented toward the hunting of large herding animals, then sites of this type have not been found in an undisturbed context in the Piedmont. Fluted points have been found individually on the surface throughout most of the Atlantic Coastal area and sites like the Williamson Site in Virginia [1] and the Quad Site in Alabama [2] have been reported, but, in every case, they were eroded remnants, and there was no way of distinguishing the Paleo-Indian complex from materials that certainly represented later Archaic occupations. Since the associated faunal remains have been destroyed, the presence of the fluted point appears to be the sole criteria for identifying a Paleo-Indian component in the east. At the Hardaway Site, three reasonably good Clovis-like points have been found on the surface, and this is what led Witthoft to place the Hardaway Component in his Enterline chert industry before the excavated data were available for the site. [3] It is interesting, though, that many of the Hardaway type points were facially fluted, and, in cases where the side-notches or basal portions were missing, they could be mistaken for fluted points of the Paleo-Indian period. Finally, the earliest C-14 date for this general area is 7061 ± 350 B.C. This was based on charcoal found at the twenty-three-foot level in Russell Cave, Alabama, which, according to Miller, was from a hearth associated with "a point with the outline of a Folsom fluted blade, but lacking the fluting. . . ." [4] Recently, however, the National Park Service has completed additional work in Russell Cave, and it is now known that its lowest level of occupation is very similar to the Kirk horizon in the Piedmont. Since both the Hardaway and the Palmer

components are stratigraphically older, we can assume that there must have been major occupations in this area at a time earlier than 7000 B.C.

A. HARDAWAY COMPLEX

The earliest material yet excavated in the Piedmont consists of a series of large, thin projectile points that began with a very simple form and evolved into a very unique side-notched type (fig. 58). Associated with these points was a series of chipped stone scrapers that differed little from those found on most Paleo-Indian sites. There did occur, however, in this period a number of projectile points that were similar in style to what has been called Dalton west of the Mississippi. [5] This is of special interest since it suggests that the Hardaway Complex had its cultural affinities to the west, along the southern end of the Appalachian Mountains, down the Tennessee and Ohio rivers into the Missouri area but not to the north. Points of a generalized Dalton type similar to those found at the Hardaway Site have been found in Missouri, in Illinois, in Tennessee, and in northern Alabama.

At Graham Cave, Missouri, Dalton-like points and blades with flaring bases like the Hardaway Blade were found in the lowest level of the deposit. These were associated with fragments of charcoal and bone that have been dated at 7744 ± 500 B.C. [6] During the excavation of the Modoc Rock Shelter, Illinois, similar points were found, and they have been associated with a radiocarbon date of 7922 ± 392 B.C. [7] The Nuckolls Site is situated along the shore of Kentucky Lake in western Tennessee. The collection of material was mainly from the surface, but it shows the occurrence of a number of Dalton-like specimens together with a local specialization of side-notching that suggests a parallel development to what was found at the Hardaway Site. [8] Finally, in northern Alabama several Dalton-like points were found at the Quad Site along with a number of blades that resembled the Hardaway type; [9] and at Russell Cave, one Dalton type was reported to have been found in the lower level, while a second example was found washed out of the fill at the mouth of the cave. [10]

II. BEGINNING OF THE ARCHAIC

A. PALMER COMPLEX

Following the Hardaway occupation, the dominant style of projectile points was a small corner-notched

[1] McCary, 1951.
[2] Soday, 1954.
[3] Witthoft, 1952.
[4] Crane and Griffin, 1959; 187.

[5] Bell and Hall, 1953: 6–7; Wormington, 1957; 113–114.
[6] Logan, 1952: pl. 4; Crane, 1956: 665.
[7] Fowler, 1959; 259–263.
[8] Lewis and Kneberg, 1958: figs. 12–23.
[9] Soday, 1954: figs. 7–12.
[10] Miller, personal communication.

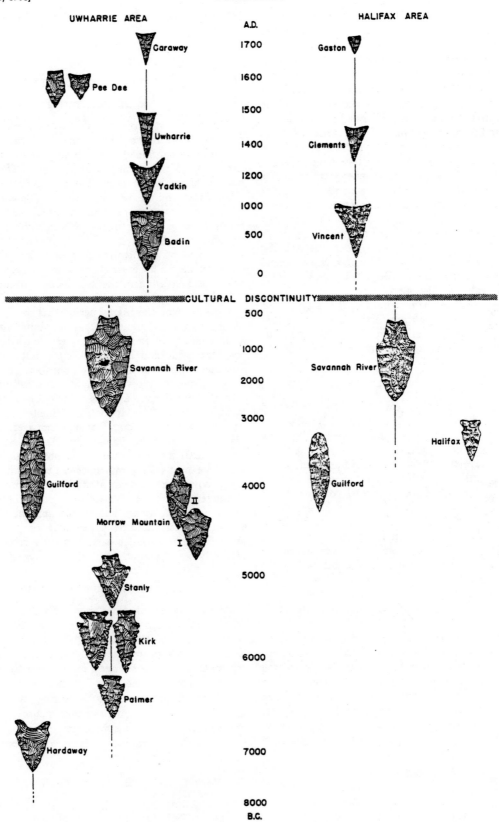

FIG. 116. The projectile point traditions of the Carolina Piedmont.

serrated variety with extensive grinding along the base. Along with this, the use of the small hafted snub-nosed scraper increased considerably, but no other change in the cultural inventory was discernible on the basis of the evidence available.

It is possible that this change in the projectile point form reflects a time break in the occupation of the Hardaway Site rather than the diffusion or migration of the trait from the outside. Some of the Hardaway Side-Notched points are very similar to the Palmer type both as to size and shape. On the other hand, there is considerable difference in the technique of manufacture of the Palmer and Hardaway points, and the Palmer type represents a fairly widespread style that occurs early throughout the East, especially in the northern area. Points of this type were found at the Camp Creek Site in Tennessee [11] and northward along the Atlantic Coast into New England.[12] Although these small corner-notched points have not been isolated as an early Archaic cultural unit elsewhere, future work will undoubtedly help explain the distribution of this type. At the present time, the significant factor seems to be that this type represents a relationship to the north of the Piedmont rather than to the south or west.

B. KIRK COMPLEX

During this period the projectile point type increased in size, but it did not greatly alter its form. Basal grinding, however, did decline and there developed a new type in the form of a broad-stemmed, deeply serrated blade. This development in the corner-notched points seemed to be consistent with a general trend throughout the East. At Graham Cave the broad corner-notched point was common in Level 3.[13] At the Modoc Rock Shelter points of this type occurred in the upper part of Zone I as well as elsewhere in the deposit, and at the Ferry Site, also in Illinois, these points were found on the surface along with a great deal of other Archaic material. A recent, and as yet unpublished, date on carbonized acorns from this site was 6201 ± 400 B.C.[14] This compares very favorably with the estimate made for the Kirk occupation in the Piedmont.

The transition to the broad-stemmed point was made locally and it was well illustrated by the materials recovered from the Hardaway Site, but the source of the idea for this style is not well known. None of the points illustrated for Graham Cave or Modoc Rock Shelter were of this type. At the Ferry Site, however, several specimens were illustrated.[15] Typologically, they resemble the San Jose points in New Mexico [16]

and the Concho points in Arizona.[17] In other words, the new innovation in the Kirk Complex appears to have been oriented toward the west.

III. THE LATER ARCHAIC

A. STANLY COMPLEX

The change in projectile point style from the corner-notched to the broad-stem form that began during the Kirk period continued in the Stanly period to the total exclusion of the corner-notched type. The form remained basically the same, but the blade tended to be made wider and the stem narrower. The concave bases tended to become more definitely notched, and the serration became less distinct. Although the Stanly occupation at the Hardaway Site continued in strength, it was also found to form the first definable period of occupation at the Doerschuk Site and served as an excellent link to connect the sequences at these two sites (see fig. 27).

It was during the Stanly period that the first evidence of polished stone appeared. A semilunar or pick-type atlatl weight was found in considerable quantity at both the Hardaway and Doerschuk sites, but there was no evidence of any other type of polished stone artifact. At Graham Cave, it was thought that a full-grooved axe was associated with Level 4 which was dated at 5944 ± 500 B.C.[18] At the Modoc Rock Shelter a full-grooved axe was found at a depth of nineteen feet, and its age was estimated to be 5000 B.C.[19] At the Ferry Site, a date of 6201 B.C. was obtained, as previously mentioned, for some part of a complex of traits that included the full-grooved axe and an atlatl weight similar to those characteristic of the Stanly Complex.[20] There appears to have accumulated a substantial amount of data that would suggest that the appearance of polished stone artifacts occurred much earlier in the Archaic than had formerly been thought.

B. MORROW MOUNTAIN COMPLEX

At the Doerschuk Site, there appeared without any background in the area a cultural unit that made relatively small projectile points with short tapering stems. These points appeared to be identical in size, shape, and workmanship to those found in Gypsum Cave, Nevada, and they have a wide distribution from the West into the Piedmont and north into New England. According to Kelley, the "Gypsum Cave type of projectile point is one variation of a widespread dart point pattern which appears, in some localities at least, to represent an early phase of the Desert cultures. . . ." [21] In Nevada, the

[11] Lewis and Kneberg, 1957: fig. 20, a–b.
[12] Bullen, 1949: 11.
[13] Logan, 1952: pl. 12, l–q.
[14] Griffin, James B., personal communication.
[15] Fowler, 1957: fig. 5, k, o, q, pls. i, k.
[16] Bryan and Toulouse, 1943.

[17] Wendorf and Thomas, 1951: fig. 49, a–h.
[18] Crane, 1956: 667.
[19] Fowler, 1959: 262.
[20] Fowler, 1957: fig. 8, a.
[21] Kelley, 1959: 279.

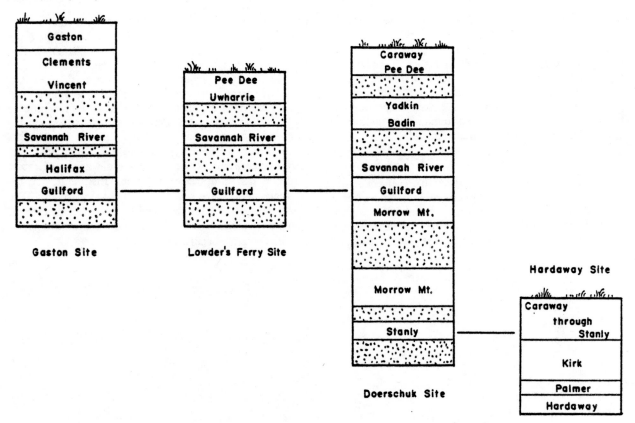

FIG. 117. Synoptic profiles of the Gaston, Lowder's Ferry, Doerschuk, and Hardaway sites.

Gypsum Cave material has been dated between 6000 and 8000 B.C.,[22] but in North Carolina it is not believed to have occurred much before 4500 B.C.

C. GUILFORD COMPLEX

Artifacts of this period, especially the long, thick lanceolate points are very widespread throughout the Piedmont, but, apparently, they are not so common outside of this area. They do not have a distribution much north of Virginia or south of Piedmont Georgia. In Tennessee and the Midwest, they are also relatively rare. Yet, like the Morrow Mountain point, they appear to have their origin to the west. Jennings has pointed out a parallel between the Guilford type and his types W8, W9, and W11 from Danger Cave.[23] There is also a fairly close typological association between the Guilford Complex, and the assemblage found at Nebo Hill in Missouri. Since these cultural units appear to have occurred later in the East, they must have diffused from the Central Plains, around the southern end of the Appalachian Mountains, into the Piedmont. This complex was represented at both the Doerschuk Site on the Yadkin River and the Gaston Site on the Roanoke River.

[22] Johnson, 1951.
[23] Jennings, 1957: 108–111.

D. HALIFAX COMPLEX

This occupation was found only at the Gaston Site on the Roanoke River, and it was defined on the basis of a small elliptical side-notched point, usually made of quartz. This material was found to overlie the Guilford occupation and was dated at 3484 B.C. (see table 15). The Halifax type seems to represent a northern influence and the point forms strongly suggest a relationship to the Lamoka and Orient Fishtail types of the New York area.[24] The Halifax Complex does not extend much farther south in the Piedmont than the Roanoke Basin.

E. SAVANNAH RIVER COMPLEX

In the Piedmont, the Archaic cultures terminate with the close of the Savannah River occupation. In North Carolina this period began as a continuation of the earlier Stanly Complex, and it continued the development of a broad-bladed, broad-stemmed point tradition along with polished stone atlatl weights and grooved axes. In the central Piedmont, however, it did not develop gradually into an early ceramic period as was true to the north and to the south.[25] The stemmed

[24] Ritchie, 1959; pl. 20.
[25] Manson, 1948; Fairbanks, 1942.

projectile points and the stone vessels appear to have been replaced abruptly by large triangular points and well-made cord- and fabric-marked pottery. It is unlikely that there could have been such a widespread replacement of a population in such a short time and the explanation must be sought elsewhere. Perhaps this period of transition simply did not exist at the sites that have been studied and will be found when further explorations are completed in this area.

IV. THE WOODLAND TRADITION

Following the end of the Savannah River occupation there occurred an abrupt change in the complexion of the observed artifactual remains. The ceramic tradition, when it first appeared, was a fully developed technology and introduced along with it were large triangular projectile points. Both of these traits have their associations to the north in the Piedmont, rather than to the south, and from this time to the protohistoric period there was virtually no interaction evident with the more southern cultural groups. It was not until after A.D. 1500, when the intrusive Pee Dee Culture appeared in the Uwharrie area, that any of the styles common to Georgia and South Carolina began to appear in the Piedmont. Soon after this, however, certain elements of the Lamar ceramic style began to be adapted to the local pottery, and by A.D. 1700 the old cord and fabric tradition had disappeared from the Piedmont. In the Roanoke area, there was no direct contact with the Pee Dee Complex, and the diffusion of the southern ceramic elements reached this area just prior to the termination of the aboriginal occupation.

BIBLIOGRAPHY

BELL, ROBERT E., and ROLAND S. HALL. 1953. Selected projectile point types of the United States. *Bulletin of the Oklahoma Anthropological Society* 1: 1-16. Norman.

BOWMAN, FRANK O., JR. 1954. The Carolina slate belt near Albemarle, North Carolina. Doctoral dissertation, University of North Carolina. Chapel Hill.

BRYAN, KIRK, and JOSEPH H. TOULOUSE, JR. 1943. The San José non-ceramic culture and its relation to Puebloan culture in New Mexico. *American Antiquity* 8(3): 269-280. Menasha.

BULLEN, RIPLEY P. 1949. Excavations in northeastern Massachusetts. *Papers of the Robert S. Peabody Foundation for Archaeology* 1(3). Andover.

—— 1958. Six sites near the Chattahooche River in the Jim Woodruff reservoir area, Florida. *Bureau of American Ethnology Bulletin* 169: 315-358. Washington.

BUSHNELL, DAVID I., JR. 1935. The Manahoac tribes in Virginia, 1608. *Smithsonian Miscellaneous Collection* 94(8). Washington.

—— 1937. Indian sites below the falls of the Rappahannock, Virginia. *Smithsonian Miscellaneous Collection* 96(4). Washington.

BYERS, DOUGLAS S. 1954. Bull Brook—a fluted point site in Ipswich, Massachusetts. *American Antiquity* 19(4): 343-351. Salt Lake City.

—— 1959a. An introduction to five papers on the archaic stage. *American Antiquity* 24(3): 229-232. Salt Lake City.

—— 1959b. The Eastern Archaic: Some problems and hypotheses. *American Antiquity* 24(3): 233-256. Salt Lake City.

CALDWELL, JOSEPH R. 1954. The old quartz industry of piedmont Georgia and South Carolina. *Southern Indian Studies* 6: 37-39. Chapel Hill.

CALDWELL, JOSEPH, and CATHERINE MCCANN. 1941. The Irene Mound Site, Chatham County, Georgia. Athens, The University of Georgia Press.

CLAFLIN, WILLIAM H., JR. 1931. The Stallings Island Mound, Columbia County, Georgia. *Papers of the Peabody Museum of American Archaeology and Ethnology* 14(1). Cambridge.

COE, JOFFRE L. 1937. Keyauwee—a preliminary statement. *Bulletin of the Archaeological Society of North Carolina* 3(1). Chapel Hill.

—— 1939. Status of North Carolina archaeology. *Journal of the Elisha Mitchell Scientific Society* 55(2). Chapel Hill.

—— 1940. The Frutchey Mound, Montgomery County, North Carolina. Occasional Contribution of the Laboratory of Anthropology, University of North Carolina 1. Chapel Hill.

—— 1952. Culture sequence of the Carolina Piedmont. *In: Archaeology of Eastern United States*. James B. Griffin, editor. Chicago, University of Chicago Press.

—— n.d. The Pee Dee pottery series. Unpublished manuscript. Research Laboratories of Anthropology, University of North Carolina. Chapel Hill.

COE, JOFFRE L., and ERNEST LEWIS. 1952. Dan River series statement. *Prehistoric pottery of the Eastern United States*, Museum of Anthropology, University of Michigan. Ann Arbor.

CORBITT, DAVID L. 1950. *The formation of the North Carolina counties, 1663-1943*. Raleigh, State Department of Archives and History.

CRANE, H. R. 1956. University of Michigan radiocarbon dates I. *Science* 124: 664-672. Washington.

CRANE, H. R., and JAMES B. GRIFFIN. 1958a. University of Michigan radiocarbon dates II. *Science* 127: 1098-1105. Washington.

CRANE, H. R., and JAMES B. GRIFFIN. 1958b. University of Michigan radiocarbon dates III. *Science* 128: 1117-1123. Washington.

CRANE, H. R., and JAMES B. GRIFFIN. 1959. University of Michigan radiocarbon dates IV. *American Journal of Science Radiocarbon Supplement* 1: 173-198. New Haven.

CROSS, DOROTHY. 1941. *The archaeology of New Jersey* 1. Trenton, The Archaeological Society of New Jersey and the New Jersey State Museum.

CRUXENT, J. M., and IRVING ROUSE. 1956. A lithic industry of Paleo-Indian type in Venezuela. *American Antiquity* 22(2): 172-179. Salt Lake City.

DAVIS, E. MOTT. 1953. Recent data from two Paleo-Indian sites on Medicine Creek, Nebraska. *American Antiquity* 18(4): 380-386. Salt Lake City.

EVANS, CLIFFORD. 1955. A ceramic study of Virginia archeology. *Bureau of American Ethnology Bulletin* 160. Washington.

FAIRBANKS, CHARLES H. 1942. The taxonomic position of Stalling's Island, Georgia. *American Antiquity* 7(3): 223-254. Menasha.

FORD, JAMES A. 1949. Cultural dating of prehistoric sites in Viru Valley, Peru. *Anthropological Papers of the American Museum of Natural History* 43(1). New York.

—— 1952. Mound builders of the Mississippi. *Scientific American* 186(3): 22-27. New York.

FORD, JAMES A., PHILIP PHILLIPS, and WILLIAM G. HAAG. 1955. The Jaketown Site in West-Central Mississippi. *Anthropological Papers of the American Museum of Natural History* 45(1). New York.

FORD, JAMES A., and CLARENCE H. WEBB. 1956. Poverty Point, a late archaic site in Louisiana. *Anthropological Papers of the American Museum of Natural History* 46(1). New York.

FOWLER, MELVIN L. 1957. The Ferry Site, Hardin County, Illinois. *Scientific Papers* 8(1). Illinois State Museum. Springfield.

—— 1959. Modoc rock shelter, an early archaic site in southern Illinois. *American Antiquity* 24(3): 257-270. Salt Lake City.

GRIFFIN, JAMES B. 1945. An interpretation of Siouan archaeology in the piedmont of North Carolina and Virginia. *American Antiquity* 10(4): 321-330. Menasha.

HAAG, WILLIAM G. 1958. The archeology of coastal North Carolina. *Louisiana State University Studies, Coastal Studies Series* 2. Baton Rouge.

HAWKES, E. W., and RALPH LINTON. 1916. A pre-Lenape site in New Jersey. *University of Pennsylvania University Museum Anthropological Publications* 6(3). Philadelphia.

HOLLAND, C. G. 1955. Analysis of projectile points and blades. *In: A ceramic study of Virginia archeology*, by Clifford Evans. *Bureau of American Ethnology Bulletin* 160. Washington.

JENNINGS, JESSE D. 1957. Danger Cave. *Memoirs of the Society for American Archaeology* 14. Salt Lake City.

JOHNSON, FREDERICK (Assembler). 1951. Radiocarbon dating. *Memoirs of the Society for American Archaeology* 17(1), No. 8. Salt Lake City.

JONES, CHARLES C., JR. 1873. *Antiquities of the Southern Indians, particularly of the Georgia tribes*. New York.

KELLEY, J. CHARLES. 1959. The desert cultures and the Balcones phase: Archaic manifestations in the Southwest and Texas. *American Antiquity* 24(3): 276-288. Salt Lake City.

KNEBERG, MADELINE. 1956. Some important projectile point types found in the Tennessee area. *Tennessee Archaeologist* 12(1): 17-28. Knoxville.

—— 1957. Chipped stone artifacts of the Tennessee valley area. *Tennessee Archaeologist* 13(1): 55–66. Knoxville.

KNOBLOCK, BRYON W. 1939. *Bannerstones of the North American Indian.* LaGrange, Popular Edition.

KRON, FRANCIS JOSEPH. 1875. Antiquities of Stanly and Montgomery counties, North Carolina. *Annual Report of the Smithsonian Institution* 1874: 389–390. Washington.

LEWIS, T. M. N., and MADELINE KNEBERG. 1957. The Camp Creek Site. *Tennessee Archaeologist* 13(1): 1–48. Knoxville.

LEWIS, T. M. N., and MADELINE KNEBERG. 1958. The Nuckolls Site. *Tennessee Archaeologist* 14(2): 60–79. Knoxville.

LOGAN, WILFRED D. 1952. Graham Cave, an archaic site in Montgomery County, Missouri. *University of Missouri Archaeological Society Memoir* 2. Columbia.

McCARY, BEN C. 1951. A workshop site of early man in Dinwiddie County, Virginia. *American Antiquity* 17(1): 9–17. Salt Lake City.

MANSON, CARL. 1948. Marcey Creek Site: An early manifestation in the Potomac valley. *American Antiquity* 13(3): 223–226. Menasha.

MILLER, CARL F. 1949. The Lake Spring Site, Columbia County, Georgia. *American Antiquity* 15(1): 38–50. Menasha.

NEWELL, H. PERRY, and ALEX D. KRIEGER. 1949. The George C. Davis Site, Cherokee County, Texas. *Memoir of the Society for American Archaeology* 5. Menasha.

PHILLIPS, PHILIP, JAMES A. FORD, and JAMES B. GRIFFIN. 1951. Archaeological survey in the Lower Mississippi alluvial valley, 1940–1947. *Papers of the Peabody Museum of Archaeology and Ethnology* 25. Cambridge.

POGUE, JOSEPH E. 1910. Cid mining district of Davidson County, North Carolina. *North Carolina Geological and Economic Survey Bulletin* 22. Raleigh.

RITCHIE, WILLIAM A. 1944. The pre-Iroquoian occupations of New York State. *Rochester Museum of Arts and Sciences.* Rochester.

—— 1958. An introduction to Hudson Valley prehistory. *New York State Museum and Science Service Bulletin* 367. Albany.

—— 1959. The Stony Brook Site and its relation to archaic and transitional cultures on Long Island. *New York State Museum and Science Service Bulletin* 372. Albany.

ROBERTS, FRANK H. H., JR. 1935. A Folsom Complex: Preliminary report on investigations at the Lindemeier Site in northern Colorado. *Smithsonian Miscellaneous Collections* 94(4). Washington.

SEARS, WILLIAM H. 1954. A late archaic horizon on the Atlantic Coastal Plain. *Southern Indian Studies* 6: 28–36. Chapel Hill.

SHIPPEE, J. M. 1948. Nebo Hill, a lithic complex in western Missouri. *American Antiquity* 14(1): 29–32. Menasha.

SODAY, FRANK J. 1954. The Quad Site, a Paleo-Indian village in northern Alabama. *Tennessee Archaeologist* 10(1): 1–20. Knoxville.

STEPHENSON, ROBERT L. 1959. The prehistoric people of Accokeek Creek. Accokeek, Maryland: Alice Ferguson Foundation.

SUHM, DEE ANN, and ALEX D. KRIEGER. 1954. An introductory handbook of Texas archeology. *Bulletin of the Texas Archeological Society* 25. Austin.

UNITED STATES ARMY CORPS OF ENGINEERS. 1933. Yadkin-Peedee River, N. C. and S. C. *73rd Congress, 1st Session, House Document* 68. Government Printing Office. Washington.

—— 1935. Roanoke River, Va. and N. C. *74th Congress, 1st Session, House Document* 65. Government Printing Office. Washington.

WEBB, WILLIAM S. 1939. An archaeological survey of the Wheeler Basin on the Tennessee River in northern Alabama. *Bureau of American Ethnology Bulletin* 122. Washington.

WEBB, WILLIAM S., and DAVID L. DeJARNETTE. 1942. An archaeological survey of the Pickwick Basin in the adjacent portion of the states of Alabama, Mississippi, and Tennessee. *Bureau of American Ethnology Bulletin* 129. Washington.

WENDORF, FRED, and TULLY H. THOMAS. 1951. Early man sites near Concho, Arizona. *American Antiquity* 17(2): 107–114. Salt Lake City.

WHITE, WILLIAM A. 1953. Systematic drainage changes in the piedmont of North Carolina and Virginia. *Bulletin of the Geological Society of America* 64(125): 561–580. New York.

WILLEY, GORDON R. 1939. Ceramic stratigraphy in a Georgia village site. *American Antiquity* 5(2): 140–147. Menasha.

WOLMAN, M. GORDON, and LUNA B. LEOPOLD. 1957. River flood plains: Some observations on their formation. *Geological Survey Professional Paper* 282-C: 87–109.

WITTHOFT, JOHN. 1950. Pottery types of the Lower Susquehanna valley. *Eastern States Archaeological Federation Bulletin* 9. Trenton.

—— 1952. A Paleo-Indian site in eastern Pennsylvania: An early hunting culture. *Proceedings American Philosophical Society* 96(4): 464–495. Philadelphia.

WORMINGTON, H. M. 1957. Ancient man in North America. *Denver Museum of Natural History Popular Series* 4. 4th edition. Denver.

DATE